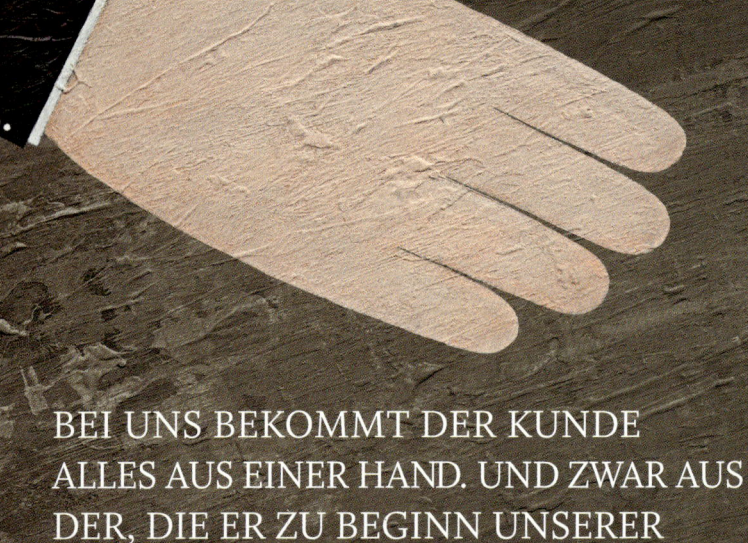

BEI UNS BEKOMMT DER KUNDE ALLES AUS EINER HAND. UND ZWAR AUS DER, DIE ER ZU BEGINN UNSERER PARTNERSCHAFT GESCHÜTTELT HAT.

Wir verstehen uns nicht nur als **unabhängige Vermögensverwaltung**, sondern leben dieses Prinzip. Intransparente Produkte lehnen wir strikt ab. Vertrauensvolle Mitarbeiter der VM Vermögens-Management GmbH finden Sie seit 1986 an Standorten wie Düsseldorf, Dortmund, München und Stuttgart. www.vmgruppe.de

Ein Unternehmen der August von Finck Gruppe

VermögensManufaktur

vm.

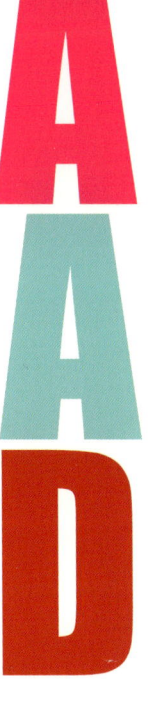

BARCELONA

edited by Patricia Massó

teNeues

ART

ARCHITECTURE

DESIGN

BARCELONA

AAD

Content

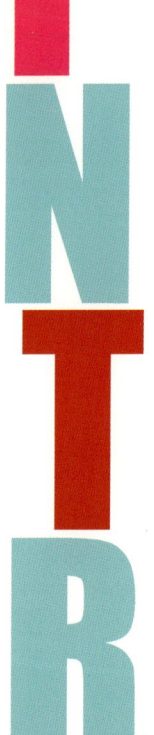

For the last 20 years, Barcelona has been undergoing changes that have been as rapid as they have been radical. Triggered by the Olympic Games in 1992, a new urban planning philosophy and a reorientation towards the oceanfront have transformed the face of the city and created new attractions: state-of-the-art sports facilities, world-class hotels, new cultural institutions, and miles of beaches right in the city. Instead of resting on their laurels, visionary politicians and ambitious entrepreneurs have kept up the tide of innovations and investments. The fusion of the old and the new has given new splendor to the cultural legacy of this city shaped by the Catalan Modernism movement without denying or obscuring it. To stay on top of what's going on, you really need to come back frequently. With blinding speed, creative minds in the fields of design, fashion, music, theater, art, media, and architecture give birth to new trends, stylish ideas, and cutting-edge concepts.

Seit zwei Jahrzehnten befindet sich Barcelona in einem rasanten Wandel. Ausgelöst wurde dieser Elan durch die olympischen Spiele 1992. Eine neue Stadtplanung und die Hinwendung zum Meer veränderten das Gesicht der Stadt und schufen neue Anziehungspunkte: hochmoderne Sportanlagen, erstklassige Hotels, neue kulturelle Einrichtungen und kilometerlange Strände im Stadtgebiet. Statt sich danach auf ihren Lorbeeren auszuruhen, übertrumpfen sich visionäre Politiker und mutige Geschäftsleute seitdem mit Innovationen und Investitionen. Die Fusion von Alt und Neu lässt dabei das kulturelle Erbe der vom katalanischen Jugendstil geprägten Stadt in neuem Glanz erstrahlen, ohne es zu verleugnen oder zu überlagern. Man muss diese Stadt häufig besuchen, wenn man auf dem Laufenden bleiben will. Die Kreativen aus Design, Mode und Musik, Theater, Kunst, Medien und Architektur bringen in schnellem Rhythmus neue Trends, stylishe Ideen und richtungsweisende Konzepte hervor.

Depuis les jeux olympiques de 1992, Barcelone vit un nouvel essor qui se maintient depuis deux décennies. Le nouvel aménagement urbain et l'ouverture vers la mer confèrent à la ville un visage nouveau et ont conduit à la création de nouveaux pôles d'attraction : complexes sportifs modernes, hôtels haut de gamme, nouvelles institutions culturelles et kilomètres de plage à l'orée de la zone urbaine. Au lieu de se reposer sur leurs lauriers, des politiciens visionnaires et entrepreneurs courageux ont continué à doter la ville d'innovations et d'investissements. La fusion de l'ancien et du moderne apporte un nouvel éclat au patrimoine culturel, tout en maintenant le style Art nouveau de la capitale catalane. Pour ne rien manquer de ses transformations, il faut visiter cette ville souvent. Les artistes du design, de la mode, la musique, le théâtre, l'art, les médias et l'architecture donnent naissance à de nouvelles tendances, de nouveaux styles et concepts novateurs à une cadence effrénée.

Desde hace dos décadas, Barcelona experimenta un cambio constante, que comenzó con la concesión de los juegos olímpicos de 1992. Un nuevo urbanismo y la apertura hacia el mar han cambiado la faz de la ciudad y han creado nuevos polos de atracción: modernísimas instalaciones deportivas, hoteles de primera, nuevas instituciones culturales y kilómetros y kilómetros de playa en el área urbana. Lejos de dormirse en los laureles, sin embargo, políticos visionarios y atrevidos empresarios compiten por la incorporación de nuevas innovaciones e inversiones. La fusión de tradición y modernidad aporta nuevos bríos a la herencia cultural de la ciudad, marcada por el modernismo catalán, sin por ello suplantarlo ni falsearlo. Es preciso visitar con frecuencia la ciudad para mantenerse siempre a la última. Diseñadores, modistos, músicos, dramaturgos, artistas, trabajadores de los medios y arquitectos conjuran nuevas tendencias, conceptos de elegancia y patrones pioneros a un ritmo endiablado.

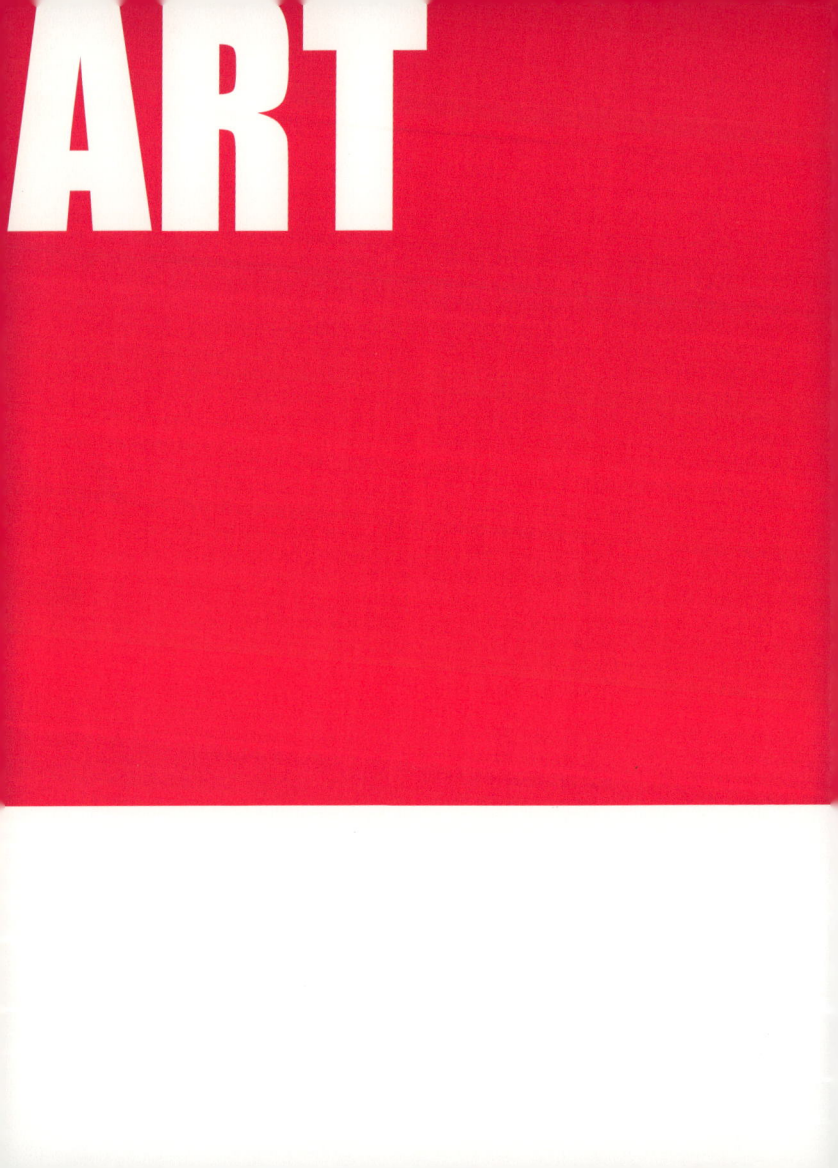

A

In Barcelona, where Picasso spent his teenage years, painting has enjoyed a long tradition which continues to this day. One of the city's oldest galleries, Sala Parés, has an impressive collection of Spanish paintings from the 19th century to the present. To honor world-renowned Catalan artists Joan Miró and Antoni Tàpies, foundations were established that show works by Spanish and international contemporary artists side by side. Within just a few years, several high-profile cultural institutions were built, including the Museu d'Art Contemporani de Barcelona (MACBA) and the Centre de Cultura Contemporània de Barcelona (CCCB) in the old city, as well as others financed by the foundations of savings banks Caixa and Caixa Catalunya. Their exhibitions push the boundaries of contemporary art, frequently supported by avant-garde exhibition design with multimedia and lighting effects. Independent galleries such as ADN, Alejandro Sales, and Estrany-de La Mota tap into international trends.

In der Stadt, in der Picasso seine Jugend verbrachte, hat insbesondere die Malerei eine lange Tradition, die gepflegt wird. Eine der ältesten Galerien der Stadt, die Sala Parés, beeindruckt mit ihrer umfassenden Sammlung spanischer Maler vom 19. Jahrhundert bis zur Gegenwart, und für das Schaffen der weltbekannten Katalanen Joan Miró und Antoni Tàpies wurden in Barcelona eigene Stiftungen eingerichtet, die parallel Ausstellungen einheimischer und ausländischer zeitgenössischer Künstler präsentieren. Mit dem Bau des MACBA (Museu d'Art Contemporani de Barcelona) und des Centre de Cultura Contemporània de Barcelona (CCCB) in der Altstadt sowie dem couragierten Engagement der Sparkassen-Stiftungen von Caixa und Caixa Catalunya entstanden darüber hinaus innerhalb weniger Jahre profilierte Kultureinrichtungen. Ihre Ausstellungen loten die Grenzen zeitgenössischer Kunst aus, häufig unterstützt durch avantgardistisches Ausstellungsdesign, in dem multimediale Effekte und Lichtinszenierungen eine große Rolle spielen. Unabhängige Galerien wie ADN, Alejandro Sales oder Estrany-de la Mota erspüren Trends und vernetzen die Kunstszene international.

Dans la ville où Picasso vécut sa jeunesse, la peinture est forte d'une longue tradition qui continue d'être entretenue. L'une des plus anciennes galeries de la ville, la Sala Parés, offre une impressionnante collection de peintres espagnols du XIXe siècle à nos jours. Pour l'œuvre de Joan Miró et Antoni Tàpies, catalans mondialement célèbres, des fondations ont été créées à Barcelone, où ont lieu en parallèle des expositions d'artistes contemporains espagnols et étrangers. Grâce à la construction du MACBA (Museu d'Art Contemporani de Barcelona) et du CCCB (Centre de Cultura Contemporània de Barcelona) dans la vieille ville et de l'engagement des fondations des caisses d'épargne Caixa et Caixa Catalunya, des institutions culturelles majeures ont été fondées en quelques années. Leurs expositions sondent les frontières de l'art contemporain et sont souvent rehaussées d'un design d'exposition avant-gardiste où effets multimédias et mises en scène de la lumière sont omniprésents. Des galeries indépendantes comme ADN, Alejandro Sales ou Estrany-de la Mota détectent les tendances et relient les artistes du monde entier entre eux.

En la ciudad en la que Picasso pasó su juventud, la pintura en particular tiene una larga y cuidada tradición. Una de las galerías más antiguas de la ciudad, la Sala Parés, impresiona con una amplia colección de pintores españoles que va desde el siglo XIX hasta la actualidad, y en la ciudad se han creado fundaciones dedicadas a la obra de los célebres catalanes Joan Miró y Antoni Tàpies, en las que en paralelo se presentan exposiciones de artistas contemporáneos locales e internacionales. Con la construcción del MACBA (Museu d'Art Contemporani de Barcelona) y del CCCB (Centre de Cultura Contemporània de Barcelona) en el casco antiguo, y a través del valiente esfuerzo de las fundaciones de las cajas de ahorros La Caixa y Caixa Catalunya, han ido surgiendo además otras instituciones culturales de perfil más modesto. Sus exposiciones exploran las fronteras del arte contemporáneo, sustentadas a menudo por un vanguardista diseño de exposición en el que los efectos multimedia y los juegos de iluminación tienen una enorme importancia. Galerías independientes como ADN, Alejandro Sales o Estrany-de la Mota identifican tendencias y tienden lazos con la comunidad internacional del arte.

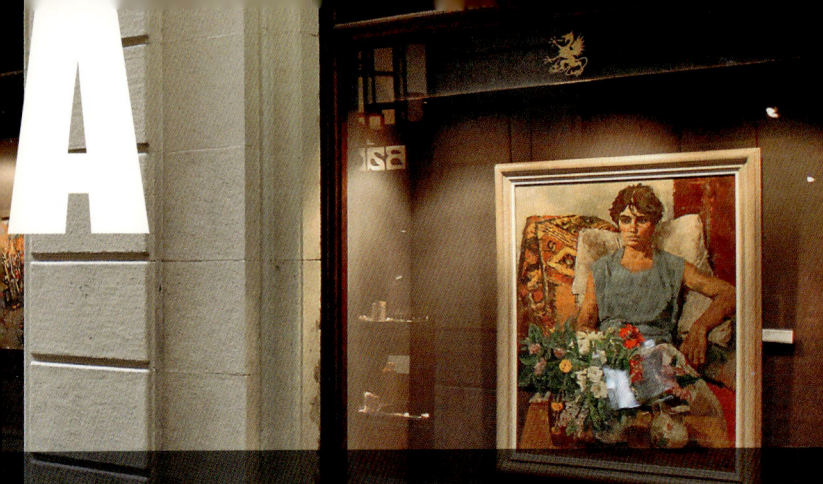

Opened 130 years ago, Sala Parés Gallery is a mecca for lovers of Spanish art. The two large exhibition spaces, designed in an industrial style and featuring a central skylight, form a perfect framework for 19th and 20th century paintings and sculptures. Currently, the gallery represents more than 40 contemporary Spanish and international artists. A private room is reserved for collectors who want to view works from the gallery's inventory, which comprises 1,000 pieces.

Die Galerie Sala Parés ist ein Mekka für Fans der spanischen Kunst. Die beiden großzügigen Ausstellungsflächen im Industriestil und mit einem zentralen Oberlicht bilden seit 130 Jahren einen perfekten Rahmen für Malereien und Skulpturen des 19. und 20. Jahrhunderts. Aktuell vertritt die Galerie mehr als 40 zeitgenössische Künstler im In- und Ausland. Sammler können sich in einem privaten Saal Werke aus dem über 1 000 Bilder umfassenden Bestand zeigen lassen.

La galerie Sala Parés est la véritable Mecque des amateurs d'art espagnol. Depuis 130 ans, les deux vastes surfaces d'exposition de style industriel avec éclairage naturel représentent un cadre attractif pour les peintures et sculptures des XIXe et XXe siècles. Actuellement, la galerie expose plus de 40 artistes contemporains du monde entier. Dans une salle privée, les collectionneurs peuvent admirer plus de 1 000 œuvres non exposées, issues de la collection de la galerie.

La galería Sala Parés es una meca para los amantes del arte español. Las dos extensas superficies de exposición de estilo industrial y luz cenital central ofrecen desde hace 130 años el marco perfecto para cuadros y esculturas de los siglos XIX y XX. En la actualidad, la galería representa a más de 40 artistas contemporáneos dentro y fuera de España. Los coleccionistas pueden evaluar en una sala privada obras de entre las más de 1 000 piezas de sus archivos.

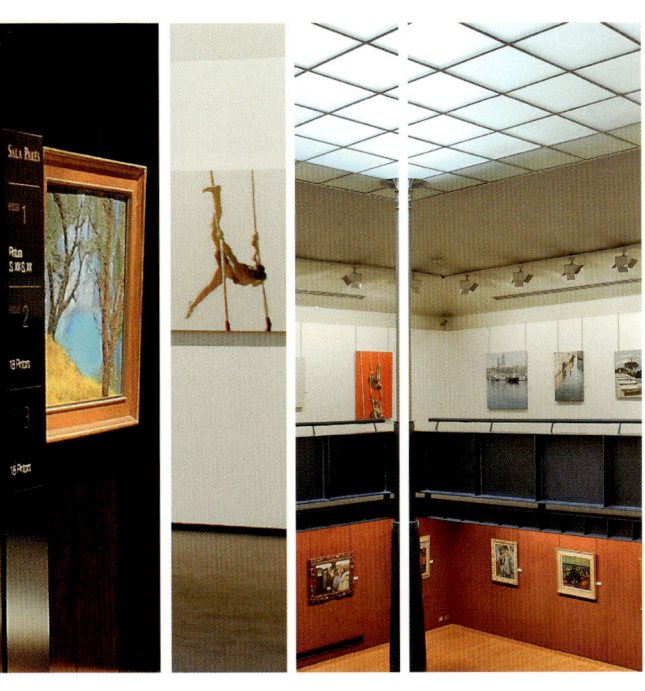

SALA PARÉS

Carrer de Petritxol, 5 // Ciutat Vella / El Barri Gòtic
Tel.: +34 93 318 70 20
www.salapares.com

Mon 4 pm to 8 pm
Tue–Sat 10.30 am to 2 pm
4.30 pm to 8 pm
Metro L1, L3, L6, L7 Catalunya

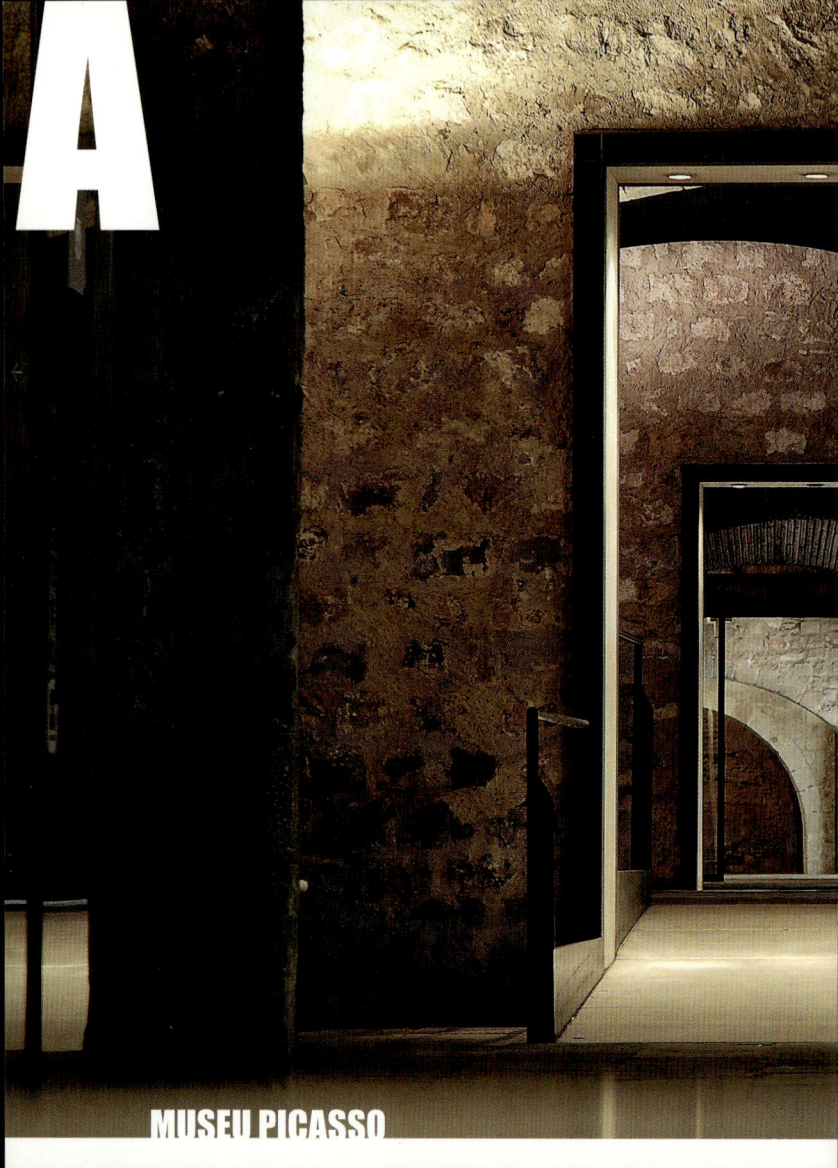

A

MUSEU PICASSO

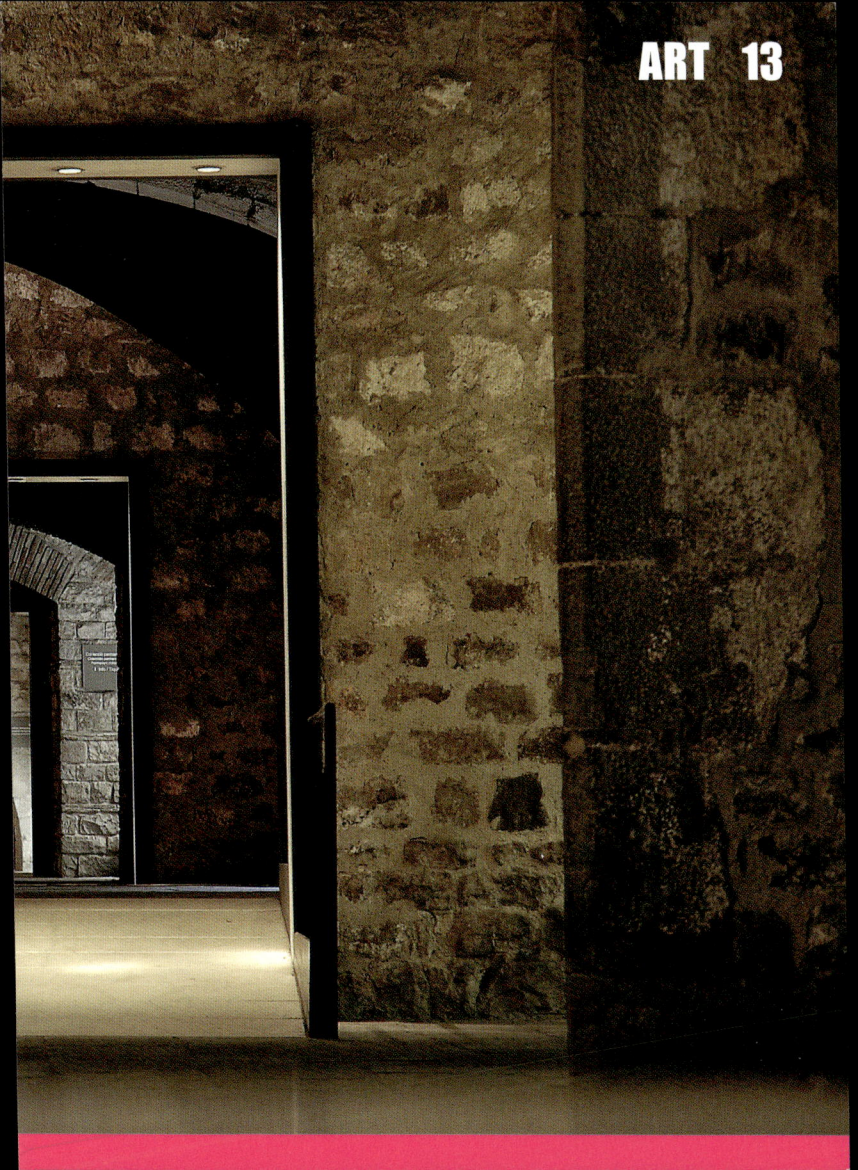

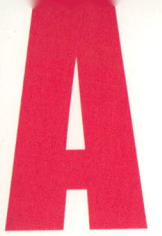

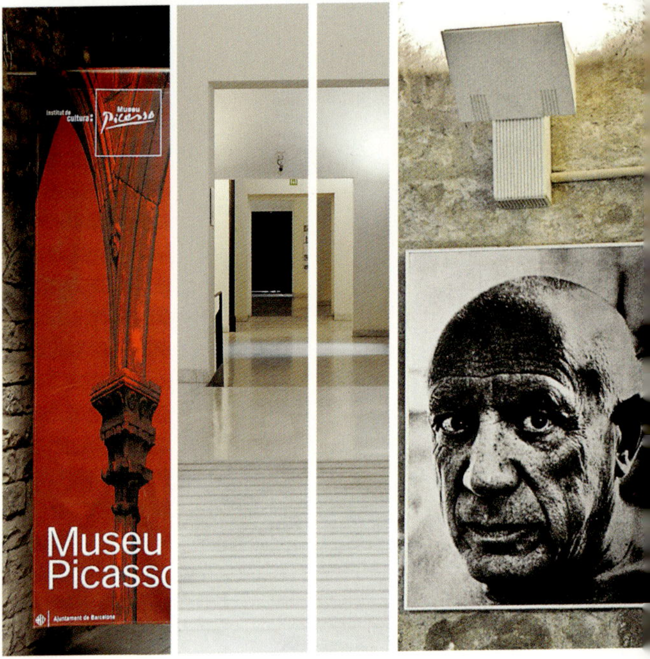

MUSEU PICASSO

Carrer de Montcada, 15-23 // Ciutat Vella / El Born
Tel.: +34 93 256 30 00
www.museupicasso.bcn.cat

Tue–Sun (including holidays) 10 am to 8 pm
Closed Apr 5th, May 1st, Jun 24th, Nov 1st, and Dec 6th
Metro L1 Arc de Triomf or L3 Liceu or L4 Jaume I

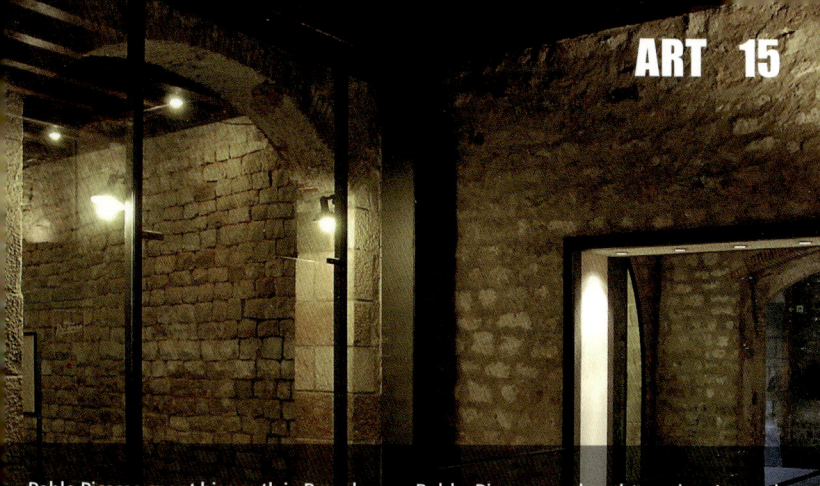

Pablo Picasso spent his youth in Barcelona and remained attached to the city for the rest of his life. The original idea for the museum came from Picasso and his friend Jaume Sabartés. Opened in 1963, it is housed in several adjoining Gothic palaces along Carrer de Montcada. The 3,800 works on display reflect Picasso's entire creative output, with a strong focus on his early years. Also shown are ceramics, etchings, and lithographs as well as the entire "Las Meninas" series.

Pablo Picasso verbrachte seine Jugend in Barcelona und blieb der Stadt stets verbunden. 1963 wurde das Museum auf Initiative des Künstlers und seines Freundes Jaume Sabartés in mehreren miteinander verbunden gotischen Stadtpalästen der Carrer de Montcada eröffnet. Die über 3 800 ausgestellten Werke spiegeln sein gesamtes Schaffen, mit deutlichem Schwerpunkt auf den Jugendjahren. Daneben sind Keramiken, Radierungen und Lithografien sowie die vollständige Serie „Las Meninas" zu sehen.

Pablo Picasso a passé une partie de sa jeunesse à Barcelone et est toujours resté très lié à la ville. À l'initiative de l'artiste et de son ami Jaume Sabartés, le musée ouvrit en 1963 dans plusieurs palais mitoyens de style gothique de la Carrer de Montcada. Plus de 3 800 travaux exposés retracent son œuvre, bien que l'accent soit mis sur ses premières années. Vous y trouverez également des céramiques, gravures et lithographies ainsi que la série complète « Las Meninas ».

La juventud de Pablo Picasso transcurrió en Barcelona y el artista siempre se sintió ligado a la ciudad. En 1963, y por iniciativa del artista y de su amigo Jaume Sabartés, se inauguró el museo en varias mansiones góticas intercomunicadas del Carrer de Montcada. Las más de 3 800 obras expuestas reflejan el conjunto de su obra, con especial énfasis en los años de juventud. Pueden también admirarse cerámicas, aguafuertes y litografías, así como la serie completa de "Las Meninas".

A

CENTRO DE CULTURA CONTEMPORÀNEA
DE BARCELONA (CCCB)

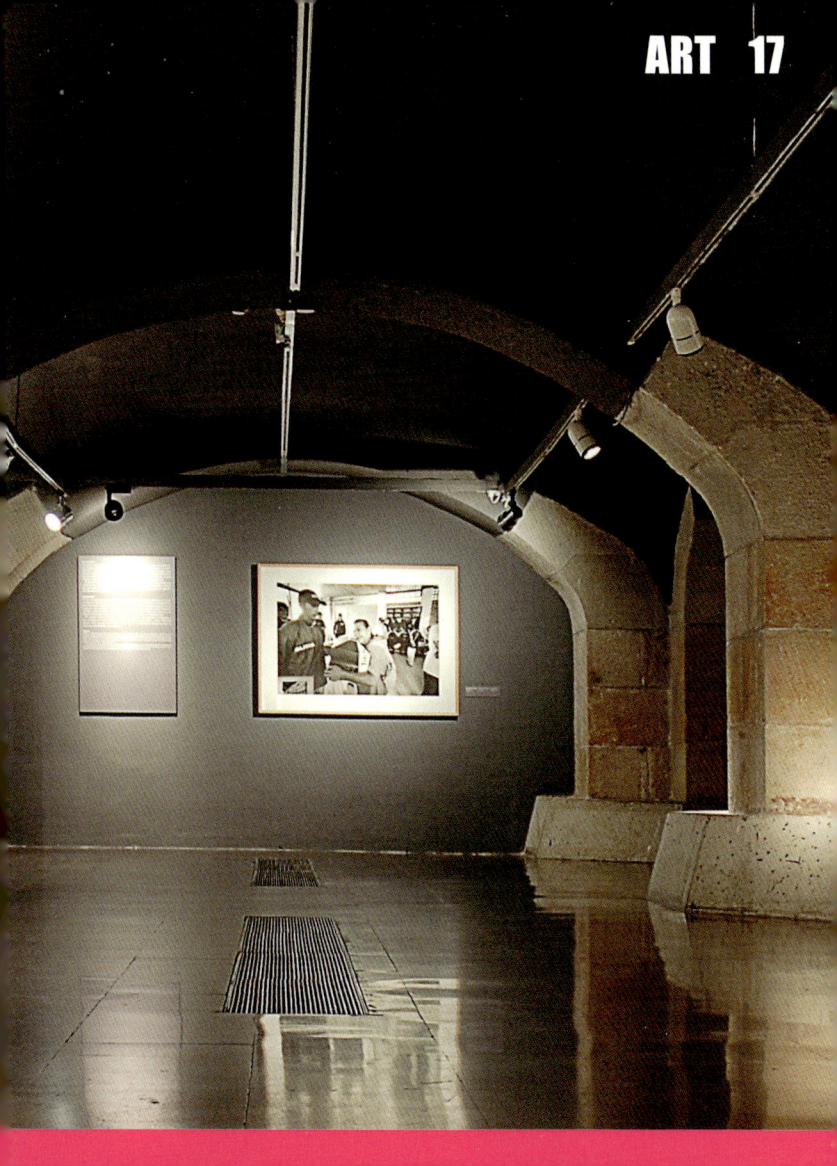

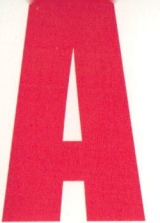

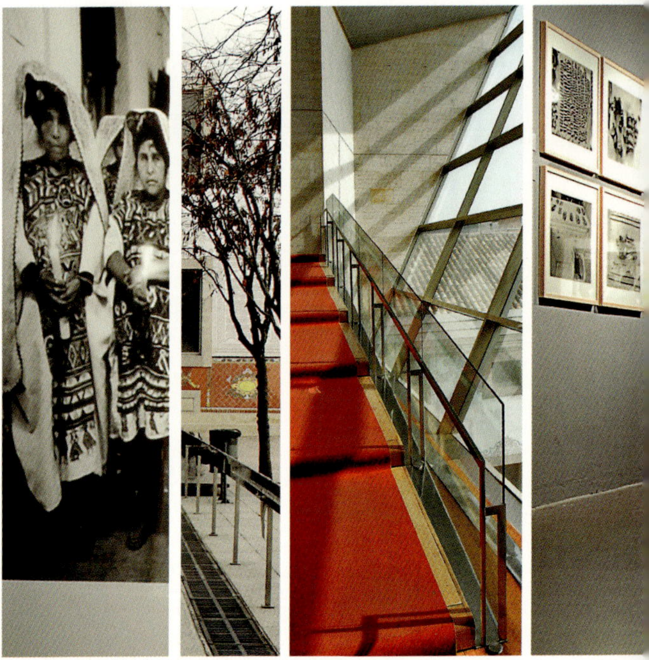

CENTRO DE CULTURA CONTEMPORÀNEA DE BARCELONA (CCCB)

Carrer de Montalegre, 5 // Ciutat Vella / El Raval
Tel.: +34 93 306 41 00
www.cccb.org

Tue–Sun 11 am to 8 pm, Thu 11 am to 10 pm
Closed Dec 25th, and Jan 1st
Special opening times: Dec 24th, 26th, 31st, and Jan 5th and 6th
11 am to 3 pm // Metro L1, L3, L6, L7 Catalunya or L2 Universitat

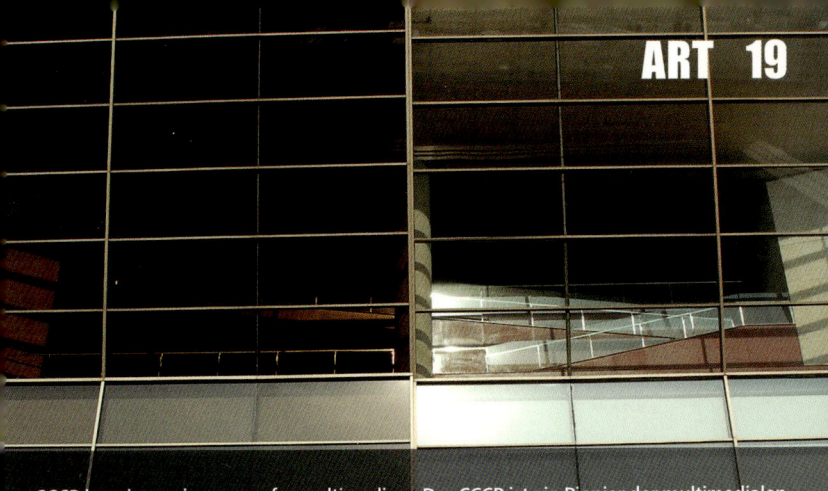

CCCB is a pioneering venue for multimedia exhibitions, and a fixture in Barcelona's art scene. Opened in 1993, CCCB offers innovative programs with exhibitions, festivals, concerts, film series, talks, and panel discussions that regularly tour Spain and other countries. Artists are encouraged to explore new technologies and forms of expression to push their creative boundaries. Helio Piñón and Albert Viaplana created CCCB's architectural framework.

Das CCCB ist ein Pionier der multimedialen Ausstellungskultur und aus der Stadt nicht mehr wegzudenken. Seit 1993 überrascht es immer wieder mit einem Programm, dessen Ausstellungen, Festivals, Konzerte, Filmreihen, Vorträge und Diskussionsforen innerhalb Spaniens und auch ins Ausland exportiert werden. Künstler werden angeregt, mit immer neuen Technologien und Ausdrucksweisen ihre kreativen Grenzen auszuloten. Helio Piñón und Albert Viaplana schufen den architektonischen Rahmen dafür.

Le CCCB est un précurseur en matière d'expositions multimédias et fait partie intégrante de la ville. Depuis 1993, il parvient constamment à nous surprendre avec des expositions, festivals, concerts, films, conférences et forums de discussions qui s'exportent en Espagne et au-delà. Les artistes y sont invités à dépasser leurs limites créatrices à l'aide de nouvelles technologies et formes d'expression. Helio Piñón et Albert Viaplana en ont défini le cadre architectural.

El CCCB es un centro pionero en la cultura de las exposiciones multimedia y forma parte ya del rostro de la ciudad. Desde 1993 no se deja de sorprender con un programa cuyas exposiciones, festivales, conciertos, retrospectivas, ponencias y foros se han exportado tanto a otros lugares de España como al extranjero. El centro anima a los artistas a explorar sus fronteras creativas con nuevas tecnologías y formas de expresión. Helio Piñón y Albert Viaplana crearon el espacio arquitectónico.

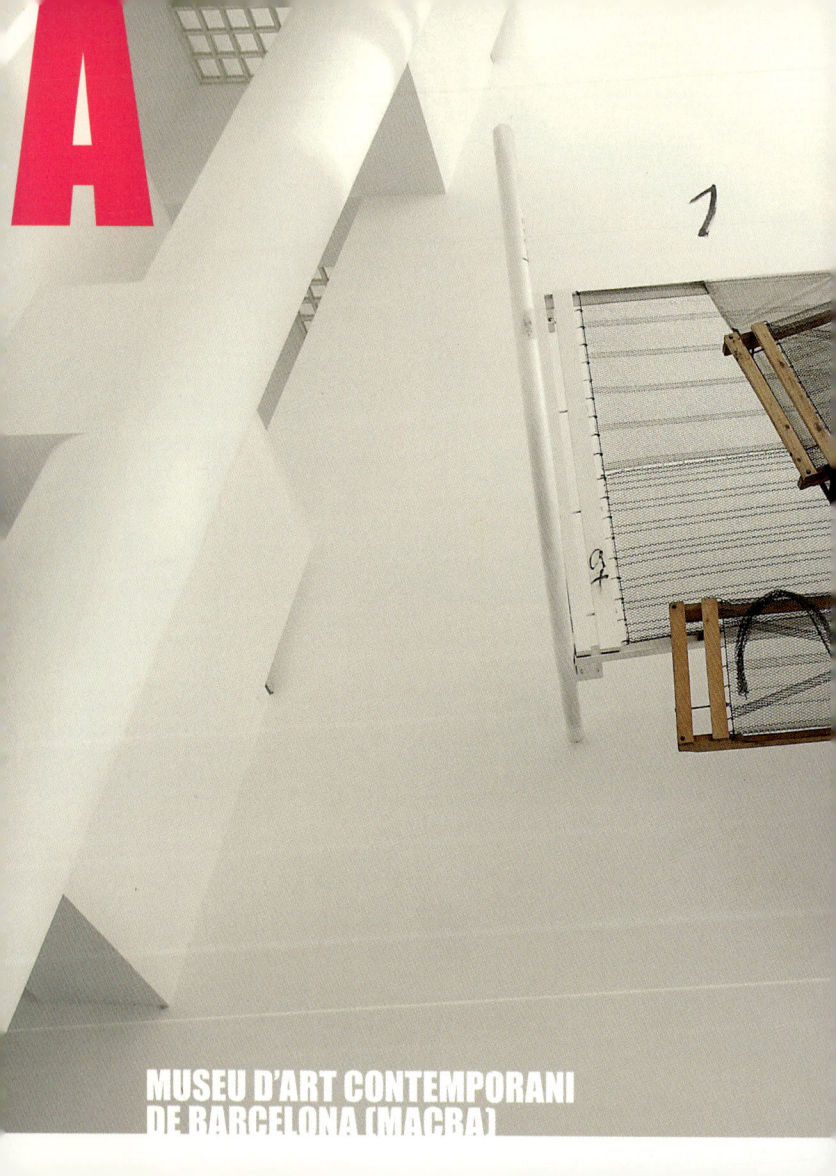

MUSEU D'ART CONTEMPORANI
DE BARCELONA (MACBA)

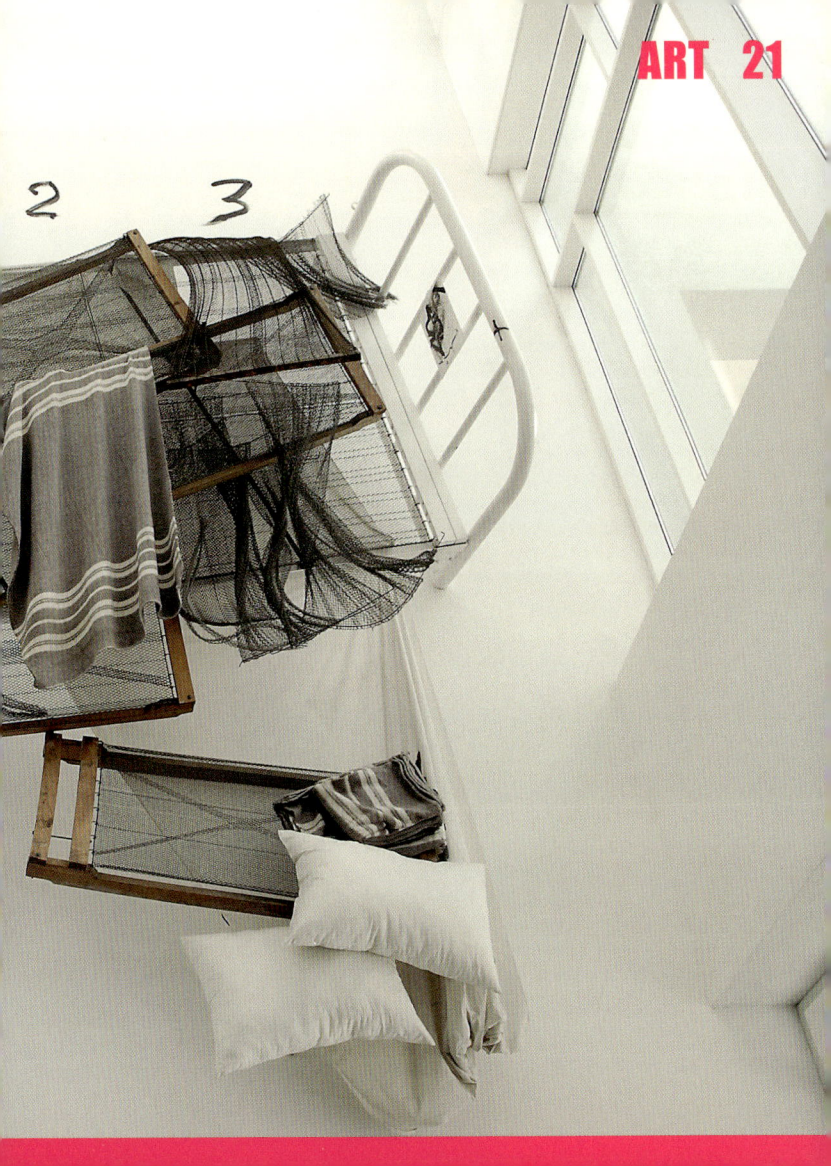

2 3

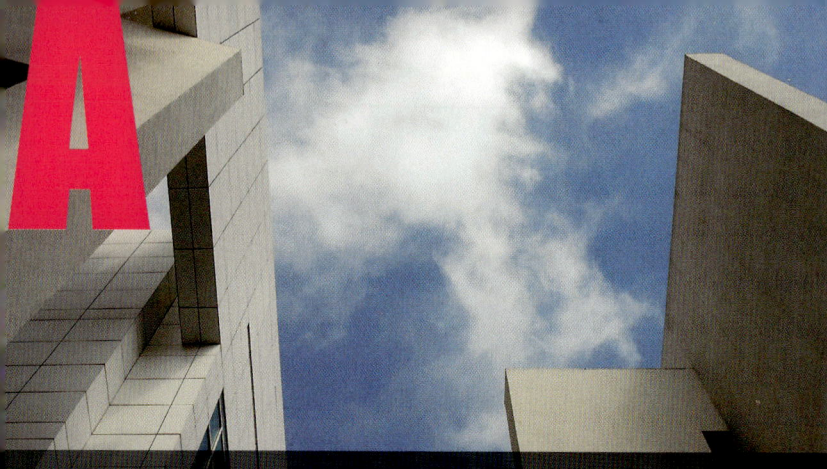

Opened in 1995, the Richard Meier-designed Museu d'Art Contemporani de Barcelona (MACBA) is located amidst the maze of streets of the El Raval neighborhood in the old city. The white, broad glass façade facing the lively Plaça dels Àngels allows views from and into the building, thus serving as a connecting element. The permanent collection has pieces ranging from the 1950s to the present, its focus being on works by Catalan artists. Changing exhibitions round out the program.

Der Architekt Richard Meier errichtete das 1995 eröffnete Museu d'Art Contemporani de Barcelona (MACBA) inmitten des Gassengewirrs des Altstadtviertels El Raval. Die weiße, breite Glasfassade zur belebten Plaça dels Àngels fungiert als verbindendes Element, indem sie Ein- und Ausblicke zulässt. Die ständige Sammlung beginnt mit Werken der 50er Jahre und reicht bis in die Gegenwart. Ihr Schwerpunkt liegt auf Arbeiten katalanischer Künstler. Wechselausstellungen ergänzen die Schau.

Le Museu d'Art Contemporani de Barcelona (MACBA), conçu par Richard Meier, a ouvert ses portes en 1995 au milieu du dédale de ruelles du quartier de la vieille ville El Raval. La large façade blanche et ses parois de verres donnent sur la Plaça dels Àngels, toujours très animée. L'exposition permanente comprend des œuvres allant des années 1950 à nos jours. L'accent est mis sur les travaux d'artistes catalans et des expositions temporaires viennent compléter l'ensemble.

En 1995 se inauguró el Museu d'Art Contemporani de Barcelona (MACBA), obra del arquitecto Richard Meier, en pleno Raval, el laberíntico casco antiguo de la ciudad. La blanca fachada vidriada que se abre al ajetreo de la Plaça dels Àngels sirve de elemento vinculador con el exterior. La colección permanente abarca desde la década de 1950 hasta la actualidad, con especial énfasis en la obra de artistas catalanes. Diversas exposiciones temporales completan la oferta.

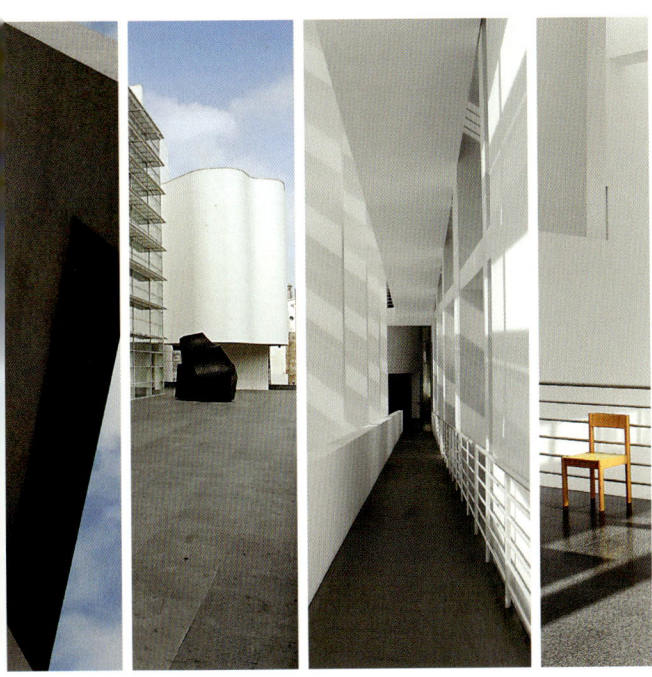

MUSEU D'ART CONTEMPORANI DE BARCELONA (MACBA)

Plaça dels Àngels, 1 // Ciutat Vella / El Raval
Tel.: +34 93 412 08 10
www.macba.cat

Mon, Wed–Sat 11 am to 7.30 pm
Sun and holidays 10 am to 3 pm
Metro L1, L3, L6, L7 Catalunya or L2 Universitat

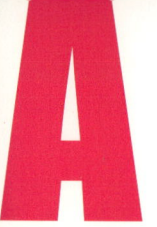

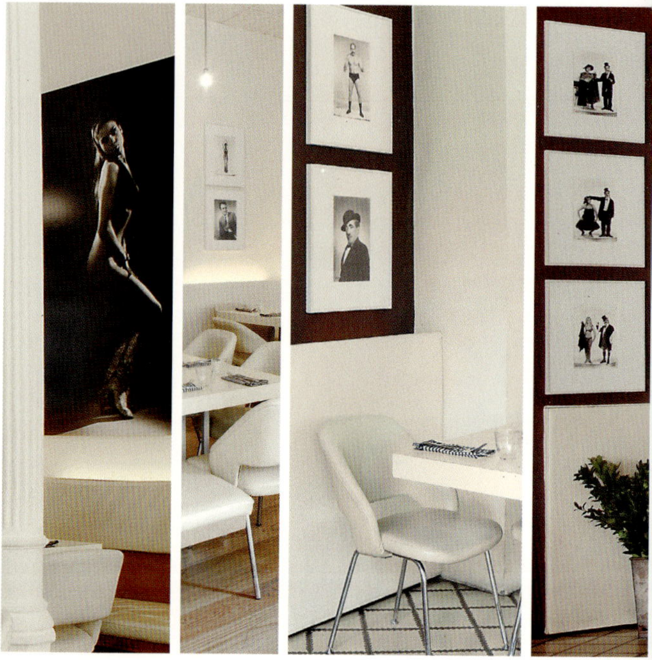

THE GALLERY AT
CARMELITAS RESTAURANT

Carrer del Doctor Dou, 1 // Ciutat Vella / El Raval
Tel.: +34 93 412 54 54
www.carmelitasgallery.com

Daily 9 pm to midnight
Metro L1, L3, L6, L7 Catalunya

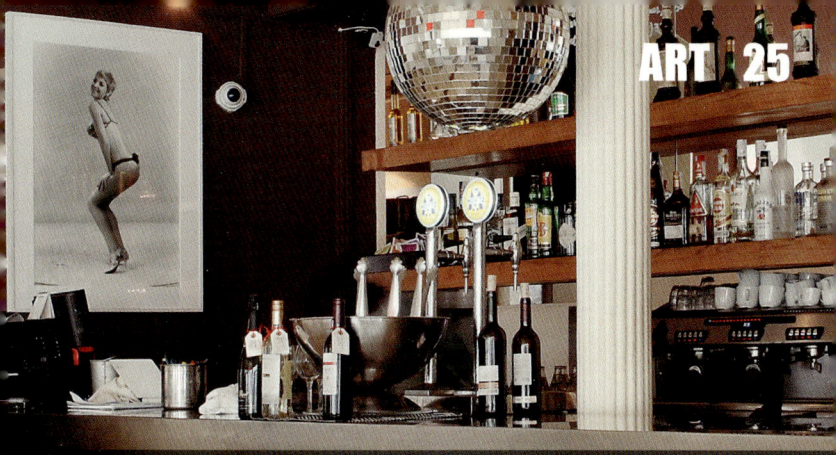

In the El Raval neighborhood of the Ciutat Vella, many new galleries have sprung up near MACBA and CCCB in recent years. Housed in a former convent, Carmelitas is a hip but friendly restaurant with an adjoining gallery specializing in video installations of international artists. The walls of the dining room on the ground floor and the large windows of the corner building are used as projection screens to create a dialog between the inside and the outside.

Um das MACBA und das CCCB herum sind im Altstadtviertel El Raval in den vergangenen Jahren viele neue Galerien entstanden. In einem ehemaligen Konvent verbindet das Carmelitas ein freundliches Szenelokal mit einer Galerie, die sich unter anderem auf Videoinstallationen internationaler Künstler spezialisiert hat. Die Wände des Speisesaales im Erdgeschoss und die großen Fenster des Eckgebäudes dienen als Projektionsflächen und inszenieren einen Dialog zwischen Innen und Außen.

Ces dernières années, dans le quartier de la vieille ville El Raval, de nombreuses galeries ont vu le jour autour du MACBA et du CCCB. Dans un ancien couvent, le restaurant Carmelitas est à la fois un local sympathique et branché et une galerie d'art dédiée aux expositions vidéos d'artistes internationaux. Les murs de la salle à manger au rez-de-chaussée et les grandes fenêtres servent d'écran de projection et mettent en scène un dialogue entre l'intérieur et l'extérieur.

Alrededor del MACBA y del CCCB han surgido en el barrio de El Raval numerosas galerías en los últimos años. En un antiguo convento, Carmelitas combina un agradable local de moda con una galería que se ha especializado en videoinstalaciones de artistas internacionales. Los muros del comedor en la planta baja y los grandes ventanales del edificio sirven como pantalla de proyección y escenifican un diálogo entre interior y exterior.

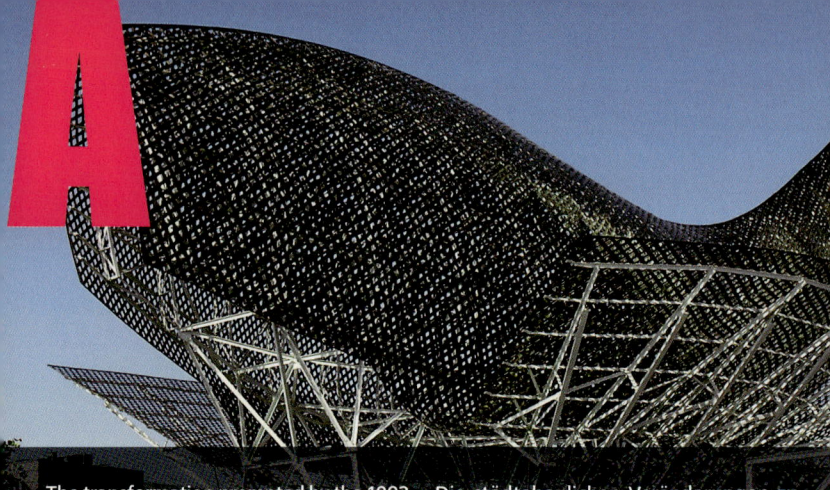

The transformation prompted by the 1992 Olympic Games gave Barcelona, which previously had directed its focus towards the mountains, a new urban space and a new orientation towards the sea, with several miles of new beaches. Located near the towers at the Olympic Harbor, architect Frank O. Gehry's monumental metal lattice fish sculpture (115 ft. tall, 164 ft. long) is visible from a distance. Other fish sculptures by Gehry are found in Kobe, Japan and Minneapolis, Minnesota.

Die städtebaulichen Veränderungen zu den olympischen Spielen 1992 haben der Stadt, die sich stets zu den Bergen orientierte, einen neuen urbanen Raum und eine neue Orientierung geschenkt: mehrere Kilometer Strand und das Meer. Bereits aus der Ferne ist der 35 m hohe, rund 50 m lange, goldglänzende Gitterfisch aus Metall des Architekten Frank O. Gehry nahe den markanten Türmen am Olympiahafen sichtbar. Weitere Fischskulpturen von Gehry stehen in Kobe, Japan, und Minneapolis, USA.

Les travaux entrepris pour les JO de 1992 ont offert un nouvel espace urbain et une nouvelle orientation à une ville qui ne jurait que par ses montagnes : plusieurs kilomètres de plages et la mer. L'énorme poisson en grillage métallique doré (35 m de haut et environ 50 m de long) de l'architecte Frank O. Gehry est visible de très loin, aux côtés des tours du Port Olympique. Gehry a réalisé d'autres sculptures en forme de poisson, à Kobe (Japon) et à Minneapolis (États-Unis).

Las modificaciones urbanísticas ocasionadas por los Juegos Olímpicos de 1992 sirvieron para que la ciudad, tradicionalmente orientada hacia la montaña, ganase un nuevo espacio urbano abierto al mar con varios kilómetros de playa. Desde muy lejos es posible ver, junto a las llamativas torres del puerto olímpico, los reflejos dorados del pez de malla metálica creado por Frank O. Gehry. El arquitecto tiene otras esculturas de peces en Kobe (Japón) y Minneapolis (EUA).

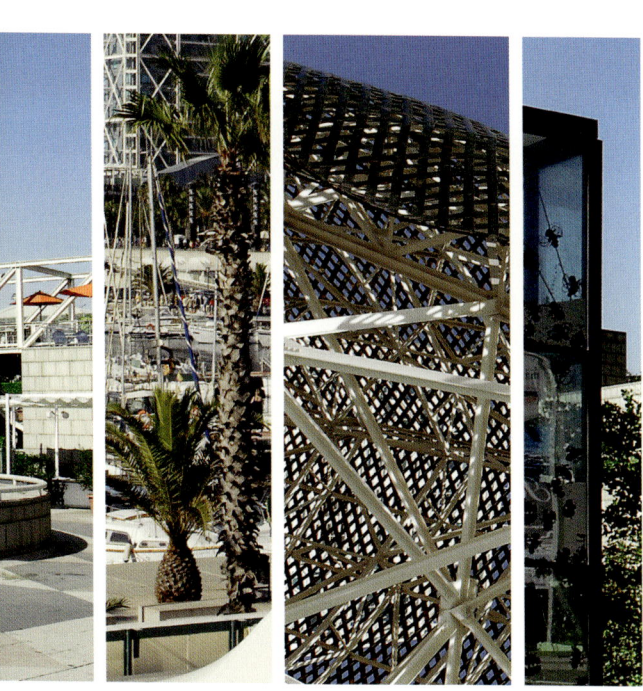

GEHRY'S FISH

Marina, Port Olímpic // Ciutat Vella / La Barceloneta

Metro L4 Ciutadella / Vila Olímpica

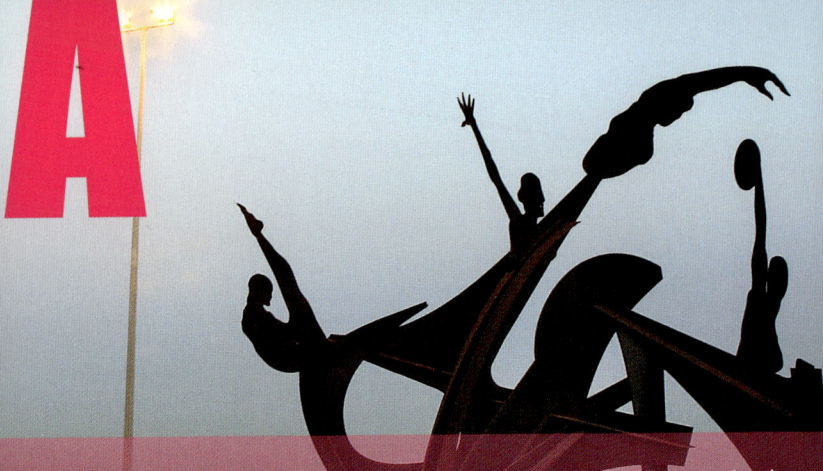

A In the past, only a couple of small seafood shacks lined what used to be a narrow stretch of beach. Today, more than six miles of beach form a unique space for recreation. The four steel-and-glass cubes, piled on top of each other in seemingly random fashion, were created by Rebecca Horn, a German artist, sculptor, and filmmaker. Her 1992 sculpture can be interpreted as an homage to these seafood shacks, an old lighthouse, and the fishing tradition of adjacent La Barceloneta.

Früher standen an dem einzigen schmalen Strandabschnitt ein paar kleine Fischrestaurants – heute bilden mehr als 10 km Strand einen einmaligen Erholungsraum. Die vier scheinbar willkürlich aufeinander gestapelten Quader aus Stahl und Glas sind ein Werk der deutschen Künstlerin, Bildhauerin und Filmemacherin Rebecca Horn. Die Skulptur von 1992 lässt sich als Hommage an die Strandbuden, einen alten Leuchtturm und das Leben der Fischer im angrenzenden Viertel La Barceloneta deuten.

Autrefois, seuls quelques petits restaurants de poisson occupaient l'unique et étroite bande de sable. Aujourd'hui, plus de dix kilomètres de plage forment un espace de détente unique. Les quatre cubes d'acier et de verre, qui semblent posés les uns sur les autres à la va-vite, sont une œuvre de l'artiste, sculptrice et cinéaste allemande Rebecca Horn. Cette sculpture de 1992 est un hommage aux cabanes sur la plage, à un vieux phare et à la vie des pêcheurs de La Barceloneta voisine.

En otra época, un par de restaurantes de pescado jalonaban el único y estrecho tramo de playa: hoy, más de diez kilómetros de playa ofrecen un espacio único de ocio y diversión. Los cuatro sillares aparentemente apilados al azar son obra de la artista, escultura y cineasta alemana Rebecca Horn. La escultura de 1992 puede interpretarse como un homenaje a los chiringuitos de playa, un antiguo faro y la vida de los pescadores en el vecino barrio de La Barceloneta.

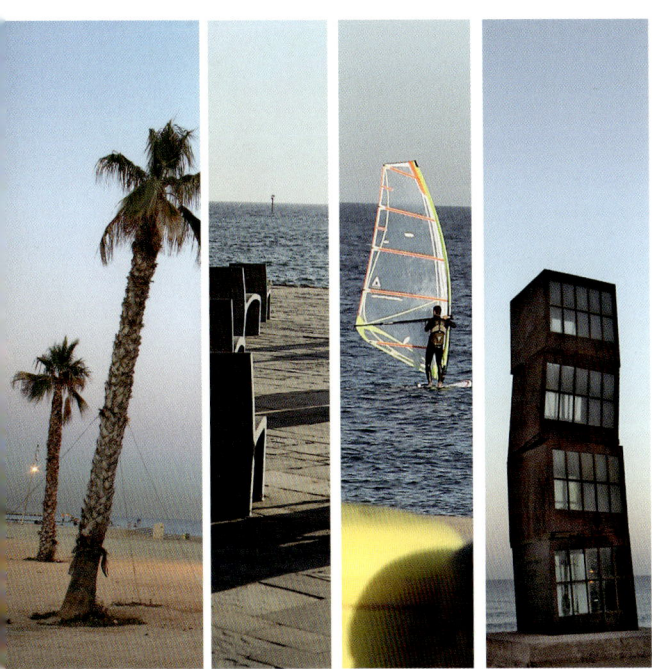

L'ESTEL FERIT –
PLATJA DE LA BARCELONETA

Platja de la Barceloneta // Ciutat Vella / La Barceloneta

Metro L4 Barceloneta

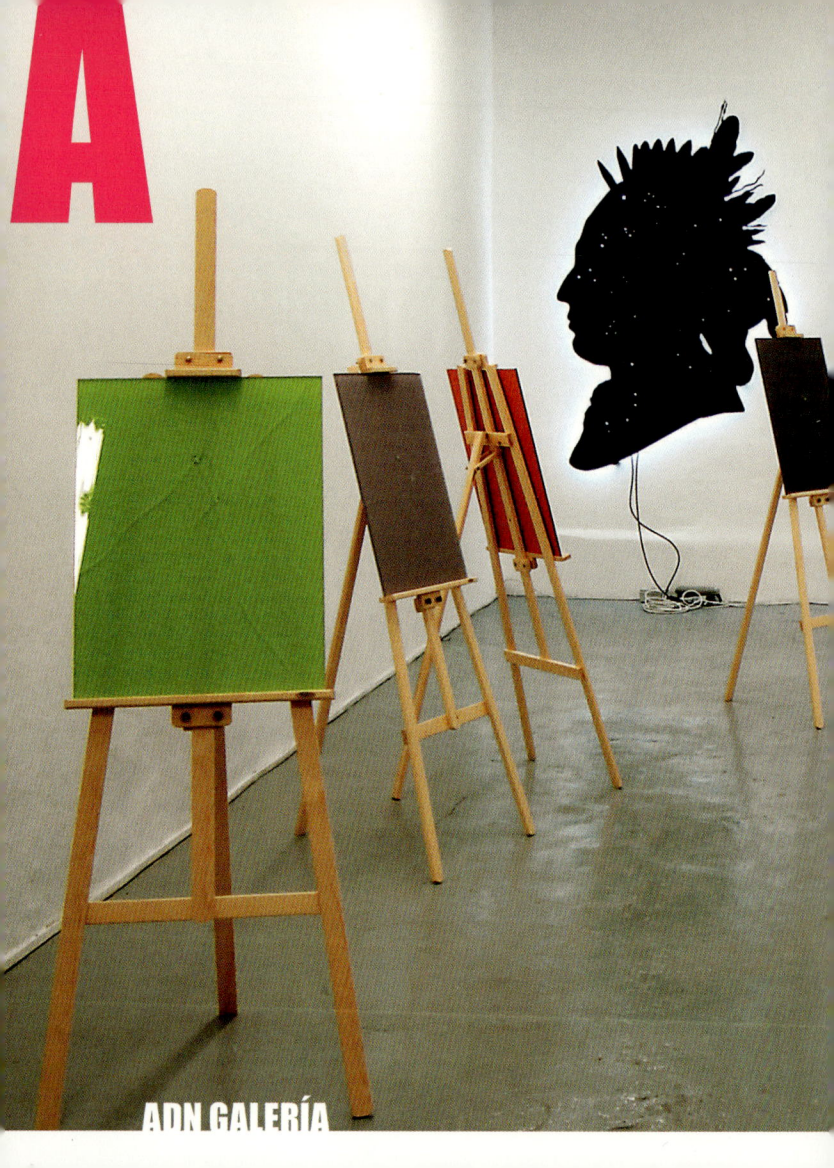

A

ADN GALERÍA

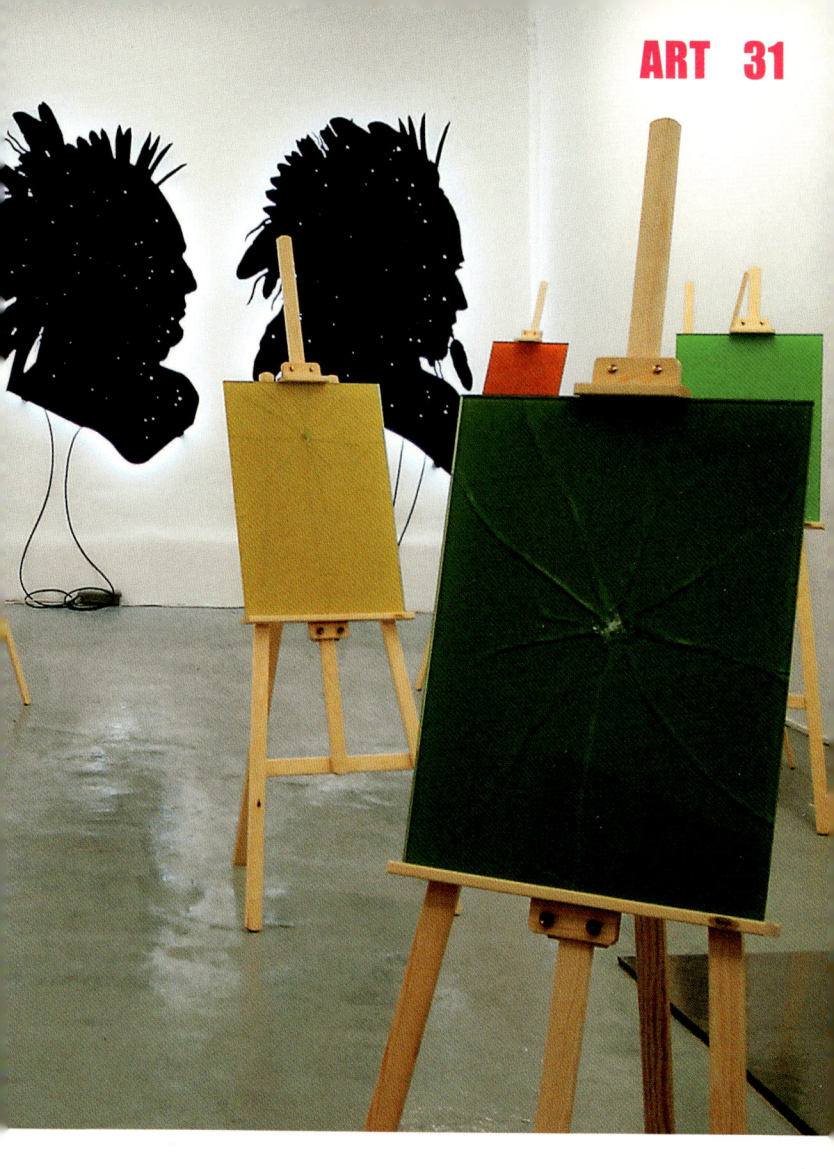

A

Miguel Ángel Sánchez has created a modern 2,600 sq. ft. gallery in a classic storefront on Carrer d'Enric Granados. With his knack for discovering new talent and a well-connected network, he offers emerging artists such as Bruno Peinado and Tobias Bernstrup not only two rooms of exhibition space, but also solid representation in international markets. For its work, the gallery was honored with an award from the Catalan association of gallery owners.

In einem klassischen Ladenlokal in der Straße Enric Granados richtete Miguel Ángel Sánchez auf 240 m² eine moderne Galerie ein. Mit seinem guten Gespür für Nachwuchstalente und einem fein gestrickten Netzwerk bietet er jungen Künstlern wie Bruno Peinado und Tobias Bernstrup nicht nur Ausstellungsfläche in zwei Räumen, sondern auch eine fundierte Vertretung auf internationalen Märkten. Dafür wurde die Galerie vom katalanischen Galeristenverband ausgezeichnet.

Un local classique de 240 m² de la Carrer d'Enric Granados a été aménagé en une galerie moderne par Miguel Ángel Sánchez. Sa faculté à dénicher de jeunes talents et son réseau très développé permettent à de jeunes artistes tels que Bruno Peinado et Tobias Bernstrup de bénéficier de surfaces d'exposition ainsi que d'une représentation établie sur les marchés internationaux. À cet effet, la galerie s'est d'ailleurs vue remettre un prix par l'association catalane des galeries d'art.

Miguel Ángel Sánchez instaló una moderna galería sobre los 240 m² de un local clásico de la Carrer d'Enric Granados. Dotado de olfato para el talento joven y de una amplia red de contactos, ofrece a jóvenes artistas como Bruno Peinado y Tobias Bernstrup no solo espacio de exposición en sus dos salas, sino también experimentada representación en el mercado internacional. Por esta labor, la galería ha merecido un premio de la asociación catalana de galeristas.

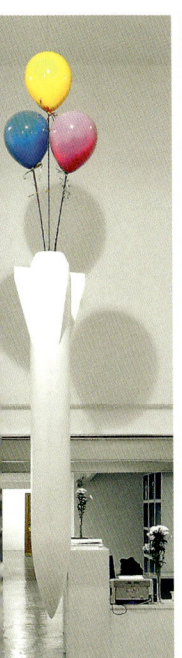 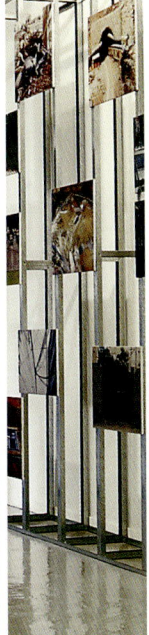 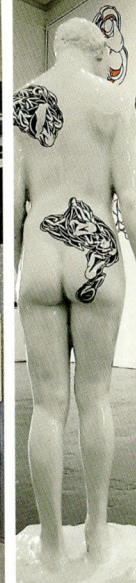 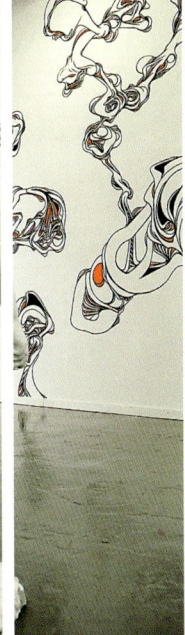

ADN GALERÍA

Carrer d'Enric Granados, 49 // Eixample
Tel.: +34 93 451 00 64
www.adngaleria.com

Tue–Sat 11 am to 2 pm, 5 pm to 8 pm
Mon on appointment
Metro L6, L7 Provença

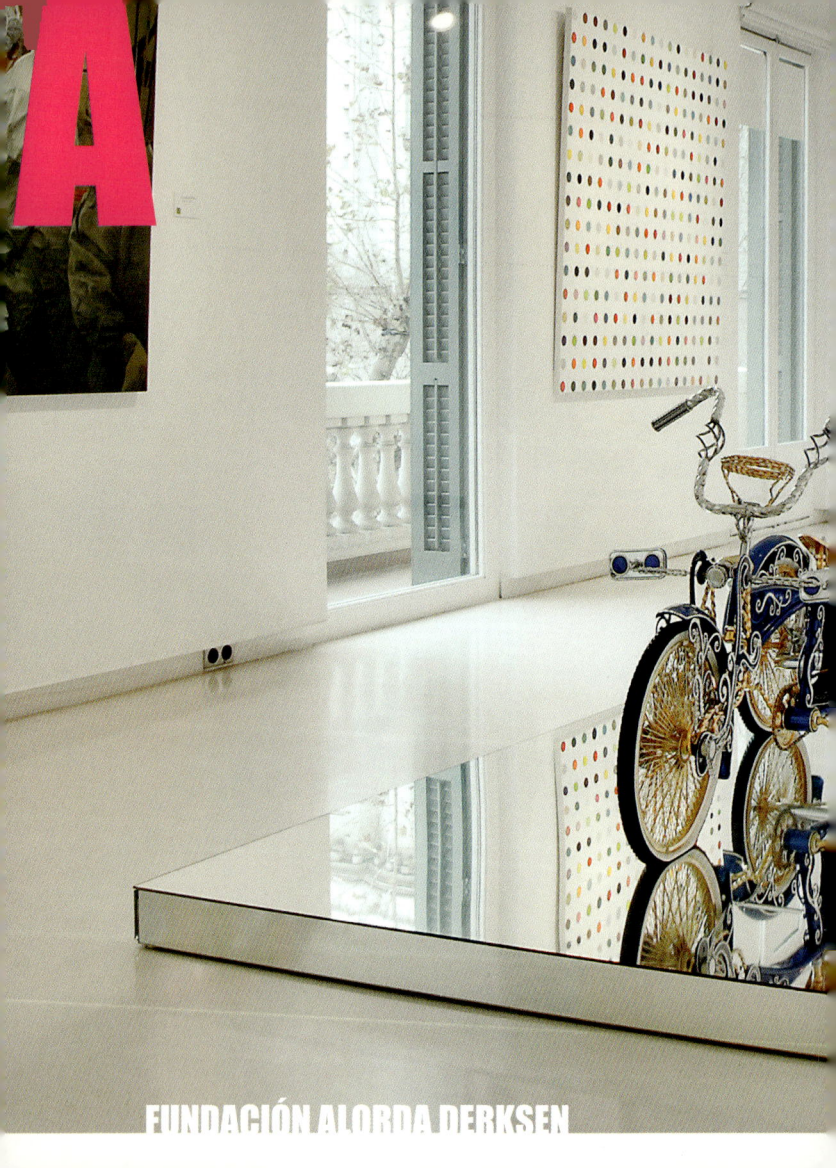

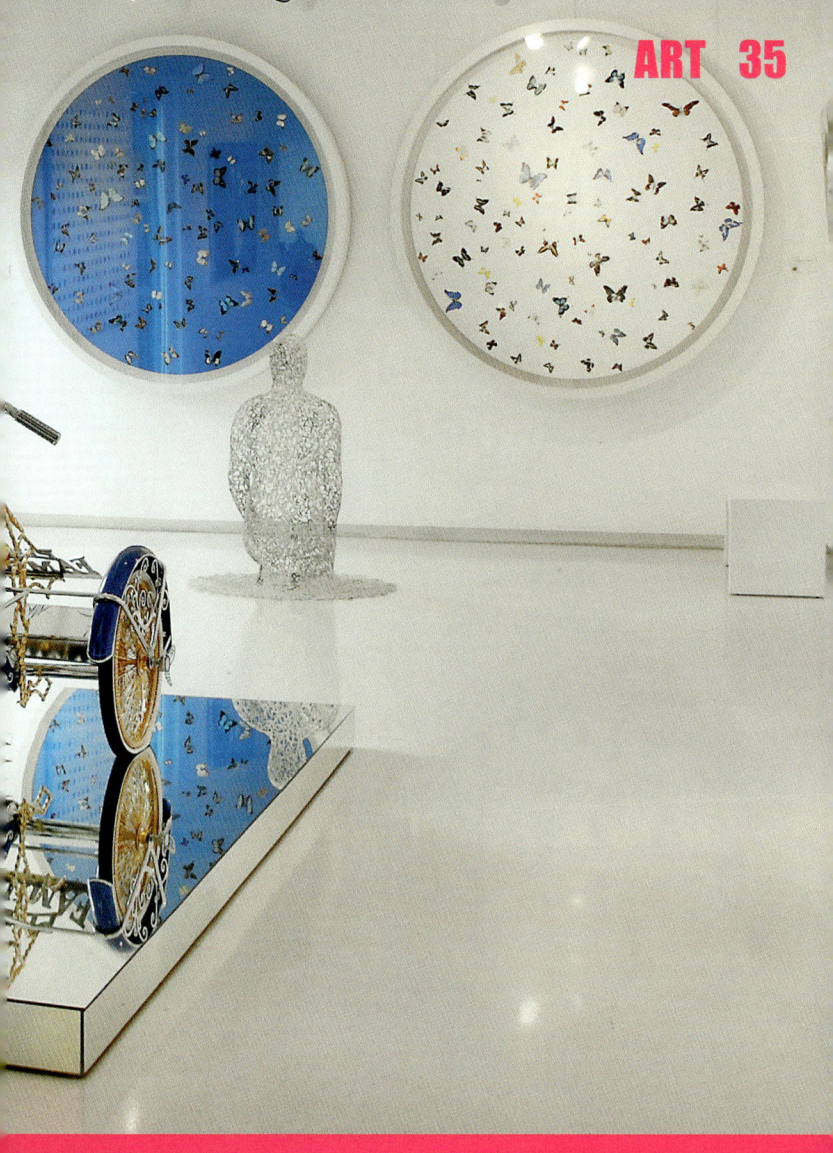

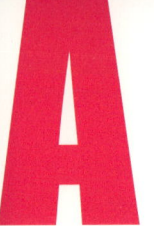

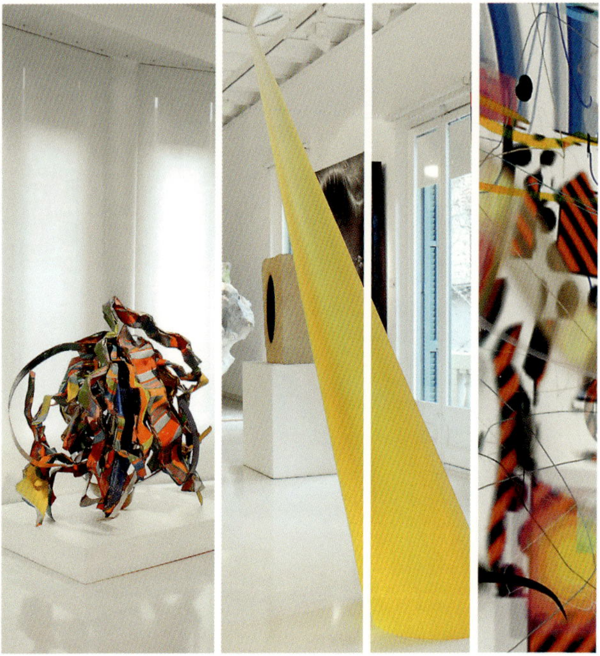

**FUNDACIÓN
ALORDA DERKSEN**

Carrer d'Aragó, 314 // Eixample
Tel.: +34 93 272 62 50
www.fundacionad.com

on appointment
Metro L4 Girona

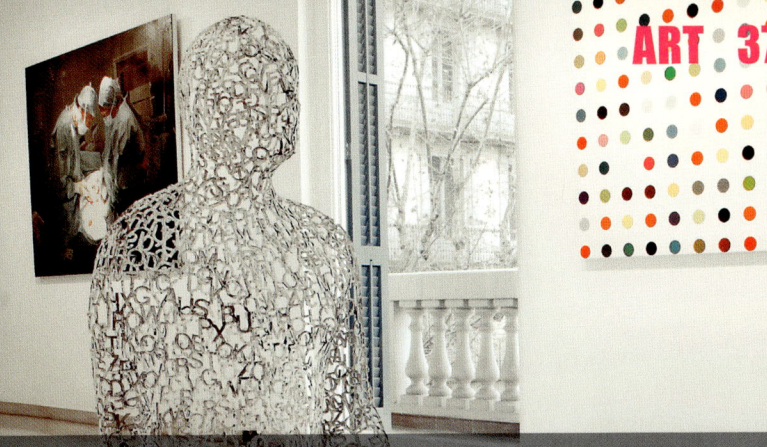

Manuel Alorda and Hanneke Derksen have been collectors for over 40 years: first Old Master paintings, now modern art. In an effort to share their enthusiasm for the avant-garde with the public, they established a foundation which has given Barcelona a new point of reference for contemporary art. Creations of young British artists, such as the brilliant but controversial Damien Hirst or Tracey Emin, engage in an exciting dialog with works by Anish Kapoor, Tom Friedman, and Anselm Kiefer.

Manuel Alorda und Hanneke Derksen sammeln seit über 40 Jahren: zunächst alte Meister, heute moderne Kunst. Ihre Begeisterung für die Avantgarde möchten sie mit anderen teilen und so entstand ihre Stiftung, die der Stadt Barcelona eine neue Referenz für zeitgenössische Kunst beschert. Schöpfungen junger britischer Künstler, der YBAs, wie des brillanten, nicht unumstrittenen Damien Hirst oder Tracey Emins, gehen mit Werken von Anish Kapoor, Tom Friedman oder Anselm Kiefer spannende Dialoge ein.

Depuis plus de 40 ans, Manuel Alorda et Hanneke Derksen collectionnent : des Maîtres d'autrefois avant et des objets d'art moderne maintenant. Leur enthousiasme pour les formes avant-gardistes les a conduit à créer leur fondation, qui dote Barcelone d'une nouvelle référence en art contemporain. Des créations de jeunes artistes britanniques, comme le génial et controversé Damien Hirst, ou Tracey Emin, se mélangent à des œuvres d'Anish Kapoor, Tom Friedman ou Anselm Kiefer.

Manuel Alorda y Hanneke Derksen son coleccionistas desde hace más de 40 años: en un primer momento pintura antigua, hoy arte moderno. Deseosos de compartir con otros su pasión por la vanguardia crearon una fundación propia, nueva referencia en Barcelona en lo tocante a arte contemporáneo. La obra de jóvenes artistas británicos como los polémicos Damien Hirst y Tracey Emin entablan un electrizante diálogo con las creaciones de Anish Kapoor, Tom Friedman o Anselm Kiefer.

MANUEL
+HANNE

Armed with an intuitive sense of aesthetics and acute business acumen, Catalonian Manuel Alorda founded Kettal in 1964. The company's innovative outdoor designer furniture became a worldwide success. Alorda not only recruited the best design talent to create trend-setting new furniture, but he and his wife Hanneke Derksen, originally from Holland, also expanded their art collection into what it is now. It all started the day after their wedding when they bought their first painting. "Art is addictive," he says. "It gives you a different view of the world." For the last several years, he has been devoting his entire time to art. With their foundation, which is co-administered by their daughter Laura, Alorda and Derksen aim to close a gap in Barcelona and show international contemporary art that is little seen elsewhere. International connoisseurs and galleries help them with the selection. With its focus on quality and selectiveness, this gallery is a treasure.

Mit einem sicheren Gespür für Ästhetik und einem ausgeprägten Geschäftssinn gründete der Katalane Manuel Alorda 1964 das Unternehmen Kettal, dessen innovative Designermöbel von Katalonien aus Terrassen und Gärten weltweit eroberten. Er rekrutierte jedoch nicht nur die besten Designtalente für wegweisende Entwürfe neuen Mobiliars, sondern erweiterte seit den 1960er Jahren kontinuierlich seine heute bedeutende Kunstsammlung, für die er mit seiner Frau, der Holländerin Hanneke Derksen, den Grundstock schon einen Tag nach ihrer Hochzeit legte, als sie ihr erstes Bild erwarben. „Kunst macht süchtig", sagt er, „sie gibt dir eine andere Sicht auf die Welt." Seit wenigen Jahren widmet er sich nun ausschließlich der Kunst. Mit der Einrichtung ihrer Stiftung, in der auch Tochter Laura aktiv ist, will das Paar Alorda-Derksen in Barcelona eine Lücke schließen und internationale zeitgenössische Kunst zeigen, die sonst wenig präsent ist. Bei der Auswahl der Werke stehen ihnen internationale Kenner und Galerien beratend zur Seite. Höchste Qualität und Selektivität machen die Galerie zu einem Kleinod.

ALORDA
KE DERKSEN

Doté d'un sens aigu pour l'esthétique et d'un sens prononcé des affaires, le catalan Manuel Alorda fonda en 1964 l'entreprise Kettal dont les meubles au design innovant envahissent les terrasses et jardins du monde entier. Il recruta les designers les plus talentueux pour concevoir un mobilier novateur et depuis les années 60, il ne cesse d'agrandir son importante collection d'art qu'il commença à constituer avec son épouse hollandaise, Hanneke Derksen, le lendemain de leur mariage, en acquérant leur premier tableau. « L'art rend accro », déclare-t-il, « il apporte un regard différent sur le monde. » Depuis quelques années seulement, il se consacre exclusivement à l'art. Avec la création de leur fondation, à laquelle leur fille Laura apporte aussi sa participation active, le couple Alorda-Derksen veut combler un vide à Barcelone et exposer de l'art contemporain international, sinon si peu représenté. Des connaisseurs internationaux et des galeries les assistent lors de la sélection des œuvres. Qualité et sélectivité sont les maîtres mots de cette galerie qui est un véritable petit bijou.

Armado con un ojo infalible para la estética y un fino sentido empresarial, el catalán Manuel Alorda puso en marcha en 1964 la empresa Kettal, cuyos innovadores muebles de diseño han conquistado las terrazas y jardines de todo el mundo. Alorda, sin embargo, no se limitó a reclutar a los mejores diseñadores con los que continuar su labor pionera en la creación de muebles, sino que desde la década de 1960 ha ido ampliando constantemente su considerable colección de arte, cuyos cimientos plantó junto con su mujer, la holandesa Hanneke Derksen, con la compra del primer cuadro al día siguiente de casarse. "El arte es adictivo", señala, "te ofrece otra visión del mundo". Desde hace pocos años se dedica en exclusiva al arte. Con la creación de su fundación, en la que también participa su hija Laura, la pareja Alorda-Derksen quiere cubrir un hueco existente en Barcelona y exponer arte contemporáneo internacional que de otro modo no encontraría eco en la ciudad. Para la selección de las obras cuenta con el asesoramiento de expertos y galerías internacionales. La extrema calidad y selectividad de su criterio hacen de la galería una verdadera joya.

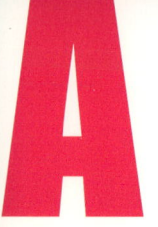

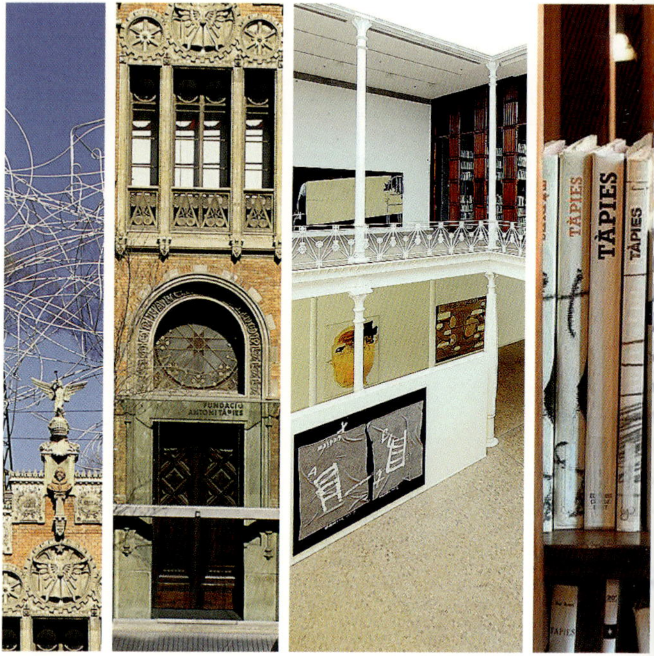

FUNDACIÓ ANTONI TÀPIES

Carrer d'Aragó, 255 // Eixample
Tel.: +34 93 487 03 15
www.fundaciotapies.org

Tue–Sun 10 am to 7 pm
Metro L2, L3, L4 Passeig de Gràcia

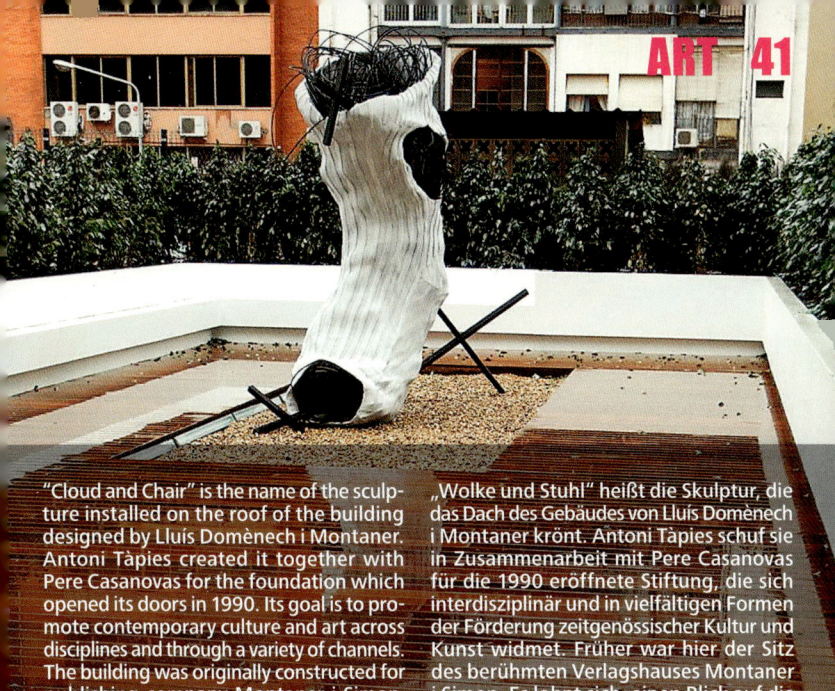

"Cloud and Chair" is the name of the sculpture installed on the roof of the building designed by Lluís Domènech i Montaner. Antoni Tàpies created it together with Pere Casanovas for the foundation which opened its doors in 1990. Its goal is to promote contemporary culture and art across disciplines and through a variety of channels. The building was originally constructed for publishing company Montaner i Simon. Don't miss the extensive library housed in historical shelves.

„Wolke und Stuhl" heißt die Skulptur, die das Dach des Gebäudes von Lluís Domènech i Montaner krönt. Antoni Tàpies schuf sie in Zusammenarbeit mit Pere Casanovas für die 1990 eröffnete Stiftung, die sich interdisziplinär und in vielfältigen Formen der Förderung zeitgenössischer Kultur und Kunst widmet. Früher war hier der Sitz des berühmten Verlagshauses Montaner i Simon. Es lohnt sich, einen Blick auf die umfassende Bibliothek in den historischen Regalen zu werfen.

La sculpture qui trône sur le toit du bâtiment conçu par Lluís Domènech i Montaner se nomme « nuage et chaise ». Elle fut créée par Antoni Tàpies et Pere Casanovas pour la fondation, qui a vu le jour en 1990 et qui a pour but de promouvoir la culture et l'art contemporains à l'aide de différentes formes et disciplines. C'est là que se trouvait autrefois la célèbre maison d'édition Montaner i Simon. La vaste collection de livres sur les étagères originales vaut le détour.

"Nube y silla" es el título de la escultura que corona el edificio de Lluís Domènech i Montaner. Antoni Tàpies la creó en colaboración con Pere Casanovas para la fundación inaugurada en 1990 y dedicada de manera interdisciplinar a la promoción del arte y la cultura contemporáneos en todas sus manifestaciones. El edificio albergó en otro tiempo las oficinas de la famosa editorial Montaner i Simon. Vale la pena echar un vistazo a la extensa biblioteca reunida en los históricos aparadores.

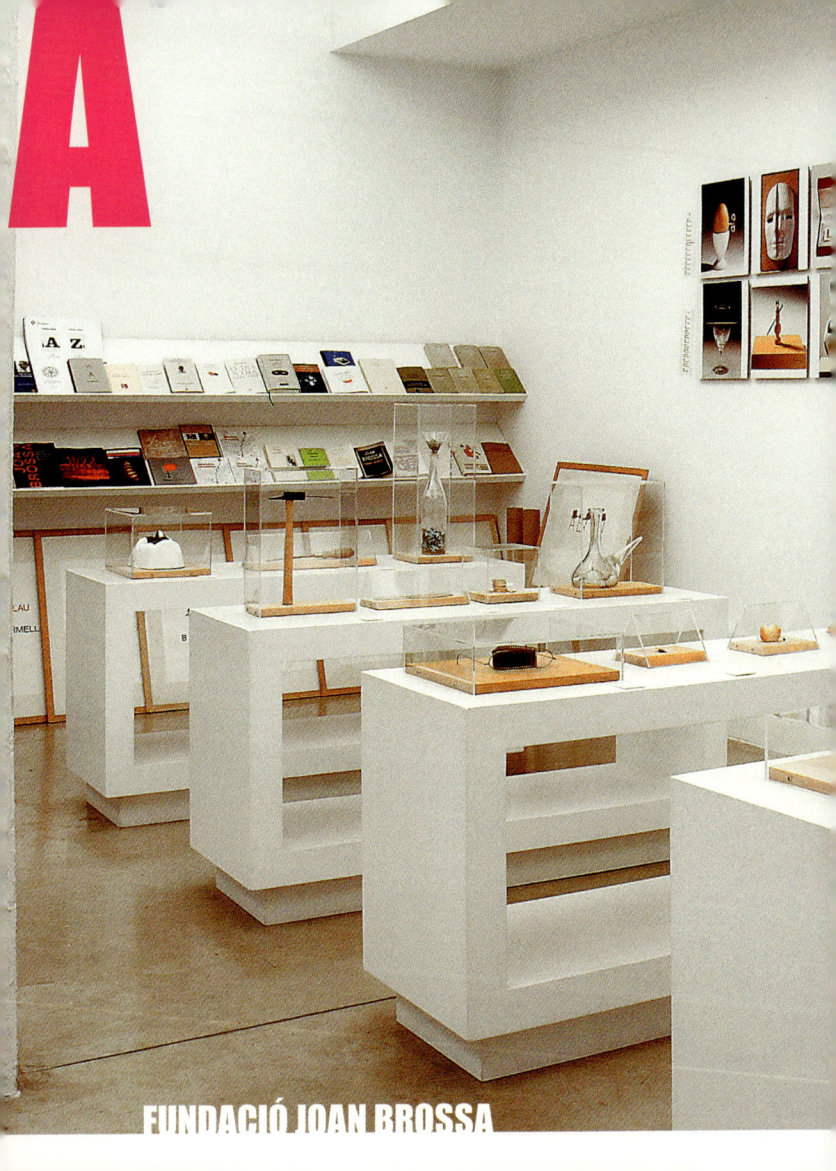

FUNDACIÓ JOAN BROSSA

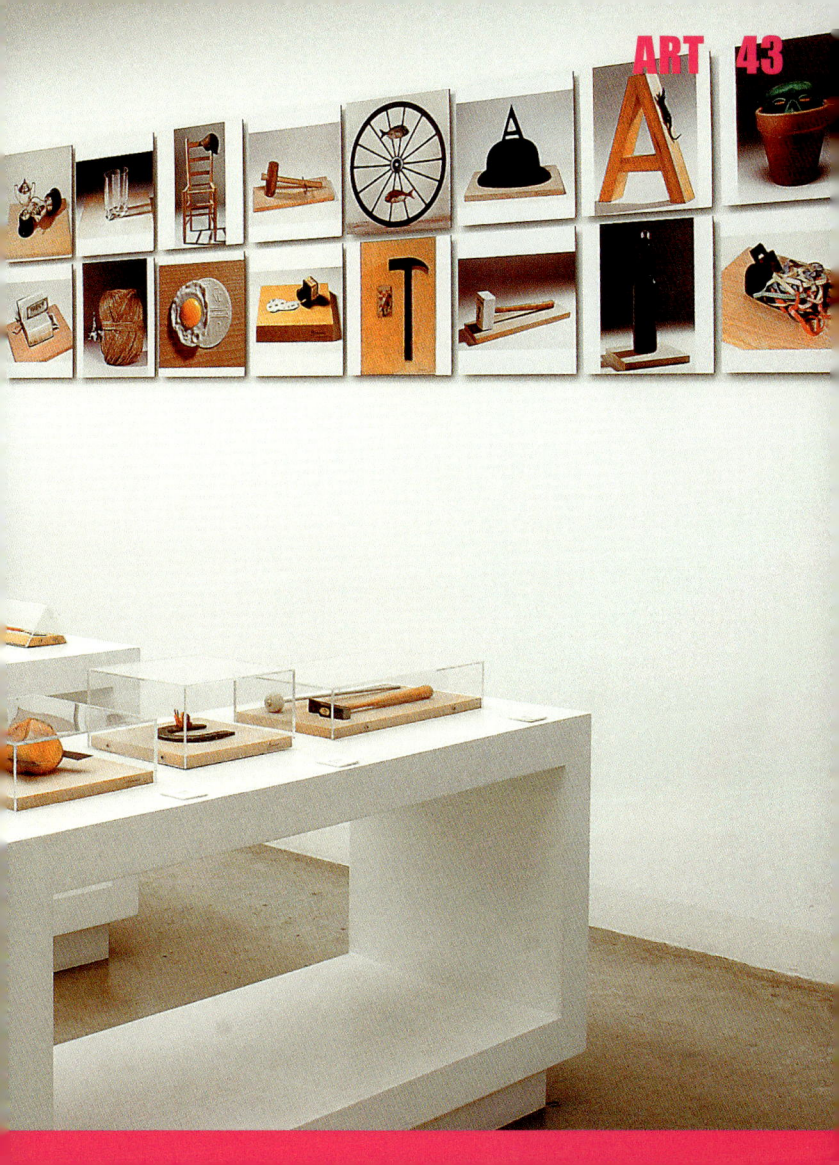

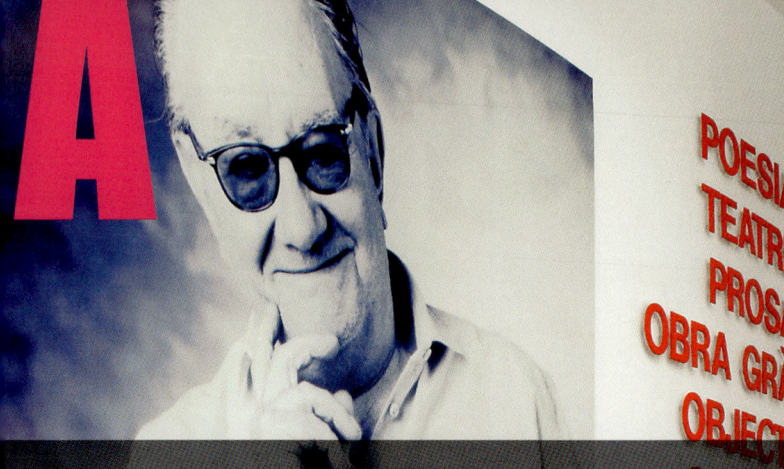

POESIA
TEATRE
PROSA
OBRA GRÀFICA
OBJECTES

In addition to poems, prose, stage and screenplays, Catalan poet Joan Brossa i Cuervo (1919–1998) also created a number of object poems, visual poems, posters, and installations over the course of his long career. In 2006, architect Albert Llorens created a space to showcase Brossa's creative output. Its restrained design is dominated by the color white and polished concrete. Audiovisual materials (films, interviews, …) complement the changing exhibitions.

Neben Gedichten, Prosa, Theaterstücken und Drehbüchern schuf der katalanische Poet Joan Brossa i Cuervo (1919–1998) im Laufe seines Lebens auch eine Vielzahl von Objektgedichten, visuellen Gedichten, Plakaten und Installationen. Der Architekt Albert Llorens hat 2006 mit einem zurück-haltenden Entwurf, in dem Weiß und polierter Beton vorherrschen, Räume für die Präsentation des Gesamtwerks Brossas gestaltet. Audiovisuelles Material ergänzt die wechselnden Ausstellungen.

Au cours de sa vie, le poète catalan Joan Brossa i Cuervo (1919–1998) n'a pas seulement composé des poèmes, de la prose, des pièces de théâtre et des scénarios de cinéma, mais aussi un grand nombre de poèmes-objets, poèmes visuels, affiches et installations. En 2006, l'architecte Albert Llorens a conçu un espace sobre où le blanc et le béton poli dominent, afin d'exposer l'œuvre complète de Brossa. Du matériel audiovisuel (films, interviews, …) permet de compléter les expositions temporaires.

Además de poemas, prosa, obras de teatro y guiones cinematográficos, el poeta catalán Joan Brossa i Cuervo (1919–1998) creó a lo largo de su vida gran cantidad de poemas escultura, poemas visuales, carteles e instalaciones. El arquitecto Albert Llorens concibió en 2006 un espacio para la presentación de la obra completa de Brossa, con un diseño comedido, en el que dominan el blanco y el hormigón pulido. Las exposiciones se completan con material audiovisual (películas, entrevistas…).

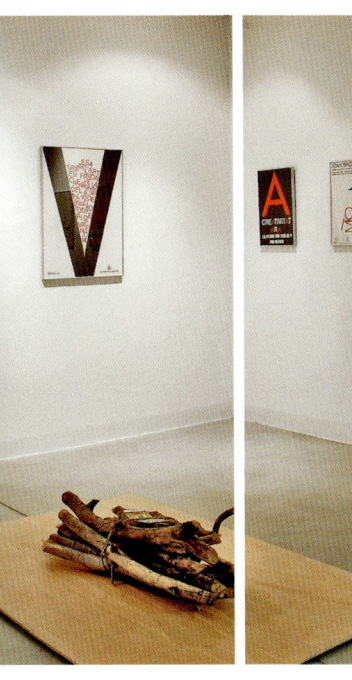
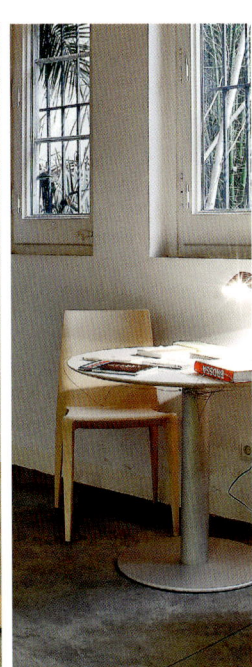

FUNDACIÓ JOAN BROSSA

Carrer de Provença, 318 // Eixample
Tel.: +34 93 467 69 52
www.fundaciojoanbrossa.cat

Tue–Fri 4 pm to 8 pm
Metro L1, L2 Universitat
L3, L5, L6, L7 Diagonal

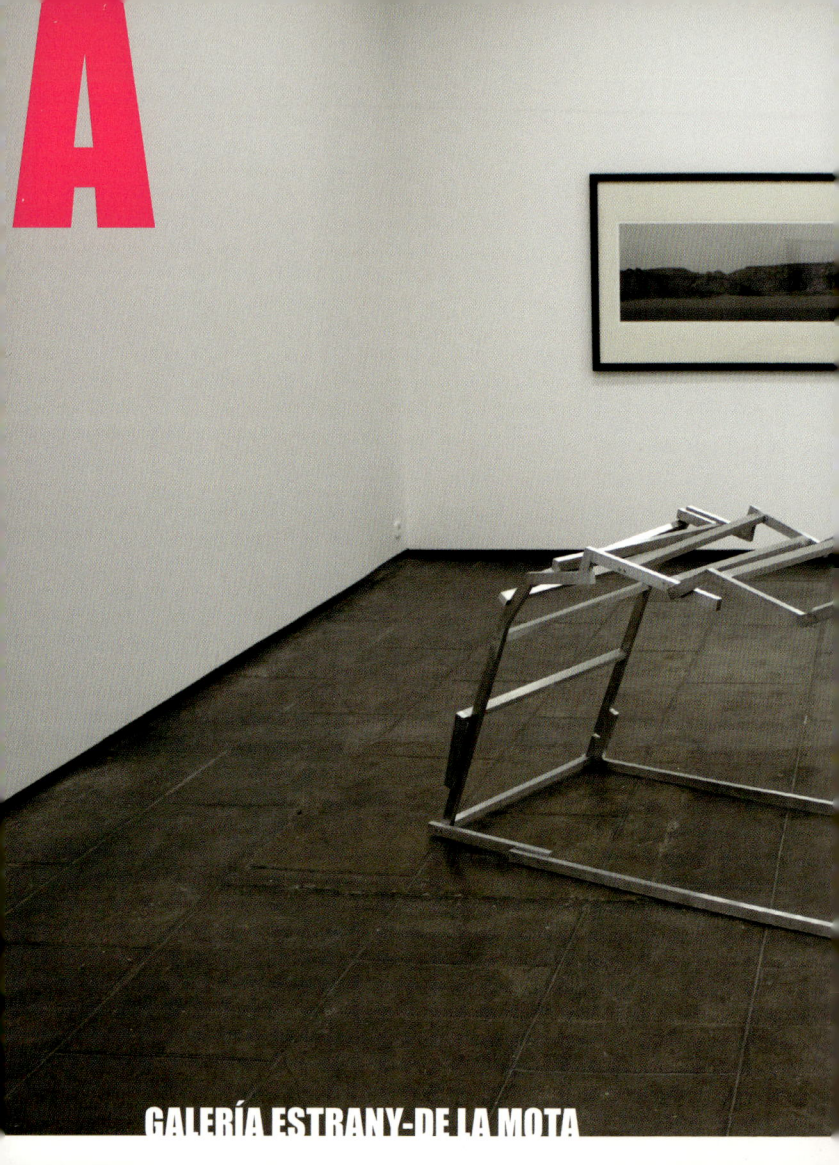

A

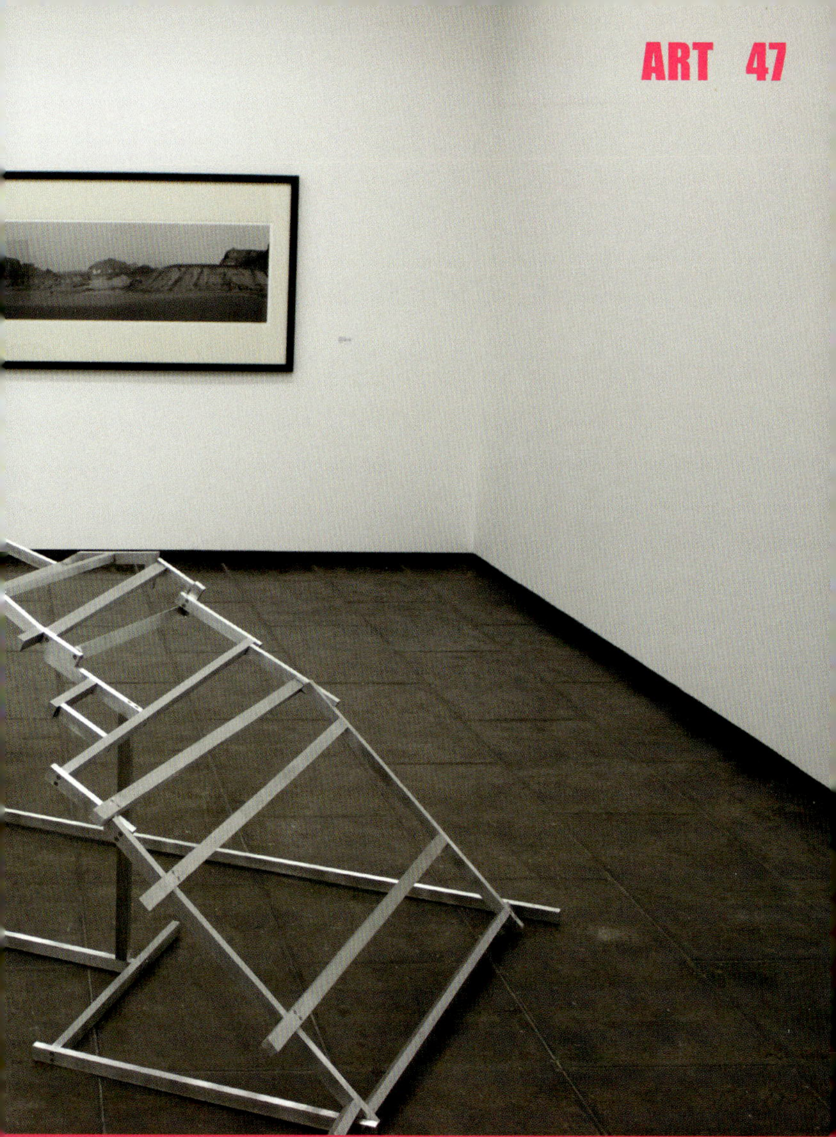

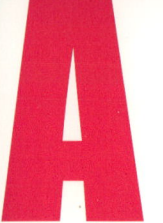

A

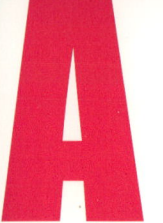

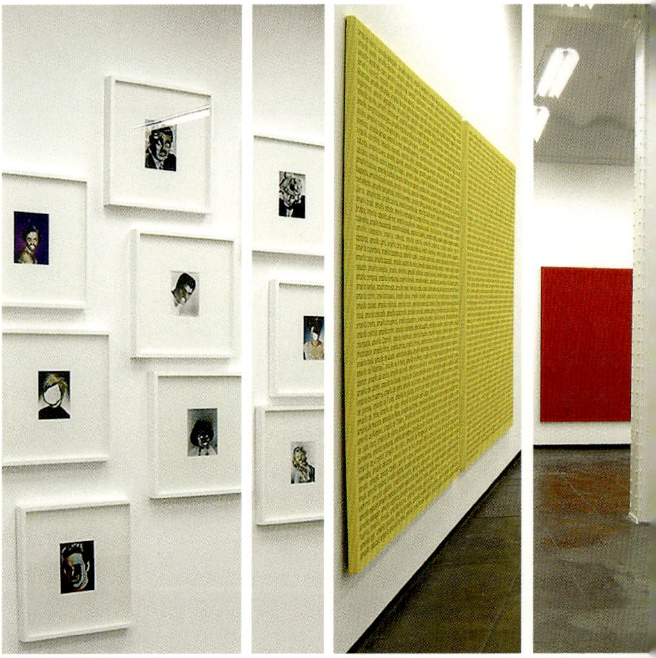

GALERÍA ESTRANY-DE LA MOTA

Passatge de Mercader, 18 // Eixample
Tel.: +34 93 215 70 51
www.estranydelamota.com

Tue–Sat 10.30 am to 1.30 pm
4.30 pm to 8.30 pm
Metro L6, L7 Provença

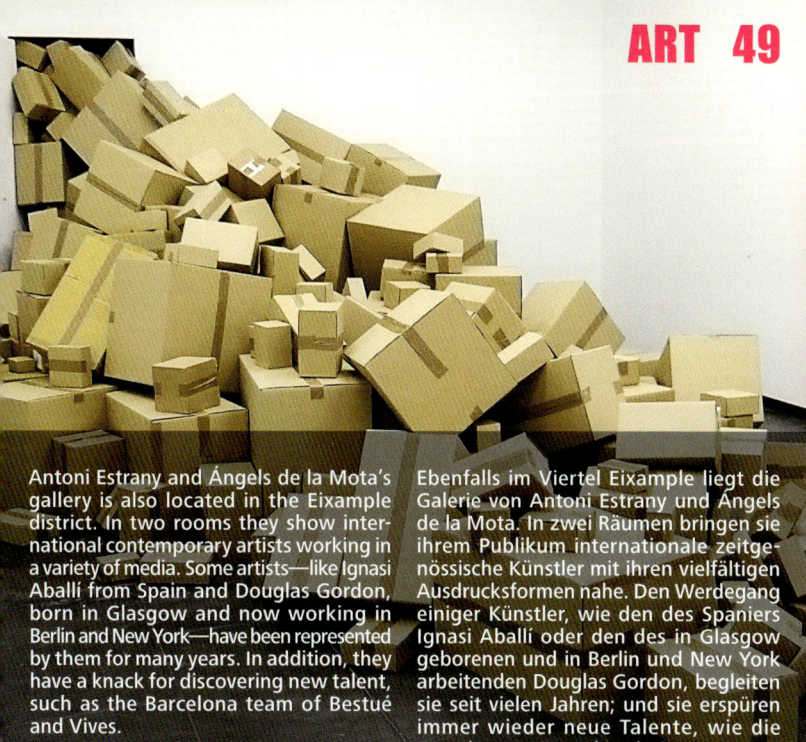

Antoni Estrany and Ángels de la Mota's gallery is also located in the Eixample district. In two rooms they show international contemporary artists working in a variety of media. Some artists—like Ignasi Aballí from Spain and Douglas Gordon, born in Glasgow and now working in Berlin and New York—have been represented by them for many years. In addition, they have a knack for discovering new talent, such as the Barcelona team of Bestué and Vives.

Ebenfalls im Viertel Eixample liegt die Galerie von Antoni Estrany und Ángels de la Mota. In zwei Räumen bringen sie ihrem Publikum internationale zeitgenössische Künstler mit ihren vielfältigen Ausdrucksformen nahe. Den Werdegang einiger Künstler, wie den des Spaniers Ignasi Aballí oder den des in Glasgow geborenen und in Berlin und New York arbeitenden Douglas Gordon, begleiten sie seit vielen Jahren; und sie erspüren immer wieder neue Talente, wie die Barceloneser Bestué und Vives.

La galerie d'Antoni Estrany et Ángels de la Mota se trouve dans le quartier de l'Eixample, où deux salles proposent au public des artistes internationaux contemporains et leurs nombreuses formes d'expression. Depuis de nombreuses années, ils accompagnent la carrière de certains artistes comme Ignasi Aballí ou Douglas Gordon, né à Glasgow et travaillant à Berlin et New York. Ce qui ne les empêche pas de continuer à dénicher de nouveaux talents tels que les Barcelonais Bestué et Vives.

También en el Eixample se encuentra la galería de Antoni Estrany y Ángels de la Mota. En sus dos salas exponen ante su público a artistas contemporáneos internacionales en sus múltiples formas de expresión. Han acompañado el devenir profesional de varios artistas, entre ellos el español Ignasi Aballí y el escocés residente en Berlín y Nueva York Douglas Gordon; y andan siempre a la búsqueda de nuevos talentos, como los barceloneses Bestué y Vives.

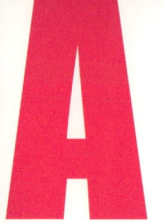

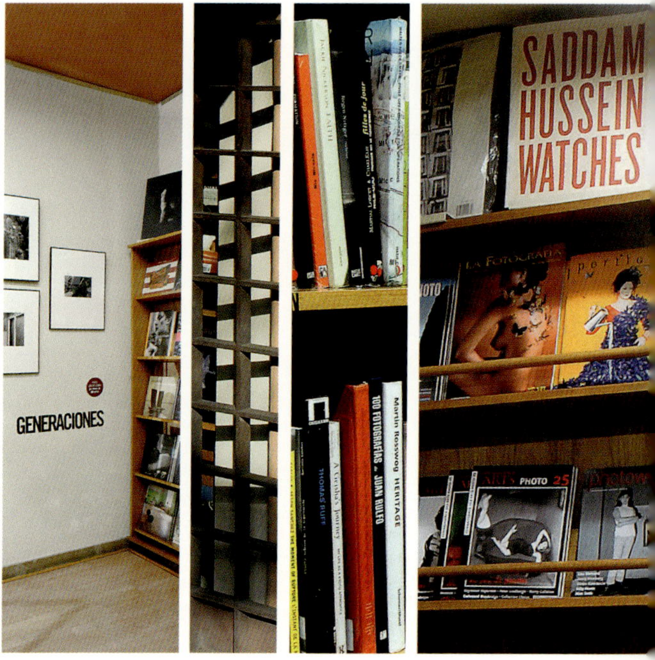

KOWASA GALLERY

Carrer de Mallorca, 235 // Eixample
Tel.: +34 93 215 80 58
www.kowasa.com

Tue–Sat 5 pm to 8.30 pm
Metro L6, L7 Provença

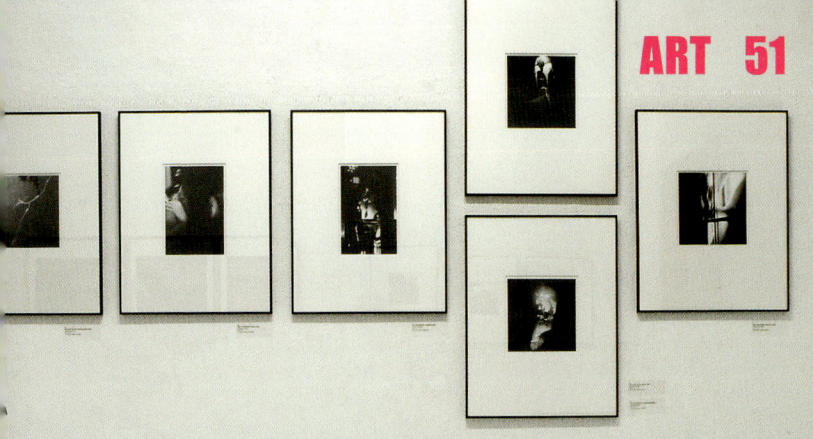

A paradise for photography lovers: two floors of photographic art. Kowasa Gallery is a Barcelona institution, and their concept is unique in Spain. Since 1997, they have been showing historical, modern, classic, and contemporary photographs by international and Spanish artists, some of them represented exclusively by them. The adjoining bookstore with its charming atmosphere has a catalog of over 10,000 titles. Could there possibly be a photographer that isn't included?

Ein Paradies für Liebhaber der Fotografie: Fotokunst auf zwei Etagen – das Konzept der Kowasa Galerie, einer Institution in Barcelona, ist einzigartig in Spanien. Seit 1997 präsentiert sie historische, moderne, klassische und zeitgenössische Fotografien internationaler und spanischer Künstler, einige darunter exklusiv. Der angeschlossene charmante Buchladen hat über 10 000 Bände in seinem Katalog, sodass man sich die Frage stellen mag, welcher Fotograf eigentlich nicht vertreten ist.

Voici un paradis des amateurs de photographie, où celles-ci s'étalent sur deux étages. Le concept de la galerie Kowasa, une institution de Barcelone, est unique en Espagne. Depuis 1997, elle présente des photographies historiques, modernes, classiques et contemporaines d'artistes internationaux et espagnols, dont certains en exclusivité. La charmante librairie attenante possède plus de 10 000 titres. On en vient à se demander s'il existe un photographe qui n'y soit pas référencé.

Un paraíso para los amantes de la fotografía: el concepto de la galería Kowasa, toda una institución en Barcelona –dos plantas dedicadas a la fotografía como arte–, es único en España. Desde 1997 expone fotografías históricas, modernas, clásicas y contemporáneas de artistas españoles e internacionales, algunas de ellas en exclusiva. La encantadora librería contigua cuenta con más de 10 000 volúmenes en su catálogo. Puede uno preguntarse: ¿hay alguien que no esté aquí representado?

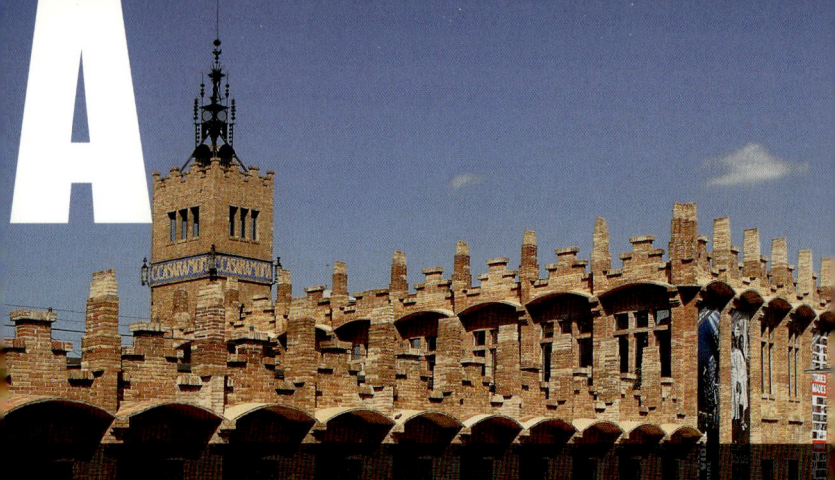

This cultural and social center in a former textile factory designed by Josep Puig i Cadafalch offers a dynamic and trendsetting program. As part of the renovations, Arata Isozaki, Francisco Javier Asarta, Roberto Luna, and Robert Brufau moved the entrance of the Modernisme building to a modern lobby on the lower level. Don't miss the temporary exhibitions on contemporary art, the multi-facetted events, and the exceptional media library.

Dynamisch und richtungsweisend ist das Programm des soziokulturellen Zentrum in der ehemaligen Textilfabrik von Josep Puig i Cadafalch. Arata Isozaki, Francisco Javier Asarta, Roberto Luna und Robert Brufau verlegten den Eingang des Modernisme-Gebäudes im Rahmen der Renovierung in eine moderne Halle im Untergeschoss. Die temporären Ausstellungen zu zeitgenössischer Kunst, die vielfältigen Veranstaltungen und die erstklassig bestückte Mediathek sollte man nicht versäumen.

Le programme de ce centre socioculturel installé dans l'ancienne usine textile conçue par Josep Puig i Cadafalch est dynamique et varié. Dans le cadre de la rénovation de ce bâtiment issu du Modernisme, Arata Isozaki, Francisco Javier Asarta, Roberto Luna et Robert Brufau ont déplacé l'entrée au sous-sol, dans un grand hall moderne. Les expositions temporaires d'art contemporain, les nombreuses manifestations ainsi que la médiathèque richement dotée sont à voir.

El programa del centro social y cultural en la antigua fábrica textil de Josep Puig i Cadafalch es a un tiempo dinámico y pionero. Arata Isozaki, Francisco Javier Asarta, Roberto Luna y Robert Brufau trasladaron la entrada del edificio modernista a una moderna sala en el sótano durante el proceso de renovación. Las exposiciones de arte contemporáneo, los numerosos eventos y la mediateca, excelentemente dotada, son algo que nadie debería perderse.

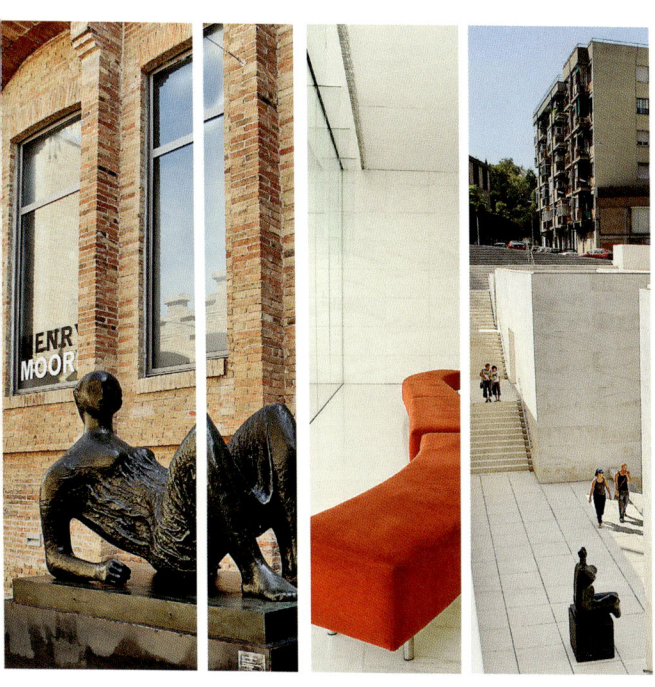

CAIXAFORUM BARCELONA

Avinguda de Francesc Ferrer i Guàrdia, 6-8
Sants-Montjuïc
Tel.: +34 93 476 86 00
www.fundacio.lacaixa.es

Mon–Sun 10 am to 8 pm, Sat 10 am to 10 pm
Closed Dec 25th, Jan 1st and 6th
Metro L1, L3, L8 Espanya

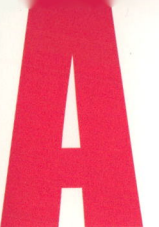

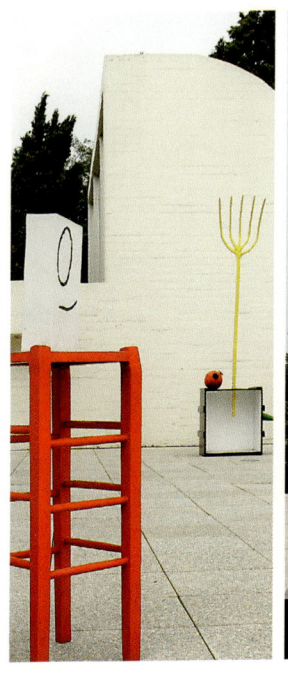

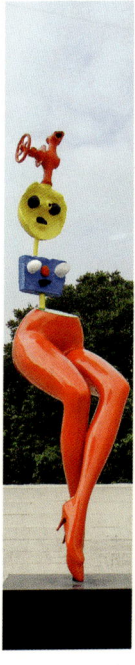

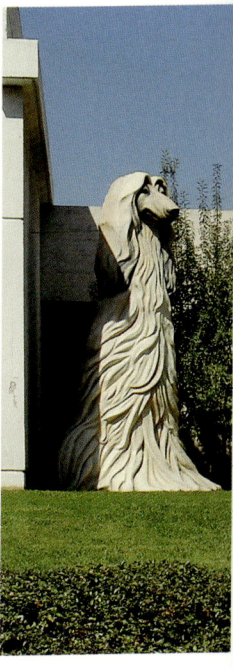

FUNDACIÓ JOAN MIRÓ

Parc de Montjuïc // Sants-Montjuïc
Tel.: +34 93 443 94 70
www.fundaciomiro-bcn.org

Thu 10 am to 9.30 pm
Sun and holidays 10 am to 2.30 pm
Oct–Jun Tue–Sat 10 am to 7 pm
Jul–Sep Tue–Sat 10 am to 8 pm

Railway Funicular de Montjuïc
(from Metro station Paral·lel)
Bus 50, 55, 193 Parc de Montjuïc

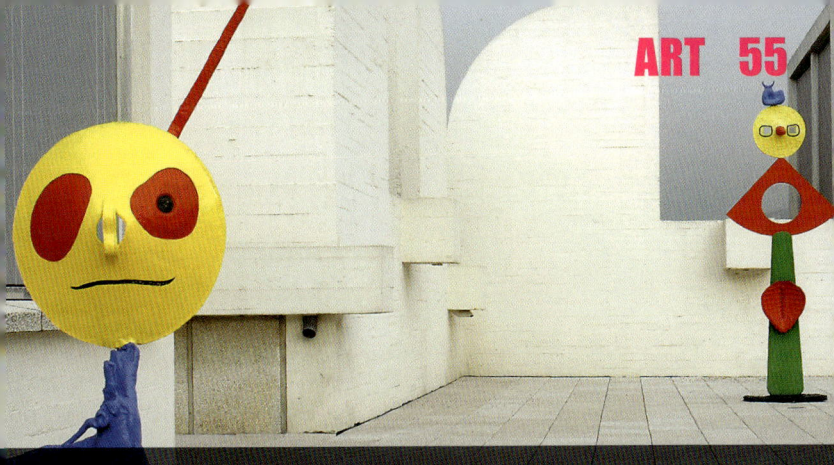

When the Miró Foundation opened its doors in 1975 on Mount Montjuïc, Barcelona was still in the middle of its cultural Sleeping Beauty slumber. The Josep Lluís Sert-designed exhibition hall whose proportions are based on Le Corbusier's Modulor caused a tremendous stir. Together with its gardens and terraces, the Foundation houses Miró's collection of 10,000 pieces from 70 years of work, donated by the artist himself. "Espai 13" is a forum for young contemporary artists.

Als die Miró-Stiftung auf dem Montjuïc 1975 ihre Tore öffnete, lag die Stadt noch in einem kulturellen Dornröschenschlaf. Umso größeres Aufsehen erregte die Ausstellungshalle von Josep Lluís Sert, deren Proportionen auf dem Modulor von Le Corbusier basieren. Zusammen mit Garten und Terrassen bildet die Stiftung den Rahmen für die vom Künstler gestiftete Sammlung mit rund 10 000 Werken aus 70 Schaffensjahren. Das Espai 13 bildet ein Forum für junge zeitgenössische Künstler.

Lorsque la fondation Miró a vu le jour en 1975 sur le Montjuïc, la ville était culturellement parlant encore en sommeil. La salle d'exposition de Josep Lluís Sert et ses proportions basées sur le modulor de Le Corbusier fit alors d'autant plus sensation. La fondation, avec ses jardins et terrasses, sert de cadre à une collection d'environ 10 000 œuvres offertes par des artistes, issues de 70 années différentes. « L'Espai 13 » est un forum pour jeunes artistes contemporains.

Cuando en 1975 la fundación Miró abrió sus puertas en Montjuïc, la ciudad vivía todavía sumida en un letargo cultural, lo que explica el revuelo causado por la sala de exposiciones de Josep Lluís Sert, cuyas proporciones se basan en las del Modulor de Le Corbusier. Junto con el jardín y las terrazas, la fundación acoge el legado del artista, compuesto por cerca de 10 000 obras creadas durante 70 años de carrera. El "Espai 13" ofrece un fórum para jóvenes artistas contemporáneos.

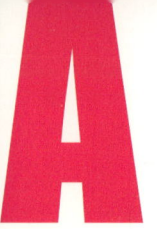
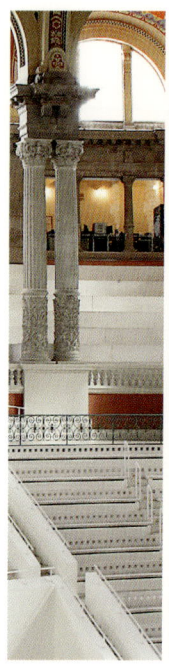
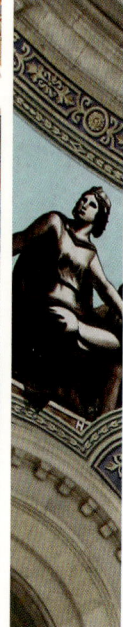
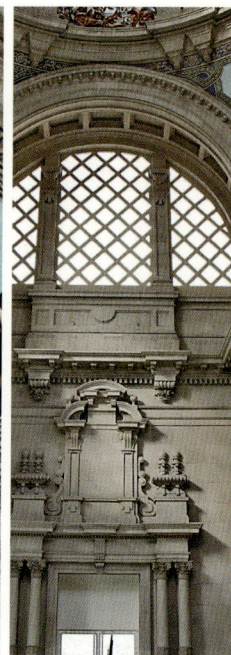
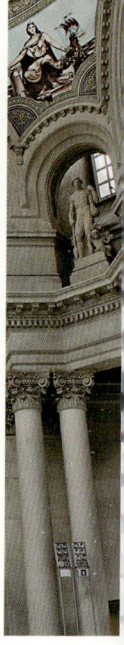

MUSEU NACIONAL D'ART DE CATALUNYA (MNAC)

Palau Nacional, Parc de Montjuïc
Sants-Montjuïc
Tel.: +34 93 622 03 76
www.mnac.cat

Tue–Sat 10 am to 7 pm
Sun and holidays 10 am to 2.30 pm
Closed Jan 1st, May 1st, and

December 25th, free entrance
1st Sun of each month

Metro L1, L3, L8 Espanya
Bus 13 Av. Marquès de Comillas-Poble
Espanyol or 50 Av. de l'Estadi-Piscines
Picornell or 55 Museu MNAC-Museu
Etnològic

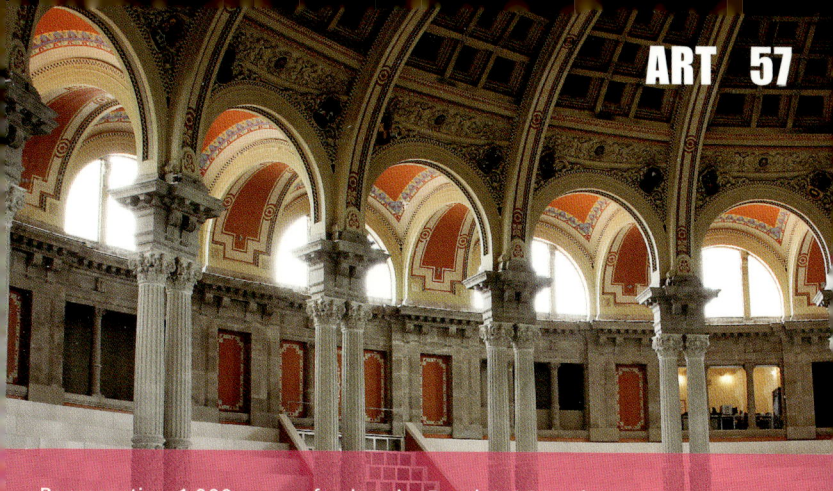

Representing 1,000 years of cultural history, the MNAC's enormous collection encompasses all forms of art, including furniture design, numismatics, and photography. The Palau Nacional, built for the 1929 International Exhibition on Mount Montjuïc above Plaça Espanya, houses works from masters as diverse as El Greco and Velázquez or Dalí and Picasso. MNAC's collection of Roman art with its murals is one of the most significant in the world.

Rund 1 000 Jahre Kunstgeschichte präsentiert das MNAC mit seiner riesigen Sammlung, zu der alle Kunstformen gehören, einschließlich Möbeldesign, Numismatik und auch die Fotografie. Werke von El Greco und Velázquez, aber auch Dalí und Picasso sind unter dem Dach des Weltausstellungspalastes von 1929 auf dem Montjuïc oberhalb der Plaça Espanya vereint. Die Sammlung romanischer Kunst mit ihren Wandmalereien gehört zu den bedeutendsten der Welt.

Le MNAC présente près d'un millénaire d'histoire de l'art grâce à sa gigantesque collection où toutes les formes d'art sont représentées, parmi lesquelles le mobilier d'artiste, la numismatique et la photographie. Des œuvres d'El Greco, Velázquez, Dalí et Picasso sont ainsi réunies sous le toit du palais de l'exposition universelle de 1929 surplombant la Plaça Espanya. La collection d'art roman et ses peintures murales compte parmi les plus importantes au monde.

La inmensa colección del MNAC recoge cerca de mil años de historia del arte: en ella tienen cabida todas las manifestaciones artísticas, incluido el diseño de muebles, la numismática y la fotografía. En Montjuïc, dominando la Plaça España, el palacio de la Exposición Universal de 1929 alberga obras de El Greco, Velázquez, Dalí, Picasso. La colección de arte románico -incluidos sus murales- se cuenta entre las más importantes del mundo.

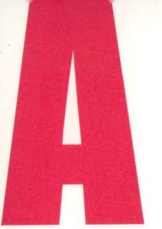

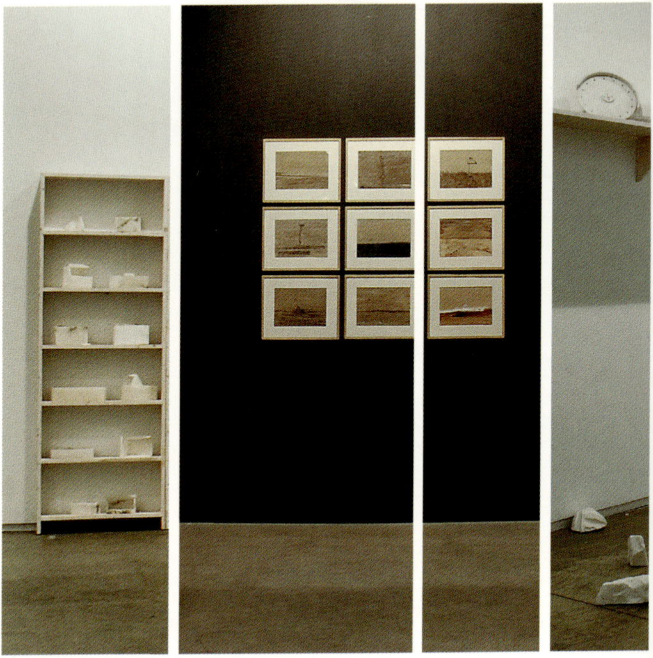

GALERÍA ALEJANDRO SALES

Carrer de Julián Romea, 16 // Sarrià-Sant Gervasi
Tel.: +34 93 415 20 54
www.alejandrosales.com

Tue–Sat 11 am to 2 pm, 5 pm to 8 pm
Jul–Sep Sat closed, Aug closed
Metro L3, L5, L6, L7 Diagonal

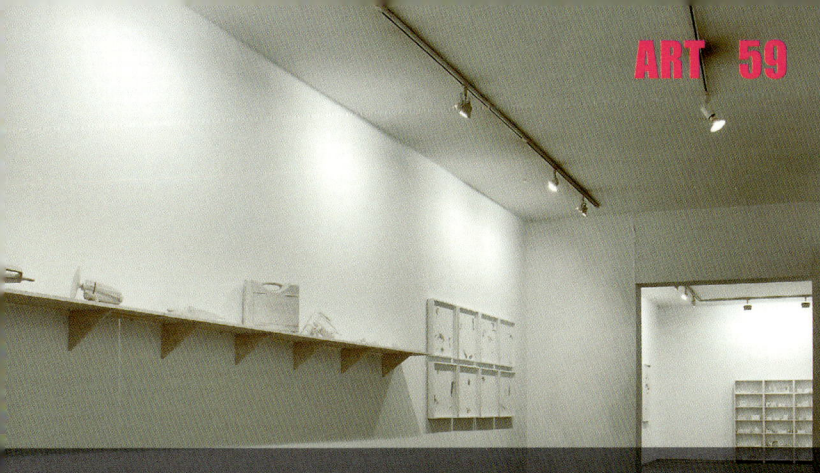

Since opening the gallery in 1985, Alejandro Sales has been presenting art at international fairs and co-organizing events such as ARCO (Madrid) and Art Chicago. After moving to a new location almost 20 years ago, he created BACKSPACE, a forum for alternative art, managed by Stefania Bortolami. In 1997, Sales added BLACKSPACE whose independent program is dedicated to showcasing internationally renowned artists whose work has rarely been exhibited in Barcelona.

Seit der Gründung der Galerie 1985 präsentiert Alejandro Sales Kunst auf internationalen Messen und gestaltete Veranstaltungen wie die ARCO und die Art Chicago mit. Nach dem Umzug in neue Räume vor knapp 20 Jahren organisierte er, mit Stefania Bortolami als Leiterin, zunächst BACKSPACE für Kunst der alternativen Szene. Seit 1997 widmet sich der Bereich BLACKSPACE mit einem unabhängigen Programm international bekannten Künstlern, die in Barcelona bisher wenig gezeigt wurden.

Depuis la fondation de la galerie en 1985, Alejandro Sales expose dans les salons du monde entier et participe à des manifestations telles que ARCO (à Madrid) ou Art Chicago. Après avoir investi de nouveaux locaux il y a tout juste 20 ans, il a d'abord ouvert l'espace BACKSPACE, dédié à la scène alternative sous la direction de Stefania Bortolami. Depuis 1997, l'espace BLACKSPACE se consacre à des artistes renommés du monde entier jusqu'à présent peu exposés à Barcelone.

Desde que en 1985 fundó la galería, Alejandro Sales presenta arte en ferias internacionales y eventos tales como ARCO (Madrid) y Art Chicago. Tras el traslado a un nuevo local hace ahora casi 20 años, organizó (con la ayuda de Stefania Bortolami como directora) BACKSPACE para las artes alternativas. Desde 1997, el programa independiente del espacio BLACKSPACE está consagrado a artistas de renombre internacional que apenas han expuesto todavía en Barcelona.

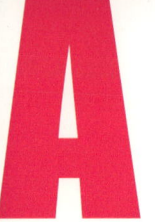

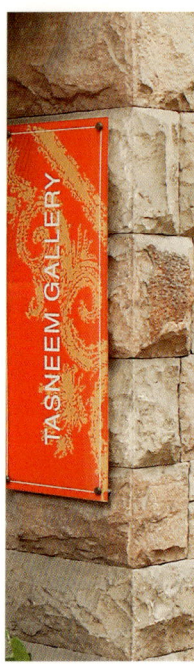

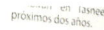

orn in 1971, is a graduate of the Art Academy
idro, Havana, Cuba. During the 80's he
the group Art Street. His work has been
nany important institutions and art events
Angeles County Museum of Art (LACMA), in
ul Biennial, at the National Museum of Fine
, in the Samuel Dorsky Museum of Art, New
useum of Modern Art (MAM), Mexico, D.F, in
f Fine Arts in Buenos Aires, Argentina, at the
ntemporary Art MARCO), Monterrey, Mexico
veral branches of the Institut fur
hungen (IFA), Germany. He has participated
ogrammes of various editions of the Havana

...nan en Tasneer
próximos dos años.

Ernesto Leal nació en 1971, e
Arte San Alejandro, La Haba
perteneció al grupo Arte Cal
en importantes institucione
County Museum of Art (LAC
el Museo Nacional de Bellas
Dorsky Museum of Art, Ne
Moderno (MAM), Mexico, D.
Buenos Aires, Argentina, el M
(MARCO), Monterrey, Mexic
Auslandsbeziehungen (IFA), /
programa colateral de varia
Habana.

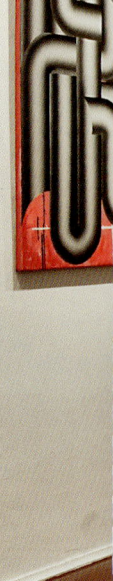

TASNEEM GALLERY

Carrer de Castellnou, 51 // Sarrià-Sant Gervasi
Tel.: +34 93 252 35 78
www.tasneemgallery.com

Tue–Fri 10 am to 2 pm, 4 pm to 8 pm
Sat 10 am to 2 pm

Metro L6 Les Tres Torres

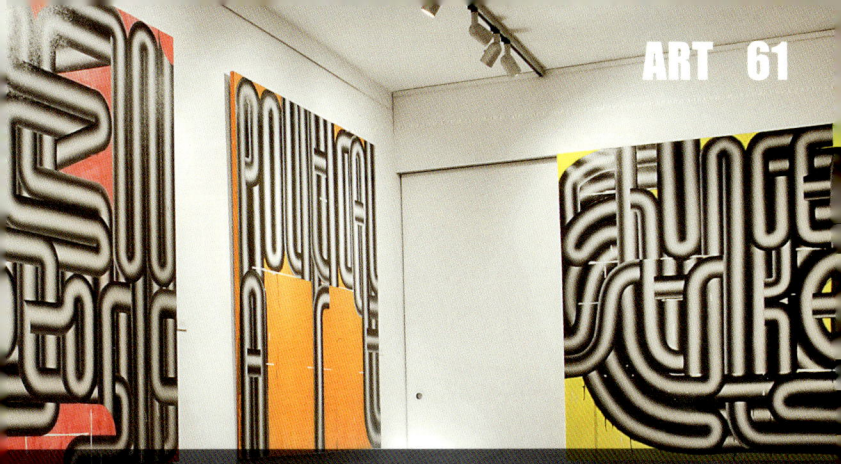

The team around Tasneem Salam, born in Bangladesh and raised in London, is as international as the emerging and established artists represented by the gallery. This includes sculptor Margarita Checa from Peru, Luis Gómez from Cuba, Htein Lin from Burma, Yoichi Tanabe from Japan, and Pape Seydi Samba from Senegal. The gallery provides consulting services for collectors and focuses on building long-term relationships in order to support artists throughout their careers.

Das Team um die in Bangladesch geborene und in London aufgewachsene Tasneem Salam ist so international wie die von der Galerie vertretenen Newcomer und etablierten Künstler. Dazu gehören unter anderem die Bildhauerin Margarita Checa aus Peru, der Kubaner Luis Gómez, Htein Lin aus Burma, der Japaner Yoichi Tanabe oder Pape Seydi Samba aus dem Senegal. Die Galerie berät Sammler und legt Wert auf langfristige Beziehungen, um die Karriereentwicklung der Künstler kontinuierlich zu begleiten.

L'équipe de Tasneem Salam, née au Bangladesh et ayant grandi à Londres, est aussi hétéroclite que la troupe d'artistes établis ou non qui sont exposés dans la galerie. On compte parmi eux la sculptrice péruvienne Margarita Checa, le Cubain Luis Gómez, le Birman Htein Lin, le Japonais Yoichi Tanabe et le Sénégalais Pape Seydi Samba. La galerie offre ses conseils aux collectionneurs et prise des relations durables avec les artistes afin d'accompagner au mieux leur carrière.

El equipo de Tasneem Salam, nacida en Bangladesh y criada en Londres, es tan internacional como los artistas, establecidos o emergentes, que representa su galería. Entre ellos se encuentran la escultura peruana Margarita Checa, el cubano Luis Gómez, Htein Lin de Birmania, el japonés Yoichi Tanabe y Pape Seydi Samba de Senegal. La galería asesora a coleccionistas y apuesta por relaciones a largo plazo para apoyar a los artistas en la evolución de sus carreras.

ARCHIT

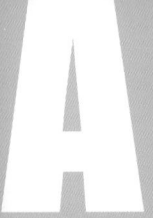

A

Ildefons Cerdà was the engineer who in the mid-1800s created the extension of Barcelona that became the Eixample district. His visionary design based on a grid pattern is still lauded today, showcasing the Modernista buildings of architects such as Antoni Gaudí, Josep Puig i Cadafalch, and Lluís Domènech i Montaner to great effect. A century after the height of Modernisme, it is the expressive contemporary architecture of talented local firms and star architects like Richard Meier, Jean Nouvel, or Toyo Ito that focus international attention on Barcelona. Visitors are captivated not only by large-scale projects that transform entire neighborhoods, like La Vila Olímpica or Diagonal Mar, but especially by myriad smaller renovation and construction projects, such as the Can Ricart sports complex by vora arquitectura, the Can Framis Museum by Studio BAAS, and the noise protection panels at the Gran Via by Enric Miralles and Benedetta Tagliabue.

Ildefons Cerdà hieß der Ingenieur, der Mitte des 19. Jahrhunderts die dringend notwendige Stadterweiterung Eixample plante. Sein visionärer Entwurf eines gleichmäßigen Straßenrasters bewährt sich bis heute und bringt die Jugendstilpaläste von Baumeistern wie Antoni Gaudí, Josep Puig i Cadafalch oder Lluís Domènech i Montaner hervorragend zur Geltung. Hundert Jahre nach der Blüte des Modernisme ist es die ausdrucksstarke zeitgenössische Architektur talentierter ortsansässiger Büros und von Stararchitekten wie Richard Meier, Jean Nouvel oder Toyo Ito, die Barcelona ins internationale Rampenlicht rücken. Dabei sind es nicht nur Großprojekte, die ganze Stadtviertel wie La Vila Olímpica oder Diagonal Mar neu entstehen lassen, sondern gerade eine Vielzahl kleinerer Um- und Neubauten, die das Auge fesseln. Hierfür stehen beispielsweise die Sportanlage Can Ricart von vora arquitectura, das Museum Can Framis vom Studio BAAS oder auch die Lärmschutzpaneele an der Gran Via von Enric Miralles und Benedetta Tagliabue.

Ildefons Cerdà est l'ingénieur qui conçut le quartier de l'Eixample, extension nécessaire de la ville au milieu du XIXᵉ siècle. Son projet visionnaire consistant en un quadrillage régulier de rues a résisté au temps et met en valeur les palais Art nouveau d'architectes comme Antoni Gaudí, Josep Puig i Cadafalch ou Lluís Domènech i Montaner. Cent ans après l'éclosion du modernisme, c'est l'architecture contemporaine très expressive de talentueux bureaux d'architecture locaux et d'architectes renommés comme Richard Meier, Jean Nouvel ou Toyo Ito qui a donné une notoriété internationale à Barcelone. Ce ne sont pas que des grands projets, des quartiers entiers comme La Vila Olímpica ou Diagonal Mar, mais aussi une multitude de restructurations et nouvelles constructions moins colossales qui attirent le regard. Le complexe sportif Can Ricart de vora arquitectura, le musée Can Framis du Studio BAAS ou le mur antibruit de la Gran Via d'Enric Miralles et Benedetta Tagliabue en sont des exemples.

Ildefons Cerdà fue el ingeniero que a mediados del siglo XIX planificó la urgente expansión urbana del Eixample. El visionario diseño de su entramado callejero de líneas regulares se conservó y su vigencia realza el atractivo de los palacetes modernistas de maestros como Antoni Gaudí, Josep Puig i Cadafalch o Lluís Domènech i Montaner. Cien años tras la eclosión del Modernismo, la expresiva arquitectura contemporánea de los audaces despachos locales y de arquitectos estrella como Richard Meier, Jean Nouvel o Toyo Ito han devuelto Barcelona a la primera línea internacional. Y no son sólo los grandes proyectos, como la Vila Olímpica o Diagonal Mar, sino precisamente las pequeñas construcciones o reconstrucciones las que concentran las miradas. A este respecto cabe destacar el pabellón deportivo Can Ricart de vora arquitectura; el museo Can Framis de Studio BAAS; e incluso los paneles de protección sonora de la Gran Via, obra de Enric Miralles y Benedetta Tagliabue.

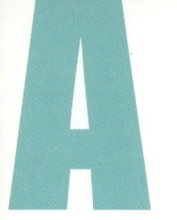

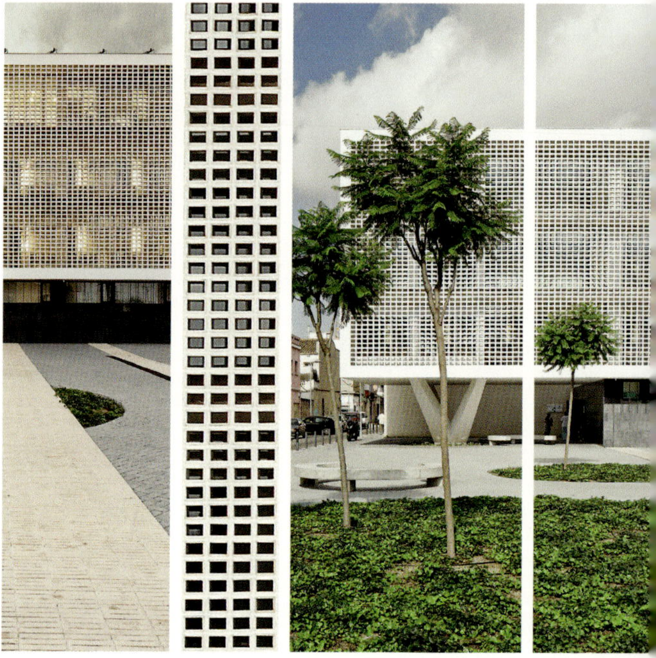

CAP PROGRÉS RAVAL DE BADALONA

Carrer del General Weyler, 44 // Badalona
www.jordibadia.com/es/equipamientos/cap-progres-
raval-badalona

Metro L2, L10 Gorg

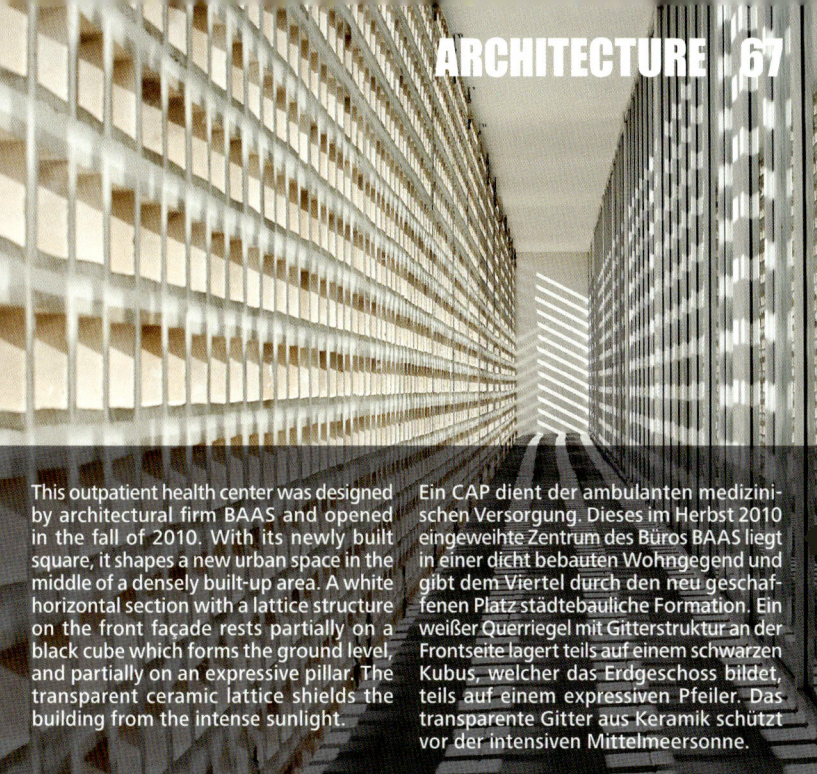

This outpatient health center was designed by architectural firm BAAS and opened in the fall of 2010. With its newly built square, it shapes a new urban space in the middle of a densely built-up area. A white horizontal section with a lattice structure on the front façade rests partially on a black cube which forms the ground level, and partially on an expressive pillar. The transparent ceramic lattice shields the building from the intense sunlight.

Ein CAP dient der ambulanten medizinischen Versorgung. Dieses im Herbst 2010 eingeweihte Zentrum des Büros BAAS liegt in einer dicht bebauten Wohngegend und gibt dem Viertel durch den neu geschaffenen Platz städtebauliche Formation. Ein weißer Querriegel mit Gitterstruktur an der Frontseite lagert teils auf einem schwarzen Kubus, welcher das Erdgeschoss bildet, teils auf einem expressiven Pfeiler. Das transparente Gitter aus Keramik schützt vor der intensiven Mittelmeersonne.

Un CAP est un centre d'assistance médicale. Celui-ci, réalisé par le bureau d'architectes BAAS, a été inauguré à l'automne 2010 et se trouve dans un quartier d'habitation auquel la création de la place a apporté un aspect plus urbain. Ce rectangle blanc à structure réticulaire sur l'avant repose sur un cube noir, qui forme le rez-de-chaussée, et sur un pilier décoratif. Le quadrillage transparent, en céramique, permet de protéger de la forte lumière du soleil.

Las siglas CAP corresponden a "Centro de Asistencia Primaria": el diseño del despacho BAAS, inaugurado en otoño de 2010, se encuentra en una zona muy poblada y el espacio que ha abierto ha modificado el urbanismo del barrio. Un bloque blanco alargado de estructura reticular sobre la fachada se sustenta sobre un cubo negro que alberga la planta baja y un pilar ramificado. La rejilla transparente de cerámica protege el interior del exceso de sol meridional.

ENRIC RUIZ-GE

With a background in theater, Enric Ruiz-Geli is a performer, loves spontaneity, and also creates stage designs and ephemeral projects. His installation "El bosque sonoro" contains an homage to composer John Cage, and for the musical "Gaudí" he cooperated with Franc Fernandez on the stage design. His buildings are imbued with a sense of weightlessness. Villa Bio seems to be on the verge of lifting off, while part of the skin of Villa Nurbs, made of state-of-the-art ETFE plastic, appears to float, especially at night. He also used ETFE to great effect in the bioclimatic façade of Media-TIC in Barcelona—an impressive building not only because of its minimal steel construction but also because of its high cost efficiency. His intent is to go beyond sustainable "green" architecture. He wants to create spaces where nature and people can meet, an architecture of empathy. To achieve this, he constantly encourages his team at Cloud9 to be daring and innovative: "Moving mountains is on our agenda every week."

Enric Ruiz-Geli kommt vom Theater, er ist ein Performer, liebt Spontaneität und realisiert auch Bühnenbilder und ephemere Projekte. Beispielsweise intonierte er in dem Stück „El bosque sonoro" eine Hommage an John Cage am Klavier und für das Musical „Gaudí" gestalte er die Bühne zusammen mit Franc Fernandez. Wenn er baut, dann drücken seine Entwürfe Leichtigkeit aus. Die Villa Bio scheint sich wie im Sprung vom Boden abzulösen, während ein Teil der Hülle der Villa Nurbs besonders am Abend zu schweben scheint, denn sie wurde bereits in dem zukunftsträchtigen Kunststoff ETFE ausgeführt. Dieses Material setzt Enric Ruiz-Geli auch in der bioklimatisch aktiven Fassade des Media-TIC in Barcelona in raffinierter Weise ein; ein Gebäude, das zugleich durch seine minimale Stahlkonstruktion und große Kosteneffizienz besticht. Sein Ziel geht über nachhaltige, grüne Architektur hinaus. Er will Räume schaffen, in denen sich Natur und Mensch begegnen, eine Art Architektur der Empathie. Dazu treibt er sein Team Cloud9 beständig zu Wagemut und Innovationen an: „Berge zu versetzen, steht jede Woche auf unserem Programm."

LI

Enric Ruiz-Geli est issu du théâtre, c'est un performer qui aime la spontanéité et réalise aussi des décors de théâtre et projets éphémères. Dans le morceau « El bosque sonoro », il entonna par exemple un hommage à John Cage au piano et conçut par ailleurs la scène de la comédie musicale « Gaudí » avec Franc Fernandez. Ses constructions expriment la légèreté. La Villa Bio a l'air de surgir du sol alors qu'une partie de l'enveloppe de la Villa Nurbs semble flotter, surtout le soir, car elle a été réalisée dans un matériau synthétique (ETFE) porteur d'avenir. Enric Ruiz-Geli a aussi intégré élégamment ce matériau à la façade bioclimatique active du Media-TIC à Barcelone ; un bâtiment qui séduit par sa construction en acier au style minimaliste et son efficacité en termes de coût. Son objectif dépasse l'architecture durable et écologique. Il veut créer des espaces où la nature et l'homme se rencontrent, une sorte d'architecture de l'empathie. Pour ce faire, il ne cesse d'inciter son équipe Cloud9 à avoir de l'audace et innover : « Déplacer des montagnes constitue le programme de chaque semaine. »

Enric Ruiz-Geli es un hombre de teatro, un intérprete amante de la espontaneidad y autor además de escenografías y proyectos efímeros. Así, por ejemplo, en la pieza "El bosque sonoro" insertó un homenaje a John Cage al piano y, junto con Franc Fernández fue el responsable de los escenarios del musical "Gaudí". Cuando construye, sus diseños expresan liviandad. La Villa Bio parece dar un brinco y alejarse del suelo, mientras que parte de la cubierta de la Villa Nurbs parece flotar, especialmente por las tardes, ya que ha sido construida con el futurista plástico ETFE. Enric Ruiz-Geli empleó también este material de manera sutil en la fachada bioclimática de la Media-TIC de Barcelona, un edificio que destaca tanto por su minimalista construcción en acero como por su alta eficiencia de costes. Su objetivo va más allá de la arquitectura verde y sostenible. Quiere crear espacios de encuentro entre el ser humano y la naturaleza, una especie de arquitectura de la empatía. Para ello anima siempre a sus colaboradores de Team Cloud9 a innovar y probar cosas nuevas: "Cada semana nos proponemos mover montañas".

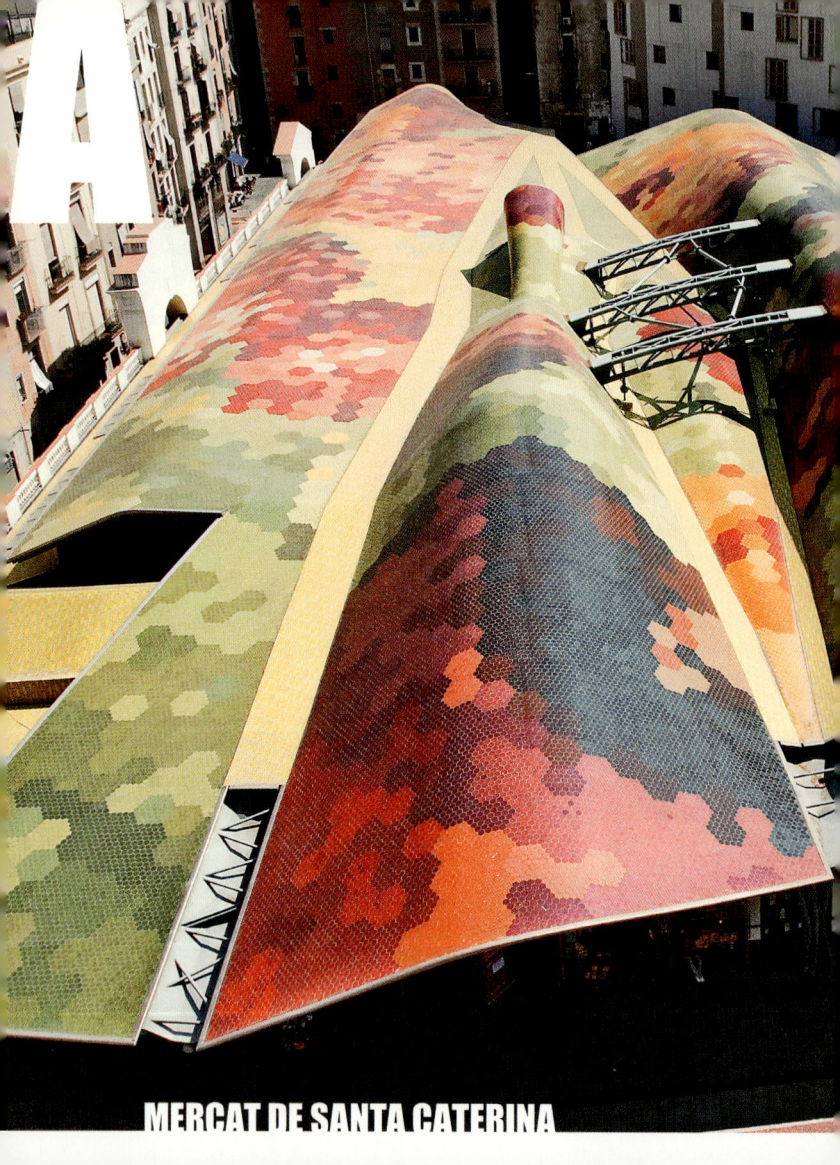

MERCAT DE SANTA CATERINA

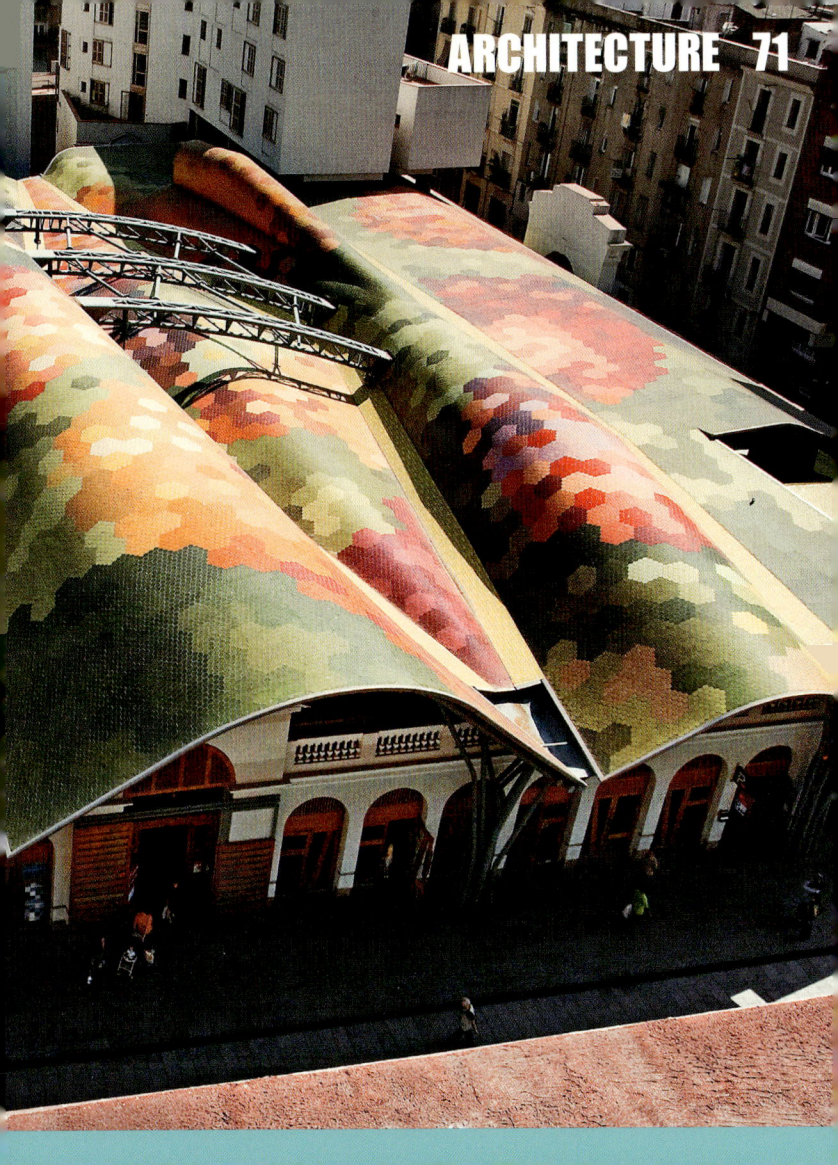

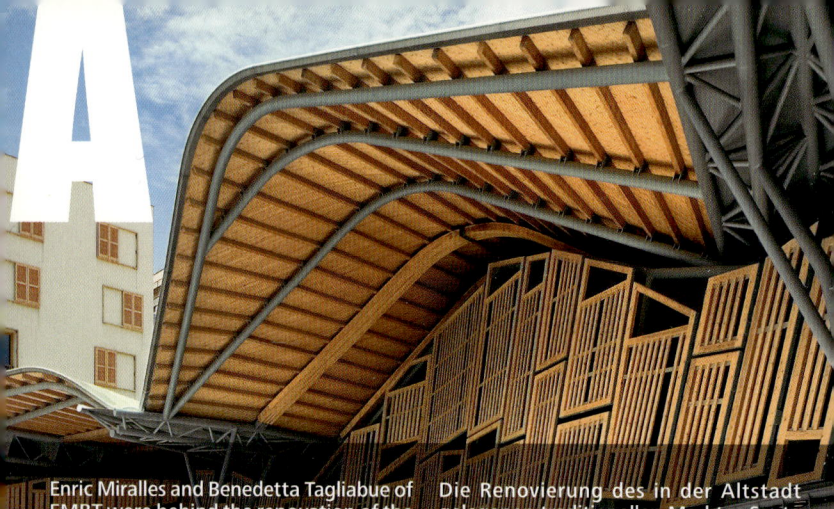

A Enric Miralles and Benedetta Tagliabue of EMBT were behind the renovation of the Santa Caterina market in the historic city center. They designed an exemplary support structure. Three projecting sheets of metal, two concrete support beams, and 109 sheets of wood in different shapes form the new wave-shaped roof. Its surface—over 45,200 sq. ft.—is covered with bright, hexagonal ceramic tiles. Open kitchens and informal counters integrate the restaurant Cuines Santa Catarina into the market stalls.

Die Renovierung des in der Altstadt gelegenen traditionellen Marktes Santa Caterina durch EMBT, Enric Miralles und Benedetta Tagliabue, ist ein Lehrstück für Tragwerkkonstruktion. Drei ausladende Metallbögen, zwei Unterzüge aus Beton und 109 Holzbögen unterschiedlicher Geometrie bilden das neue, wellenförmige Dach, dessen 4 200 m² große Oberfläche mit bunten, sechseckigen Keramikplatten gedeckt ist. Offene Küchen und informelle Tresen gliedern das Restaurant Cuines Santa Caterina in die Marktstände ein.

La rénovation du marché Santa Caterina fut entreprise par les architectes Enric Miralles et Benedetta Tagliabue (EMBT) et représente un chef d'œuvre de charpenterie. Trois larges poutrelles métalliques, deux poutres en béton et 109 arches de bois de dimensions variées supportent le toit en forme de vague, dont les 4 200 m² sont recouverts de plaques de céramique hexagonales multicolores. Le restaurant Cuines Santa Catarina est parfaitement intégré aux stands maraîchers grâce à ses cuisines ouvertes et ses agréables comptoirs.

La renovación del tradicional mercado de Santa Caterina, obra de EMBT (Enric Miralles y Benedetta Tagliabue), es un ejercicio maestro de construcción en voladizo. Tres arcos portantes de metal, dos vigas de hormigón y 109 arcos de madera de cambiante geometría sustentan el nuevo y ondulado tejado, cuyos 4200 m² están recubiertos de placas cerámicas hexagonales de colores diversos. Las cocinas abiertas y los mostradores informales integran el Cuines Santa Catarina restaurante entre los puestos del mercado.

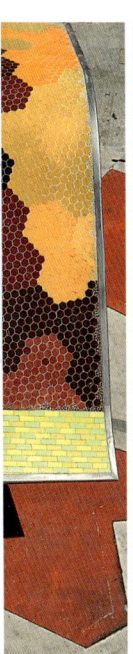
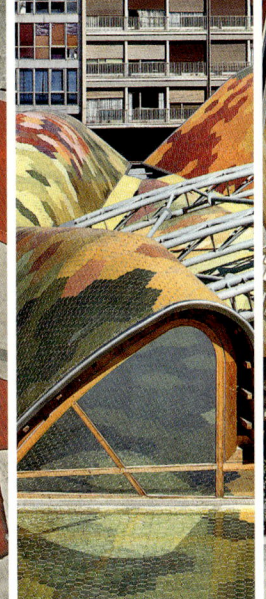
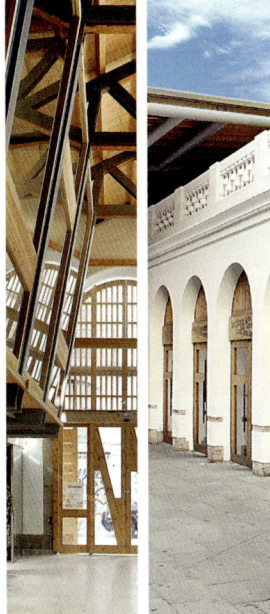

MERCAT DE SANTA CATERINA

Avinguda de Francesc Cambó, 16 // Ciutat Vella
www.mercatsantacaterina.net

Mon–Wed 7.30 am to 2 pm
Thu–Fri 7.30 am to 8.30 pm
Sat 7.30 am to 3.30 pm
Metro L4 Jaume I

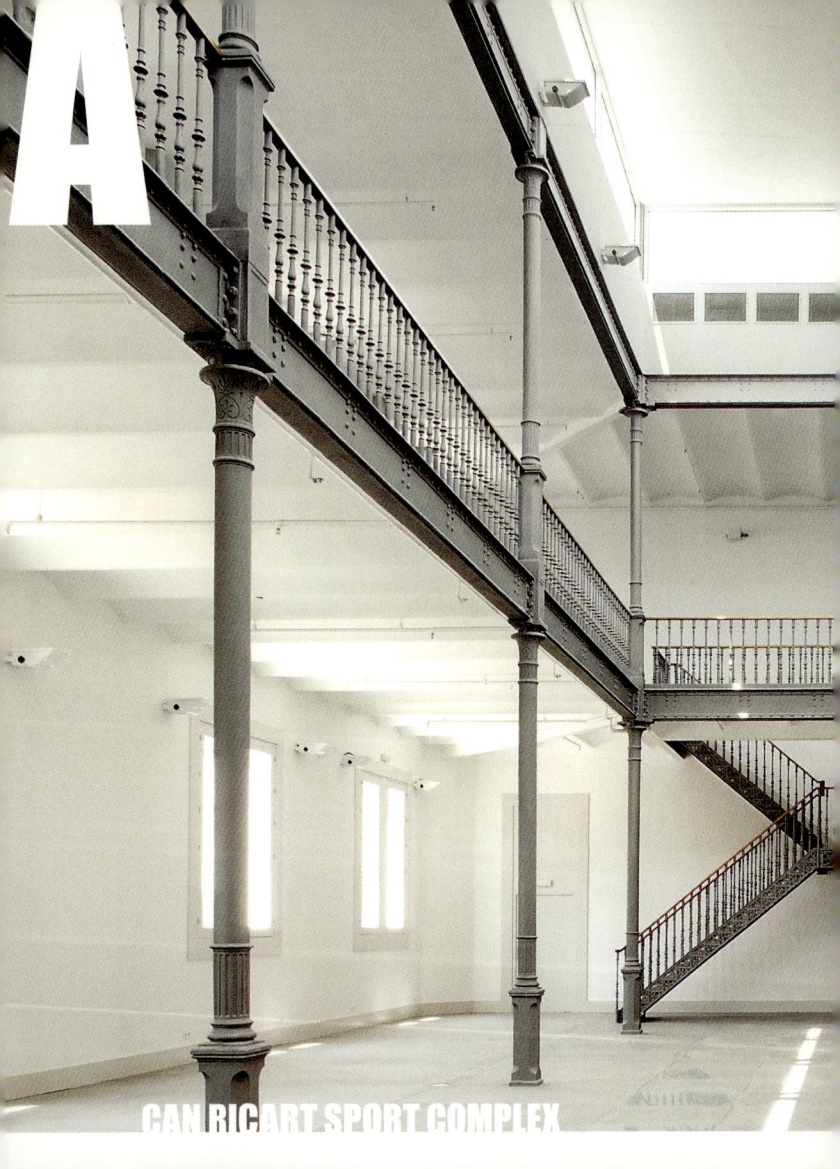

A

CAN RICART SPORT COMPLEX

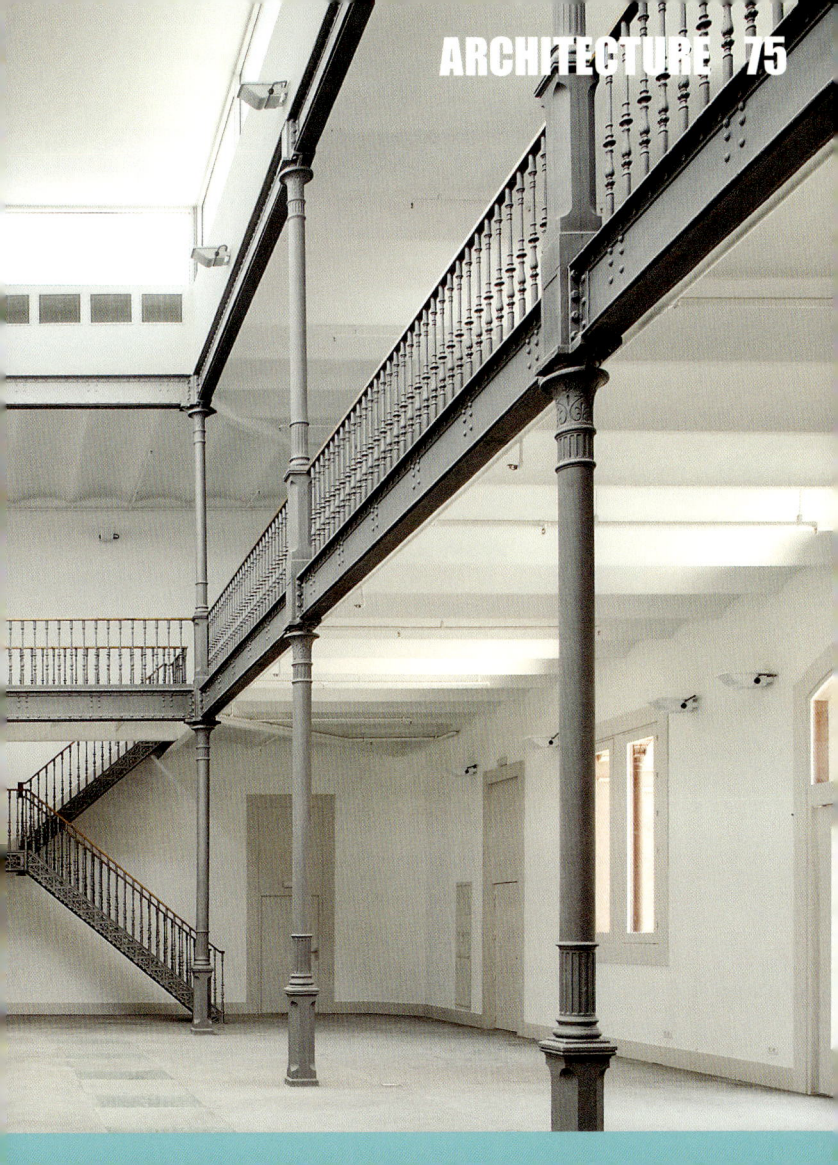

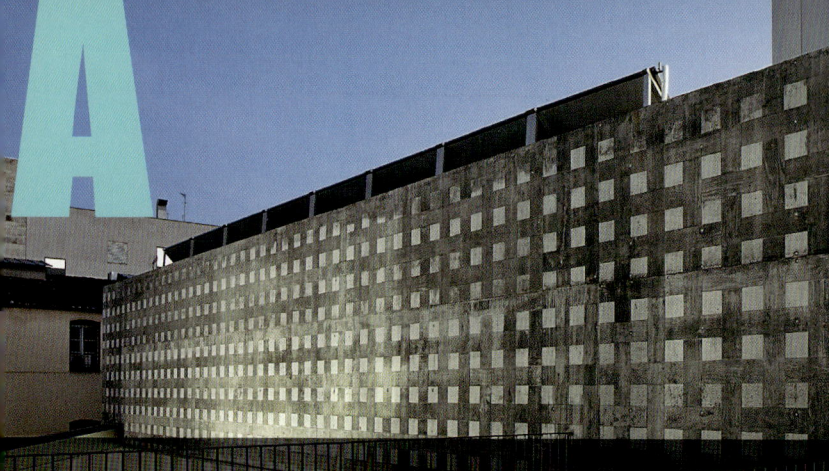

New facilities such as this sports complex are designed to revitalize run-down neighborhoods and to integrate all residents. Projects of this nature typically involve existing buildings that need to be incorporated into the design. Using austere materials and formal restraint to merge the old and the new, vora arquitectura successfully combined the new indoor swimming pool, the 1989 gymnasium, and the restored 19th century industrial facility into a functional whole.

Die Revitalisierung der Altstadt und die Integration der Bevölkerung sollen durch die Einrichtung neuer Anlagen wie dieses Sportkomplexes gefördert werden. Bauen im Bestand ist dabei eine typische Herausforderung für die Architekten. vora arquitectura fusioniert Alt und Neu durch nüchterne Materialien und formale Zurückhaltung, sodass die neue Schwimmhalle mit der Sporthalle von 1989 und der restaurierten Industrieanlage des 19. Jahrhunderts eine funktionale Einheit bildet.

La revitalisation de la vieille ville et l'intégration de sa population passe par l'aménagement de nouvelles installations, à l'image de ce complexe sportif. La transformation des bâtiments déjà existants est un des défis typiques présentés aux architectes. vora arquitectura allie ancien et nouveau à l'aide de matériaux simples et d'un style sobre, afin de faire de la nouvelle piscine, du gymnase de 1989 et de l'usine restaurée du XIXe siècle un ensemble fonctionnel.

La creación de nuevas instalaciones como este complejo deportivo pretende revitalizar el casco antiguo e integrar a sus habitantes. La construcción sobre lo ya existente suele ser el gran reto para los arquitectos. vora arquitectura fusionó lo viejo con lo nuevo mediante materiales sobrios y serenidad formal y consiguió que la nueva piscina forme una unidad funcional con el pabellón deportivo de 1989 y la restaurada nave industrial del siglo XIX.

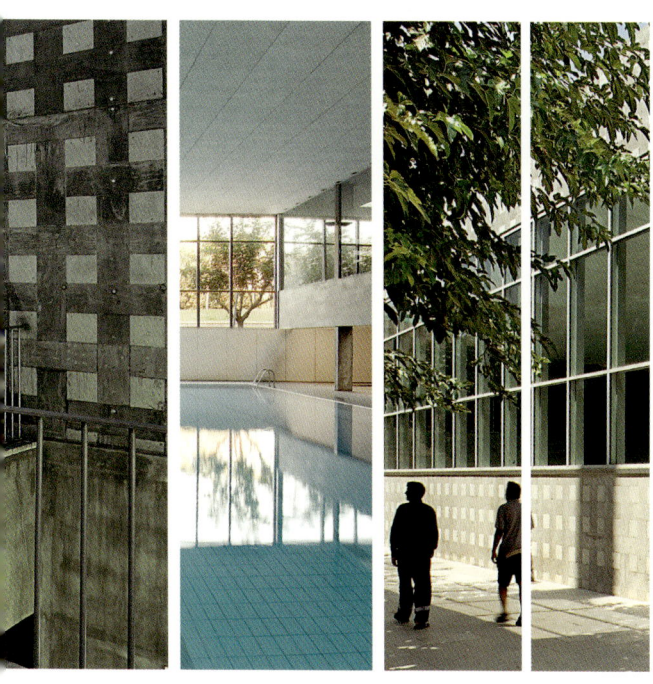

CAN RICART SPORT COMPLEX

Carrer de Sant Oleguer, 10 // Ciutat Vella / El Raval
Tel.: +34 93 441 75 26
www.canricart.com

Mon–Fri 7 am to 10.30 pm, Sat 9 am to 8 pm
Sun and holidays 9 am to 2.30 pm
Metro L2, L3 Paral·lel
Bus 120 Rambla del Raval (Sant Pau-Sant Josep Oriol)

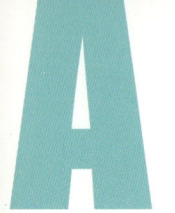

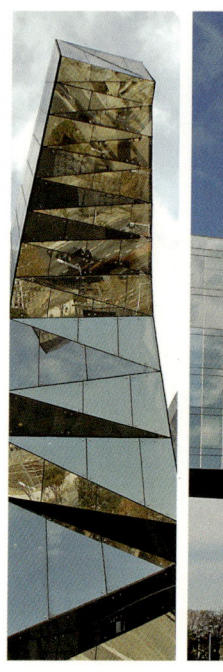

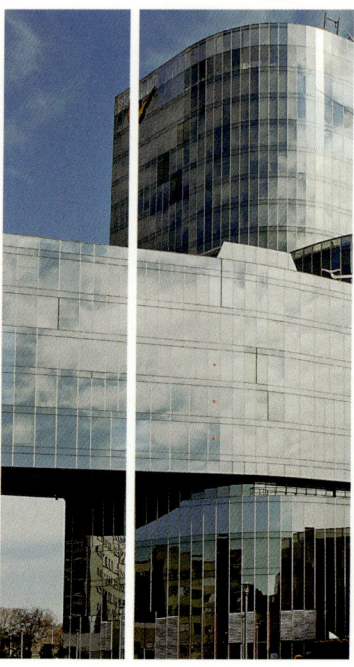

GAS NATURAL HEADQUARTERS

Plaça del Gas, 1 // Ciutat Vella / La Barceloneta
Tel.: +34 90 219 91 99
www.gasnatural.com

Metro L4 Barceloneta

The Gas Natural Fenosa energy company moved into its new headquarters in La Barceloneta in 2008. Designed by Enric Miralles and Benedetta Tagliabue, this energy-efficient building, glazed in shades of blue and brown, towers 278 ft. into the air, with another 278 ft. section branching out at a right angle like a horizontal skyscraper, fondly nicknamed the "aircraft carrier." MoMA in New York acquired the model of the building for its collection

Der Energiekonzern Gas Natural Fenosa bezog seinen von Enric Miralles und Benedetta Tagliabue geschaffenen neuen Firmensitz in La Barceloneta im Jahr 2008. Der in Blau- und Brauntönen verglaste, energieeffiziente Bau reckt sich als Turm in 85 m Höhe und kragt als eine Art horizontaler Wolkenkratzer mit einem ebenfalls 85 m langen Querriegel zu den Seiten aus. Das Element wird liebevoll der „Flugzeugträger" genannt, und das MoMA in New York erwarb das Modell des Gebäudes.

Conçu par les architectes Enric Miralles et Benedetta Tagliabue, le nouveau siège du groupe énergétique Gas Natural Fenosa a été inauguré en 2008 dans le quartier de La Barceloneta. L'édifice, économe en énergie et constitué de vitres teintées de bleu et brun, est composé d'une tour de 85 m de haut et d'une sorte de gratte-ciel horizontal affectueusement surnommé « le porte-avions », qui s'étend également sur 85 m. Le modèle du bâtiment a été acquis par le MoMA de New York.

En 2008, la compañía Gas Natural Fenosa se trasladó a su nueva sede de La Barceloneta, diseñada por Enric Miralles y Benedetta Tagliabue. El edificio, de alta eficiencia energética y vidriado en tonos azules y pardos, alcanza los 85 m de altura, y el voladizo lateral, también de 85 m, hace de él una especie de rascacielos horizontal. El modelo del edificio, conocido cariñosamente como "el portaaviones", ha sido adquirido por el MoMA de Nueva York.

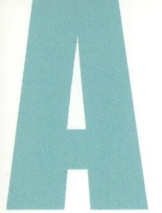

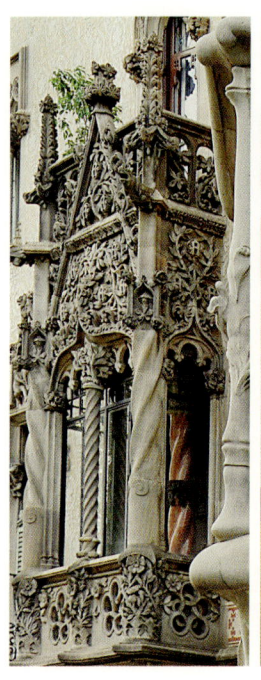
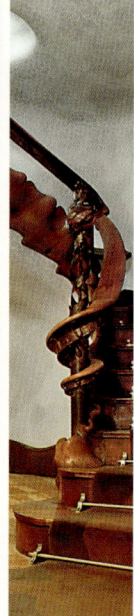
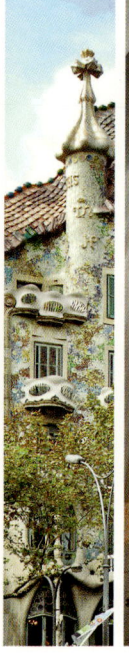
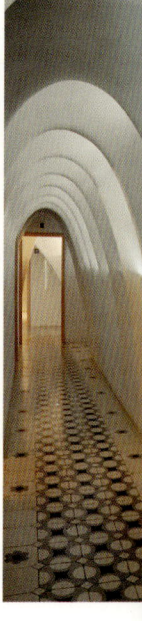

CASA BATLLÓ

Passeig de Gràcia, 43 // Eixample
Tel.: +34 93 216 03 06
www.casabatllo.es

Daily 9 am to 8 pm (last admissions)

Metro L2, L3, L4 Passeig de Gràcia

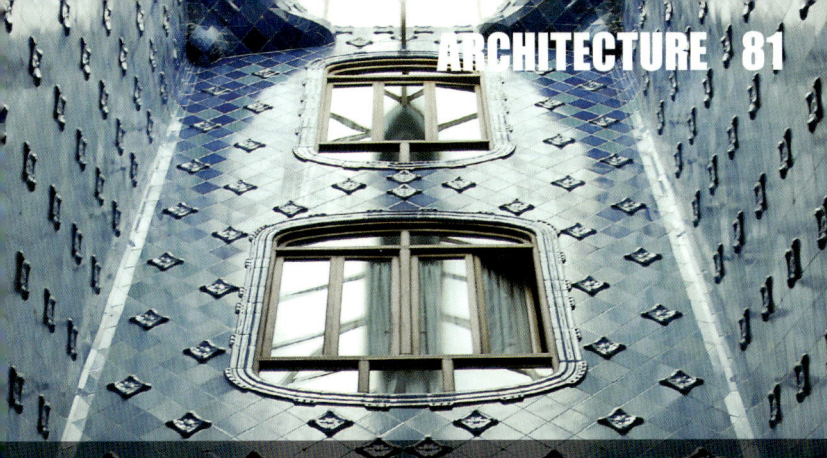

From 1904–1906, Antoni Gaudí transformed a building originally constructed in 1875 into one of Barcelona's most unique landmarks. Gaudí's idiosyncratic design language, partially inspired by the dragon from the legend of Saint George, becomes eternal poetry because of his choice of materials and colors: Tiles shimmering like scales symbolize the dragon's skin, the roof is its back. The interiors and the colorful rear façade help turn Casa Battló into a pioneering work of art.

Antoni Gaudí baute ein 1875 errichtetes Wohnhaus am Passeig de Gràcia 1904–1906 zu einem schillernden Gebäude um. Die eigenwillige Formensprache, die an den Drachen aus der Legende des Heiligen Georg erinnert, wird durch die Wahl der Materialien und Farben zu einem Ausdruck ewiger Poesie: wie Schuppen glänzende Kacheln symbolisieren die Haut, das Dach den Rücken des Drachen. Die Innenräume und die farbenfrohe rückwärtige Fassade machen das Gebäude zu einem richtungsweisenden Gesamtkunstwerk.

Entre 1904 et 1906, Antoni Gaudí transforma une maison construite en 1875 sur l'avenue Passeig de Gràcia en un édifice chatoyant. Le choix des matériaux et couleurs permet de donner vie à sa forme originale, qui rappelle le dragon de la légende de Saint Georges : les carreaux brillant de mille feux symbolisent les écailles du dragon et le toit en est le dos. Les différentes salles ainsi que la façade intérieure, très colorée, font de ce bâtiment une œuvre d'art novatrice.

La remodelación acometida por Gaudí entre 1904 y 1906 de una casa de pisos construida en 1875 en pleno Passeig de Gràcia hizo de ella un edificio sin igual. Las formas inéditas, que recuerdan entre otros al dragón de la leyenda de San Jorge, se convierten en expresión poética inmortal gracias a la selección de materiales y colores: los azulejos relucientes simbolizan las escamas, y el tejado el lomo del dragón. El interior y la colorista fachada posterior hacen del conjunto una obra pionera de arte total.

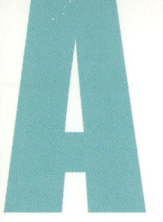

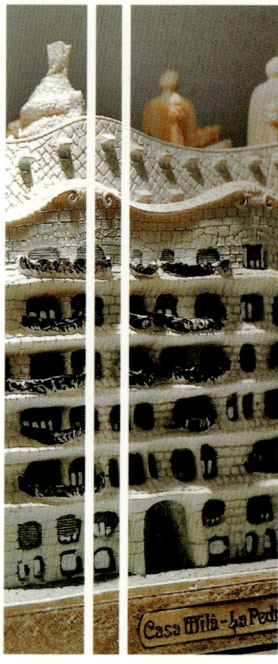

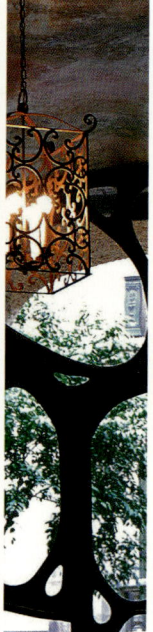

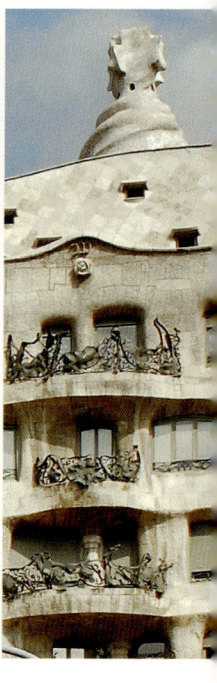

CASA MILÀ

Carrer de Provença, 261 // Eixample
Tel.: +34 90 240 09 73
www.lapedreraeducacio.org; www.gaudiclub.com

Mar–Oct daily 9 am to 8 pm
Nov–Feb daily 9 am to 6.30 pm
Metro L3, L5, L6, L7 Diagonal

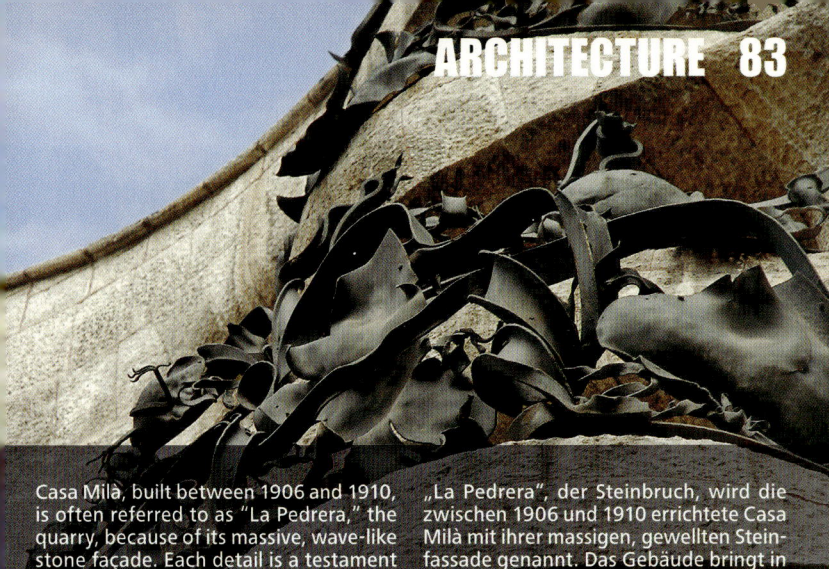

Casa Milà, built between 1906 and 1910, is often referred to as "La Pedrera," the quarry, because of its massive, wave-like stone façade. Each detail is a testament to the genius of Antoni Gaudí, whose goal was to create a synthesis between architecture and the organic shapes of nature. Museums and exhibition spaces in this apartment building with its sculptural roof (open to the public) provide fascinating insights into design and construction and showcase the whimsical furniture.

„La Pedrera", der Steinbruch, wird die zwischen 1906 und 1910 errichtete Casa Milà mit ihrer massigen, gewellten Steinfassade genannt. Das Gebäude bringt in allen Details das Genie Antoni Gaudís zum Ausdruck, der mit seinem Schaffen die Synthese der Architektur mit dem Organischen anstrebte. Museen und Ausstellungsräume in dem Mehrfamilienhaus mit begehbarem Skulpturendach erlauben erstaunliche Einblicke in Entwurf und Konstruktion und zeigen auch das verspielte Mobiliar.

La Casa Milà et sa façade de pierre massive et ondulée, construite entre 1906 et 1910, est surnommée « La Pedrera », la carrière. Le bâtiment fait ressortir tout le génie d'Antoni Gaudí, qui souhaitait créer un projet d'architecture organique. Les musées et salles d'exposition qu'on trouve dans cet immeuble au toit sculptural, auquel on peut accéder, offriront un regard étonnant sur sa conception et sa construction, sans oublier son mobilier extravagant.

La Casa Milà, construida entre 1906 y 1910, es conocida como "la Pedrera" (cantera) por su maciza y ondulada fachada de piedra. Todos los detalles del edificio exprimen la genialidad de Gaudí, quien pretendía con su obra sintetizar lo arquitectónico y lo orgánico. Los museos y salas de exposiciones del edificio, cuya azotea puede también visitarse, permiten asombrosas perspectivas en el diseño y la construcción y presentan también el caprichoso mobiliario.

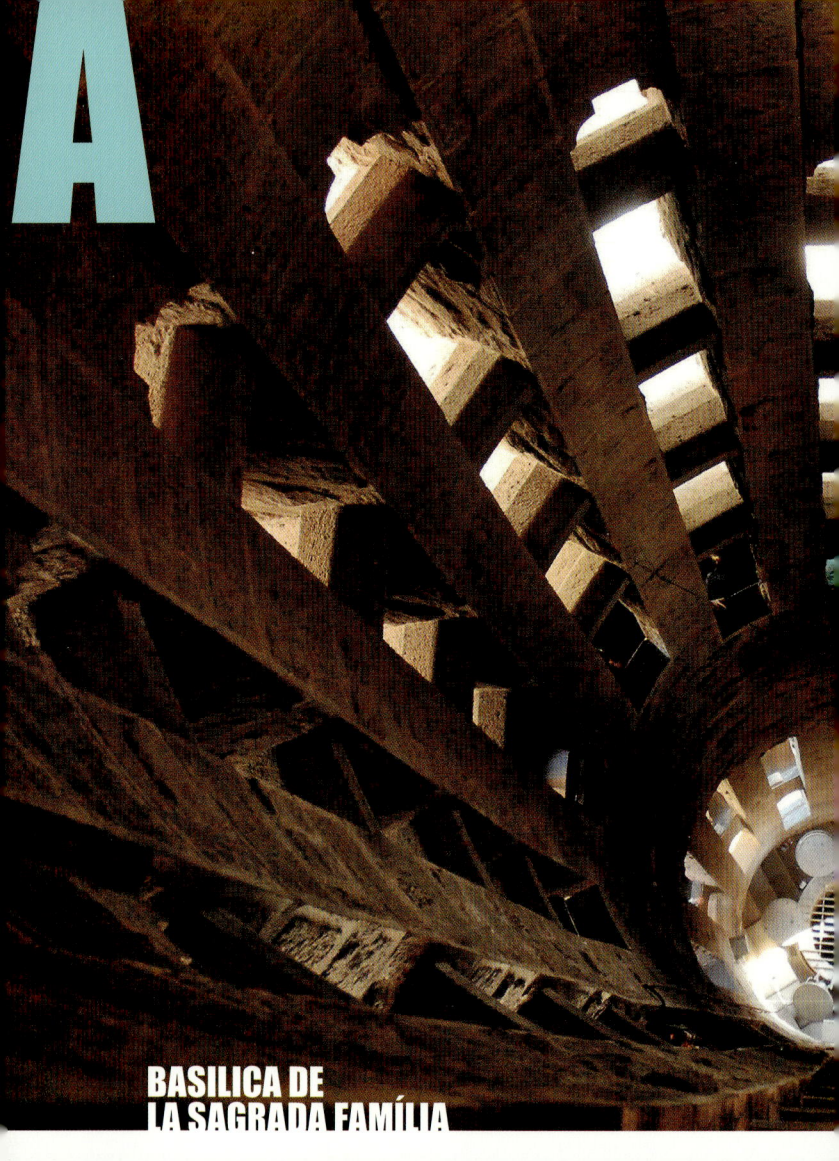

A

BASILICA DE
LA SAGRADA FAMÍLIA

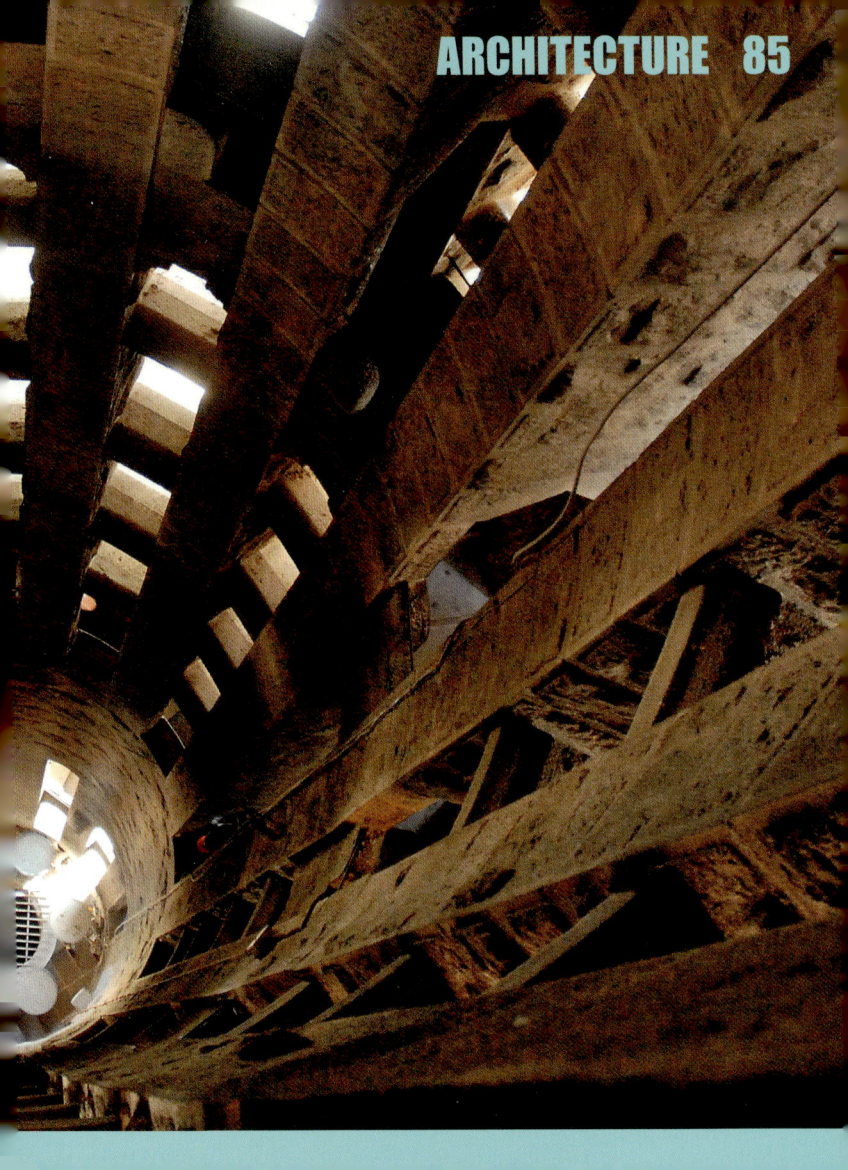

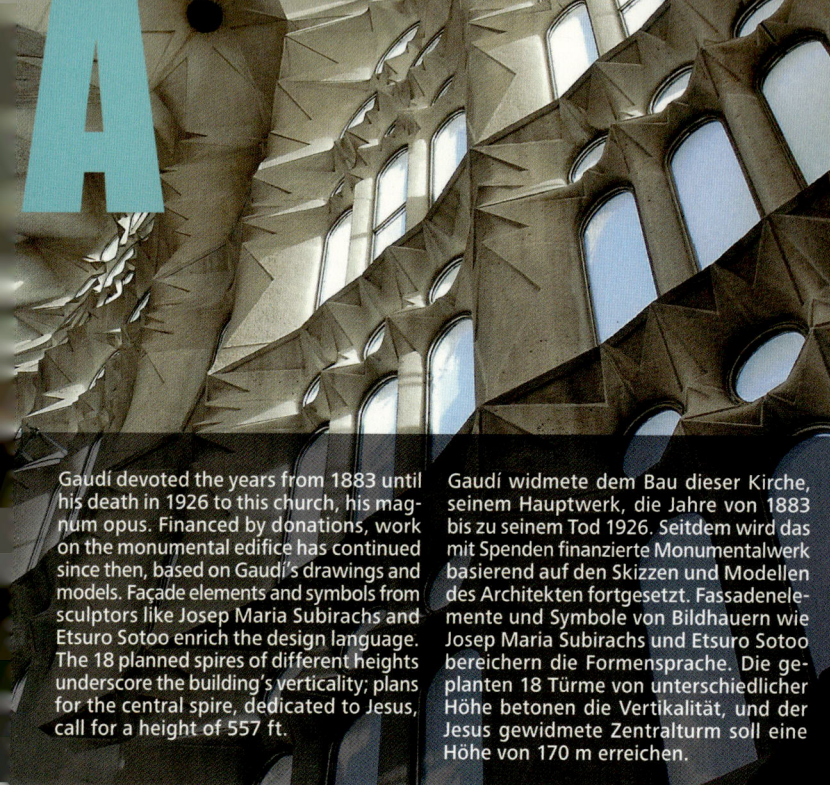

Gaudí devoted the years from 1883 until his death in 1926 to this church, his magnum opus. Financed by donations, work on the monumental edifice has continued since then, based on Gaudí's drawings and models. Façade elements and symbols from sculptors like Josep Maria Subirachs and Etsuro Sotoo enrich the design language. The 18 planned spires of different heights underscore the building's verticality; plans for the central spire, dedicated to Jesus, call for a height of 557 ft.

Gaudí widmete dem Bau dieser Kirche, seinem Hauptwerk, die Jahre von 1883 bis zu seinem Tod 1926. Seitdem wird das mit Spenden finanzierte Monumentalwerk basierend auf den Skizzen und Modellen des Architekten fortgesetzt. Fassadenelemente und Symbole von Bildhauern wie Josep Maria Subirachs und Etsuro Sotoo bereichern die Formensprache. Die geplanten 18 Türme von unterschiedlicher Höhe betonen die Vertikalität, und der Jesus gewidmete Zentralturm soll eine Höhe von 170 m erreichen.

Gaudí se consacra à la construction de cette église, son chef d'œuvre, de 1883 à sa mort en 1926. Depuis, ses croquis et ses plans servent à la poursuite de cette œuvre monumentale, financée par des dons. Des éléments de la façade et des symboles de sculpteurs tels que Josep Maria Subirachs et Etsuro Sotoo enrichissent ses formes. Les 18 tours de tailles différentes soulignent la verticalité de l'ensemble et la tour centrale, dédiée à Jésus, devrait atteindre 170 m.

Gaudí dedicó a la que sería su obra maestra los años que van desde 1883 hasta su muerte en 1926. Desde entonces, la monumental obra se ha ido completando mediante donaciones a partir de sus modelos y esbozos. El lenguaje formal de la fachada se ha visto enriquecido con obras de escultores como Josep Maria Subirachs y Etsuro Sotoo. Las 18 torres previstas a distintas alturas subrayan la verticalidad, y la torre central, consagrada a Jesús, debería alcanzar los 170 m.

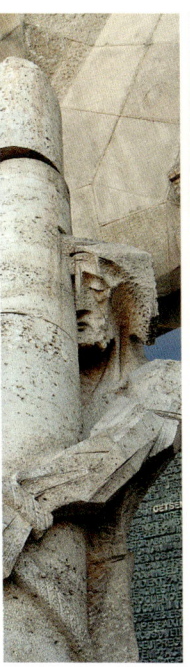
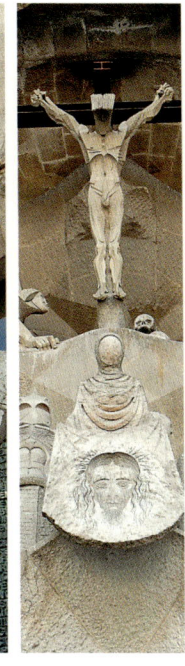
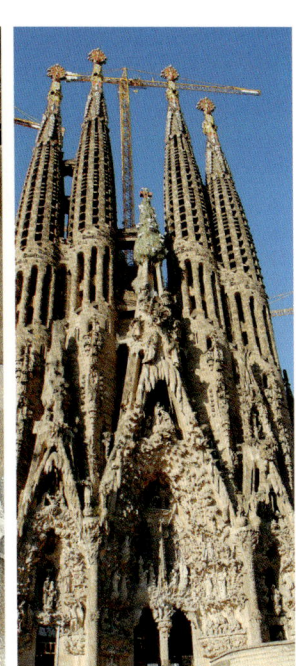

SAGRADA FAMÍLIA

Carrer de Mallorca, 401 // Eixample
Tel.: +34 93 207 30 31
www.sagradafamilia.org

Oct–Mar 9 am to 6 pm
Apr–Sep daily 9 am to 8 pm
Holidays 9 am to 2 pm
Metro L2, L5 Sagrada Família

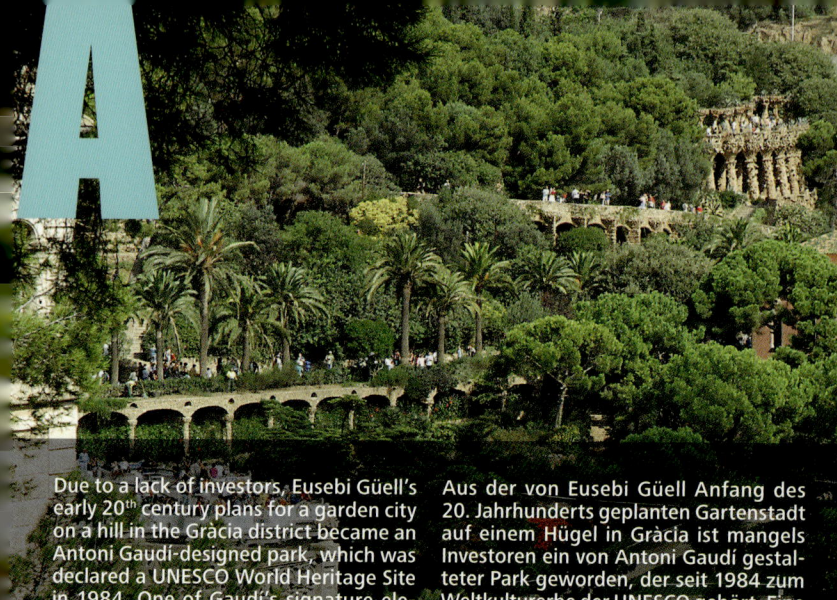

Due to a lack of investors, Eusebi Güell's early 20th century plans for a garden city on a hill in the Gràcia district became an Antoni Gaudí-designed park, which was declared a UNESCO World Heritage Site in 1984. One of Gaudí's signature elements are tile and glass mosaics known as "trencadís." They decorate the lavishly renovated buildings at the entrance, the stairs to the Sala Hipóstila with its 86 columns, and the 360 ft. bench that snakes its way around the central square.

Aus der von Eusebi Güell Anfang des 20. Jahrhunderts geplanten Gartenstadt auf einem Hügel in Gràcia ist mangels Investoren ein von Antoni Gaudí gestalteter Park geworden, der seit 1984 zum Weltkulturerbe der UNESCO gehört. Eine Spezialität Gaudís sind die „Trencadís" genannten Mosaike aus Keramik und Glas. Sie zieren die aufwendig restaurierten Gebäude am Eingang, die Treppe zum Sala Hipóstila mit ihren 86 Säulen und die 110 m lange Bank, die sich um den zentralen Platz schlängelt.

Ce qu'Eusebi Güell imaginait devenir une Cité-jardin sur une colline de Gràcia au début du XXe siècle est devenu, faute d'investisseurs, un parc aménagé par Antoni Gaudí, inscrit au patrimoine mondial de l'UNESCO depuis 1984. Les « Trencadís », mosaïques de céramique et de verre, spécialités de Gaudí, décorent les bâtiments entièrement rénovés de l'entrée, les marches menant à la Sala Hipóstila, ses 86 colonnes et le banc de 110m de long entourant la place centrale.

La falta de inversores hizo que la ciudad jardín concebida por Eusebi Güell en una colina de Gràcia a comienzos del siglo XX se convirtiese en un parque diseñado por Antoni Gaudí que desde 1984 forma parte del patrimonio universal de la UNESCO. Característicos de Gaudí son los mosaicos de "trencadís" que adornan los edificios cuidadosamente restaurados de la entrada, la escalera de la Sala Hipóstila con sus 86 columnas y el largo banco de 110 m que rodea sinuoso la plaza central.

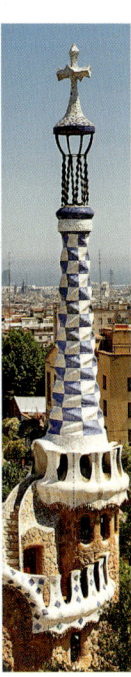 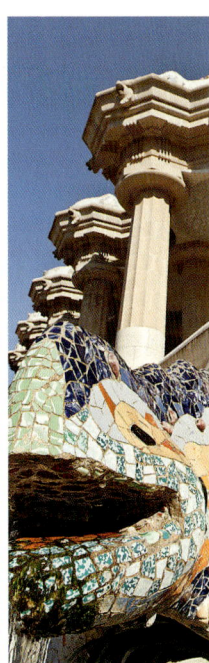 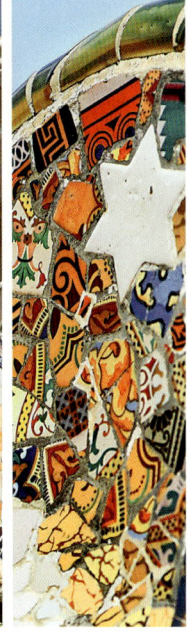 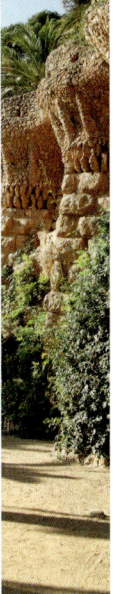

PARK GÜELL

Carrer d'Olot, 5 // Gràcia   Metro L3 Lesseps
Tel.: +34 93 413 24 00   Bus 129 Esteve Terradas (Josep
www.parkguell.es   Jover-Viaducte de Vallcarca)

Apr–Sep 10 am to 8 pm
Oct–Mar 10 am to 6 pm

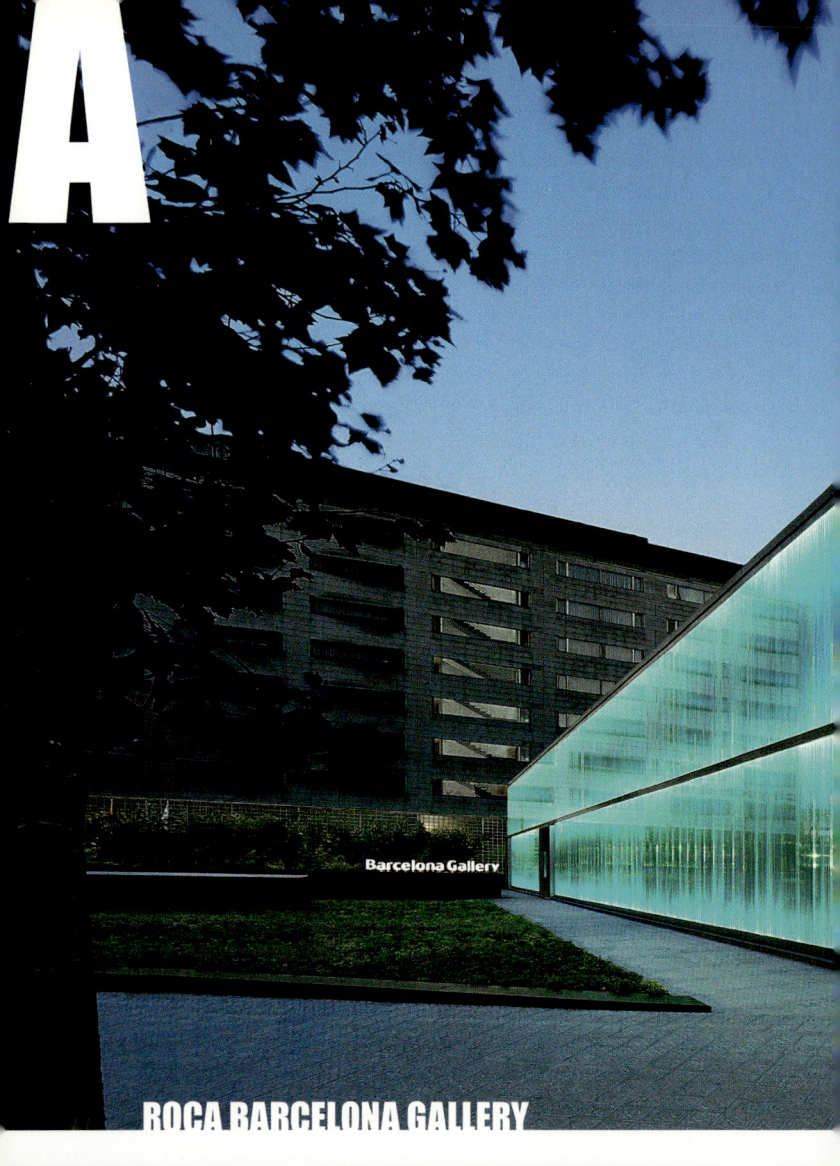

A

Barcelona Gallery

ROCA BARCELONA GALLERY

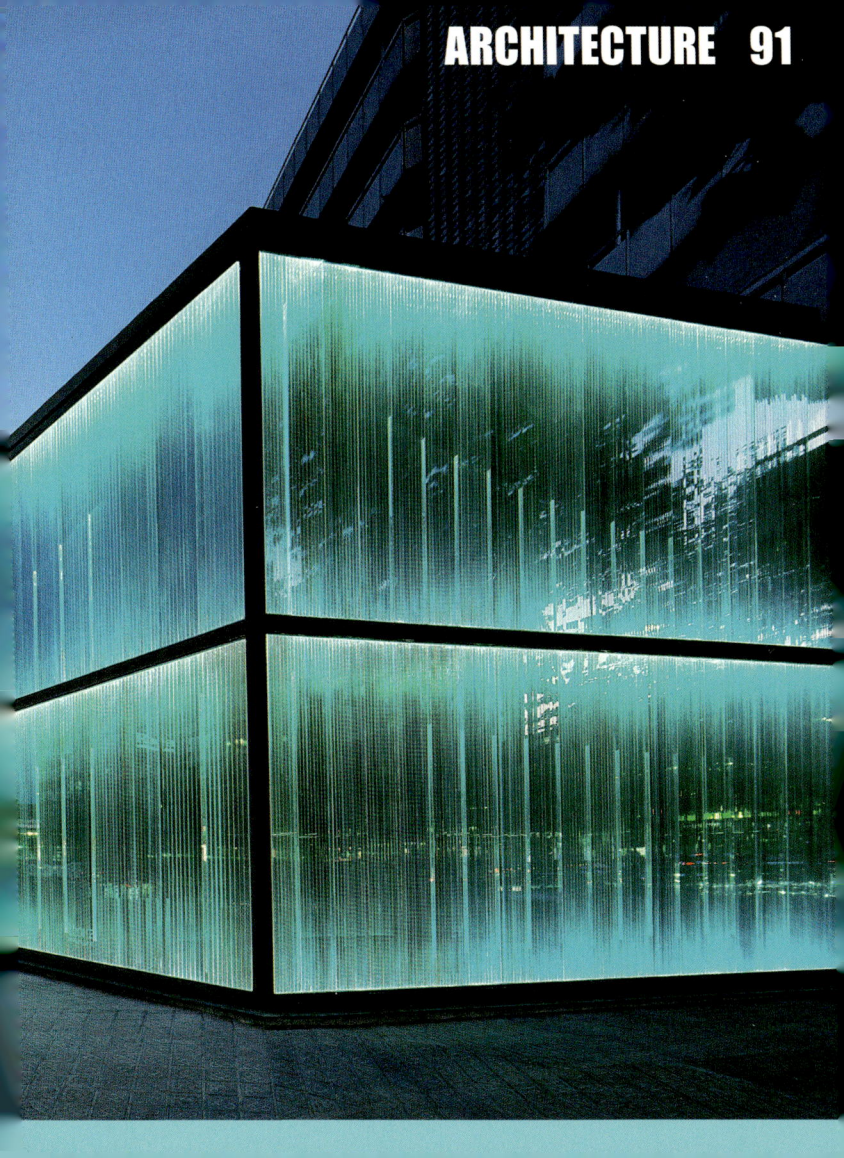

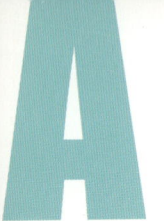

ROCA BARCELONA GALLERY

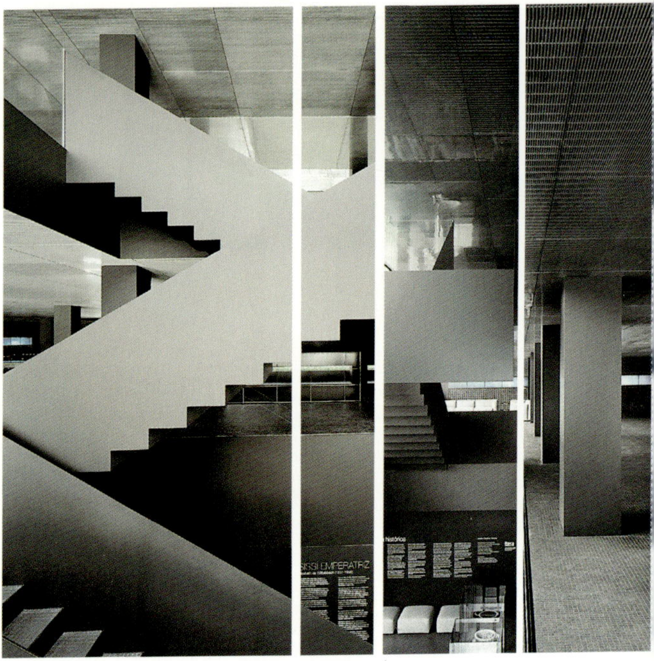

Carrer de Joan Güell, 211-213 // Les Corts
Tel.: +34 93 366 12 12
www.rocabarcelonagallery.com

Mon–Sat 10 am to 8 pm
Sun 10 am to 2 pm
Metro L3 Maria Cristina

For Roca's flagship store and showroom, Borja and Lucía Ferrater of architect Carlos Ferrater's firm OAB interpreted the aesthetic values of Roca, a leading manufacturer of bathroom fixtures, as a low-slung elongated cube. The visual character of the LED-equipped glass skin matches the sensuous interior where Roca's brand, products, and company history are presented as an interactive multimedia experience encompassing sophisticated lighting effects.

Für den Flagship-Store mit Ausstellungszentrum interpretierte das Büro des Architekten Carlos Ferrater OAB unter der Leitung von Borja und Lucía Ferrater den Wertekanon des Unternehmens Roca, eines führenden Bäderherstellers, als lang gestreckten Kubus. Der visuelle Charakter der mit LEDs bestückten gläsernen Hülle entspricht dem sinnlichen Innenraum, in dem Marke, Produkte und Firmengeschichte in einer ausgeklügelten Lichtinszenierung als interaktives Multimediaerlebnis präsentiert werden.

Sous la direction de Borja et Lucía Ferrater, le bureau d'architecture Carlos Ferrater OAB a réalisé la nouvelle boutique phare avec espace d'exposition de l'entreprise Roca, leader de l'équipement de salles de bains, en interprétant ses valeur. L'aspect extérieur de ce cube allongé composé de vitres équipées de LEDs fait écho à son charme intérieur, au sein duquel l'histoire de l'entreprise, la marque et ses produits, sont présentés de manière interactive et multimédia dans un savant jeu de lumières.

Para este "flagship" store con centro de exposiciones, el despacho OAB del arquitecto Carlos Ferrater interpretó (bajo la dirección de Borja y Lucía Ferrater) el canon de valores de la empresa de sanitarios Roca como un cubo alargado. El carácter visual de la cubierta, iluminada con LEDs, se corresponde con el sensorial espacio interior en el que marca, producto e historia de la empresa aparecen representados en una experiencia multimedia e interactiva.

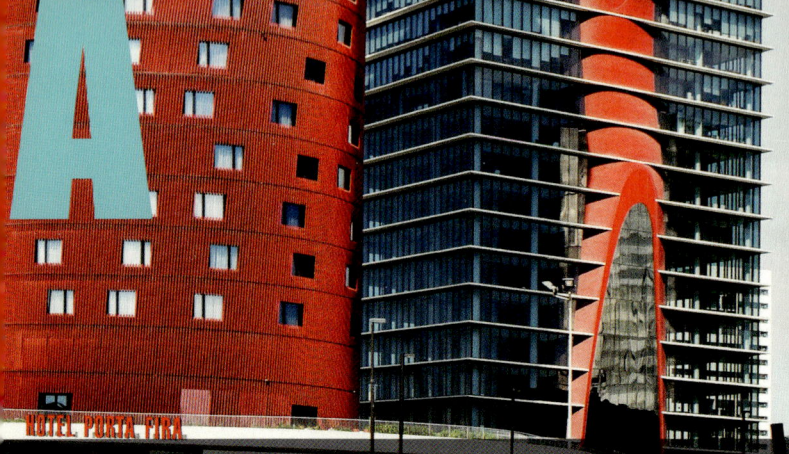

HOTEL PORTA FIRA

In addition to the master plan for the extension of the trade fair site at the Gran Via, Toyo Ito, in cooperation with Barcelona firm b720 Fermín Vázquez Arquitectos, also designed two 374 ft. towers: a hotel and an office building. The shape of the hotel's red aluminum skin is repeated by the red vertical core of the office building which breaks through its glass façade. With this emblematic ensemble, the Japanese architect takes the organic architecture developed by Gaudí into the 21st century.

Neben dem Masterplan für die Erweiterung des Messegeländes an der Gran Via entwarf Toyo Ito in Zusammenarbeit mit dem Büro b720 Fermín Vázquez Arquitectos aus Barcelona auch zwei 114 m hohe Türme: ein Hotel und ein Bürohaus. Die Form der roten Aluminiumhülle des Hotels wird im Inneren des Bürogebäudes aufgenommen und durchbricht seine gläserne Fassade als Zitat. Der japanische Architekt schreibt mit diesem emblematischen Ensemble die von Gaudí entwickelte organische Architektur im 21. Jahrhundert fort.

En parallèle à l'élargissement du parc des expositions sur l'avenue Gran Via, Toyo Ito et le bureau d'architecture de Barcelone b720 Fermín Vázquez Arquitectos ont conçu deux tours de 114 m de hauteur : l'une abrite un hôtel, l'autre des bureaux. La forme de la couche d'aluminium rouge qui recouvre la première est reprise à l'intérieur de la seconde, traversant sa façade de verre de haut en bas. Avec cette œuvre emblématique, l'architecte japonais poursuit le principe d'architecture organique de Gaudí.

Además de los planes maestros para la ampliación de los terrenos de la Fira, Toyo Ito diseñó junto al despacho barcelonés b720 Fermín Vázquez Arquitectos dos torres de 114 m de altura: un hotel y un edificio de oficinas. La forma de la fachada roja de aluminio del hotel está también presente en el interior del edificio de oficinas y se alude a ella en su fachada vidriada. El arquitecto japonés recuperaba con este emblemático conjunto la arquitectura orgánica de Gaudí para el siglo XXI.

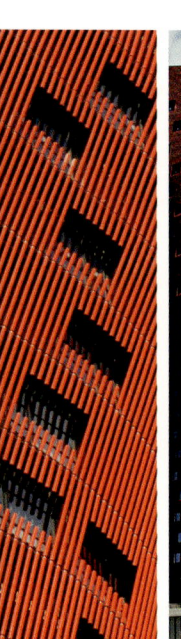
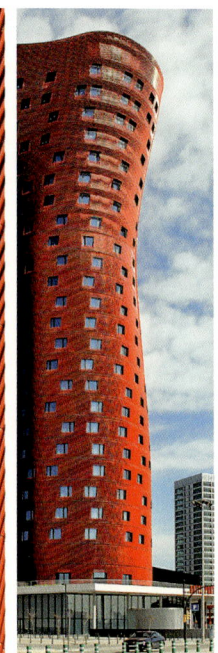
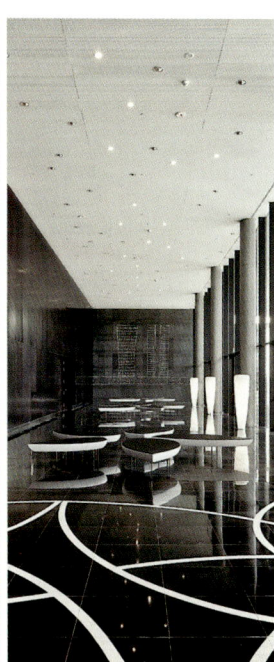

TORRES PORTA FIRA

Plaça d'Europa, 45 // L'Hospitalet de Llobregat
www.toyo-ito.co.jp; www.b720.com

Metro L8 Europa / Fira

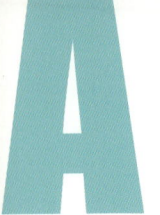

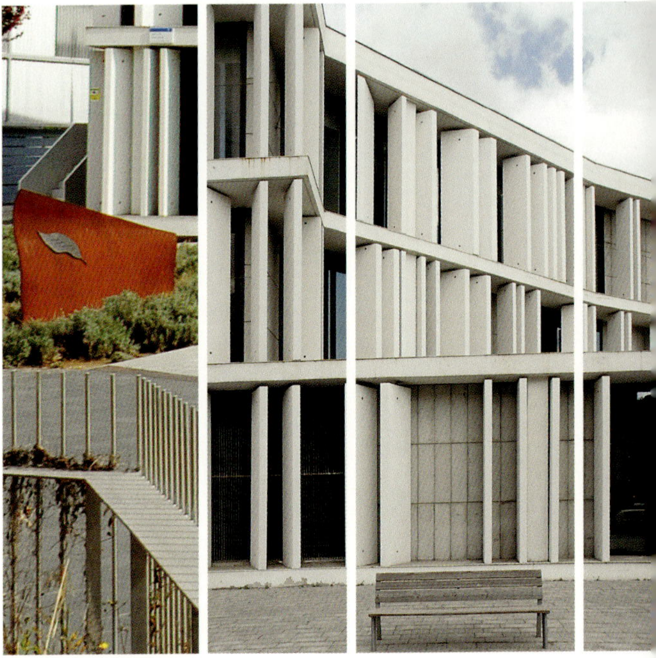

LAW COURTS, SANT BOI DE LLOBREGAT

Carrer de Carles Martí i Vilà,
Carrer de Josep Torras i Bages // Sant Boi de Llobregat
www.jordibadia.com/en/equipamientos/juzgados-de-sant-boi

Train R5, R6 (Barcelona Cercanías Network)
from Plaça d'Espanya to Sant Boi de Llobregat

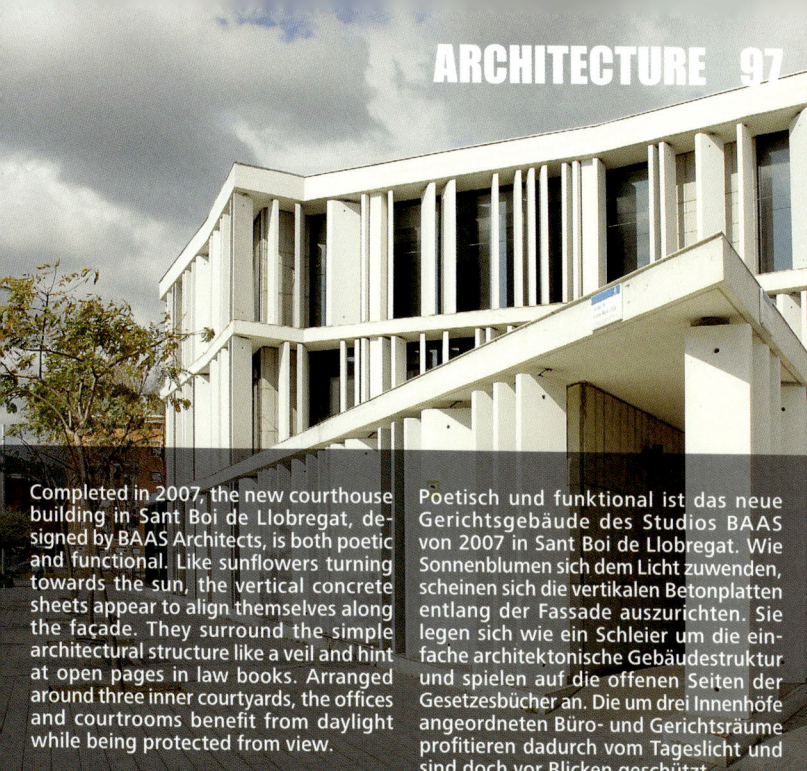

Completed in 2007, the new courthouse building in Sant Boi de Llobregat, designed by BAAS Architects, is both poetic and functional. Like sunflowers turning towards the sun, the vertical concrete sheets appear to align themselves along the façade. They surround the simple architectural structure like a veil and hint at open pages in law books. Arranged around three inner courtyards, the offices and courtrooms benefit from daylight while being protected from view.

Poetisch und funktional ist das neue Gerichtsgebäude des Studios BAAS von 2007 in Sant Boi de Llobregat. Wie Sonnenblumen sich dem Licht zuwenden, scheinen sich die vertikalen Betonplatten entlang der Fassade auszurichten. Sie legen sich wie ein Schleier um die einfache architektonische Gebäudestruktur und spielen auf die offenen Seiten der Gesetzesbücher an. Die um drei Innenhöfe angeordneten Büro- und Gerichtsräume profitieren dadurch vom Tageslicht und sind doch vor Blicken geschützt.

Le nouveau palais de justice du studio BAAS à Sant Boi de Llobregat, réalisé en 2007, est poétique et fonctionnel. Les dalles de béton verticales, sur toute la façade, s'ouvrent au soleil à la manière de tournesols. Elles forment un voile autour de l'architecture simple du bâtiment et rappellent les pages d'un code civil. Les bureaux et salles d'audition, autour de trois cours intérieures, profitent ainsi de la lumière naturelle, tout en étant protégés des regards extérieurs.

El edificio de los juzgados de Sant Boi de Llobregat, diseñado por el estudio BAAS en 2007, es poético y funcional. Las placas verticales de hormigón de la fachada parecen orientarse por el sol, como si de girasoles se tratase, y forman un velo sobre la sencilla estructura del edificio que evoca las páginas abiertas de los códigos legales. Oficinas y tribunales, distribuidos en torno a tres patios, se benefician de la luz diaria sin por ello estar expuestos al exterior.

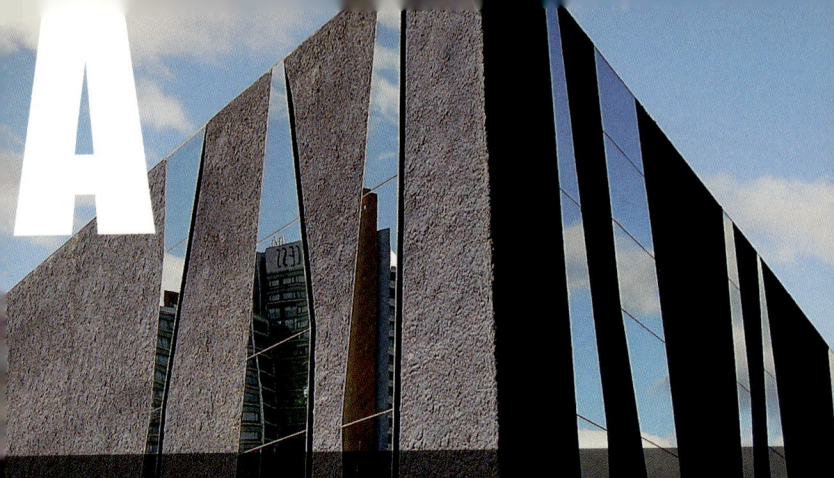

A

For the 2004 Universal Forum of Cultures, an event venue with an esplanade and a marina were built on a brownfield site where Avinguda Diagonal dead-ends at the ocean. Designed by Martínez Lapeña—Torres Arquitectos, the fingers of the expansive esplanade extend like cliffs over the water, and the gigantic concrete pergola equipped with 48,400 sq. ft. of solar panels became a symbol. Today, this area is quiet. Visitors usually only come to swim in the ocean.

Anlässlich des Forums der Kulturen im Jahre 2004 entstand dort, wo die Avinguda Diagonal am Meer endet, auf ehemaligem Brachland ein Veranstaltungsgelände mit Esplanade und Sporthafen. Martínez Lapeña – Torres Arquitectos lassen die Finger der weitläufigen Esplanade wie Klippen über dem Wasser aufragen, und die riesige skulpturale Pergola aus Beton mit 4 500 m² Solarzellen wurde zum Symbol. Heute geht es hier ruhig zu, und Besucher kommen meist, um im Meer zu baden.

Cet ancien terrain vague a été transformé en champ de foire avec esplanade et port de plaisance à l'occasion du Forum des cultures de 2004, là où la Avinguda Diagonal rencontre la mer. Martínez Lapeña et Torres Arquitectos ont laissé les extrémités de la large esplanade s'avancer sur la mer, et la gigantesque, sculpturale pergola de béton et ses 4 500 m² de panneaux solaires est devenue un symbole. L'endroit est aujourd'hui tranquille et les visiteurs viennent principalement s'y baigner.

Con ocasión del Fórum de las Culturas en 2004 se creó un espacio para eventos con explanada y puerto deportivo allí donde la Avenida Diagonal llegaba al mar. Martínez Lapeña – Torres Arquitectos consiguieron que los dedos de la extensa explanada se alcen como acantilados sobre el agua, y la enorme y escultural pérgola de hormigón, recubierta con 4500 m² de células solares, se ha convertido en un símbolo. Hoy las cosas se han calmado y los visitantes acuden sobre todo a bañarse en el mar.

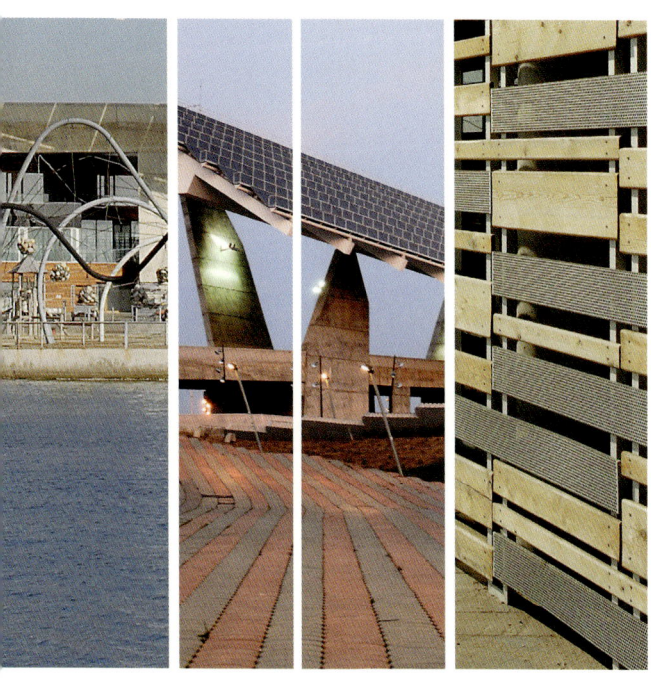

FÒRUM ESPLANADE AND PHOTOVOLTAIC POWERPLANT

Plaça de Llevant / Parc Fòrum // Sant Martí
www.barcelona2004.org

Leisure and events Jun 11th to Oct 31st
Metro L4 El Maresme / Fòrum

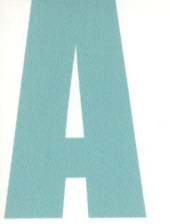

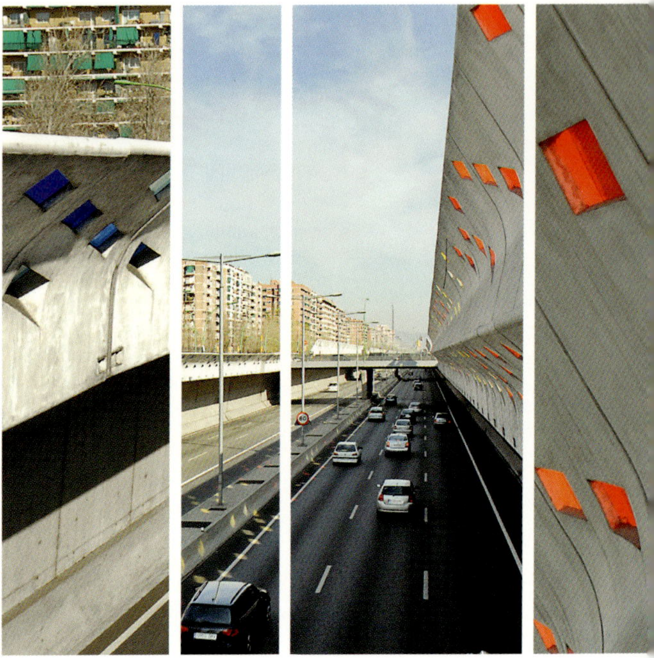

GRAN VIA ACOUSTIC PANELS

Gran Via de les Corts Catalanes // Sant Martí
www.mirallestagliabue.com

Bus 50, 60, B21 Gran Via-Bilbao or Gran Via-Monturiol

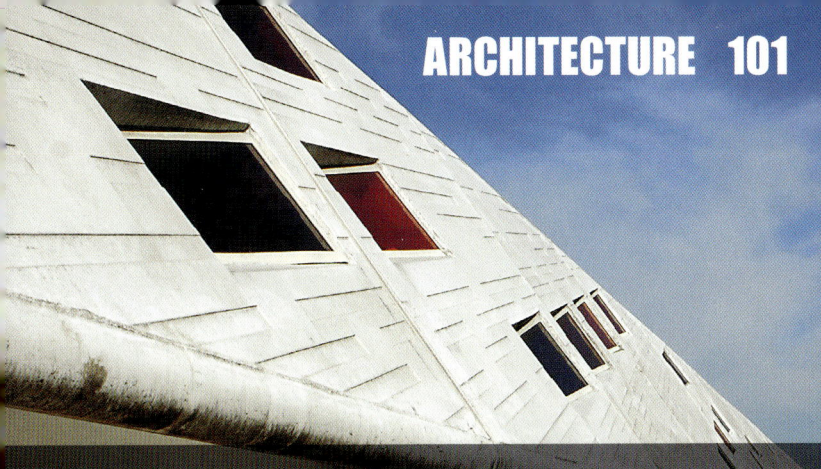

Benedetta Tagliabue has managed the successful Barcelona firm of Miralles Tagliabue EMBT since Enric Miralles' death in 2000. Many modern designs in the city carry his or their joint signature. The acoustic panels along the Gran Via, one of Barcelona's major arteries, were completed posthumously in 2007. The shape of the panels reflects the sound downward to the expressway below, and the material in their core absorbs part of the noise to create a quieter environment for residents.

Benedetta Tagliabue führt das erfolg-reiche Büro Miralles Tagliabue EMBT auch nach dem Tod von Enric Miralles im Jahr 2000 weiter, und viele moderne Entwürfe in Barcelona tragen seinen bzw. ihren gemeinsamen Stempel. Die Lärmschutzpaneele an der Gran Via, einer der Hauptverkehrsachsen, wurden erst posthum 2007 fertig gestellt. Die Form der Paneele reflektiert den Schall zur tiefer liegenden Schnellstraße, und das Material im Kern absorbiert zum Wohle der Anwohner einen Teil des Lärms.

Malgré le décès d'Enric Miralles en 2000, Benedetta Tagliabue continue de diriger Miralles Tagliabue EMBT avec succès, comme en témoignent les nombreux bâti-ments de Barcelone portant leur sceau. Les murs de protection sonore sur la Gran Vía, un axe de circulation majeur, ont été terminés posthume en 2007. La forme des panneaux renvoie le son vers la voie rapide en contrebas, et le matériau utilisé pour le cœur des panneaux absorbe une partie du bruit, pour le bien-être des riverains.

Benedetta Tagliabue sigue al frente del despacho Miralles Tagliabue EMBT tras la muerte de Enric Miralles en el año 2000, y muchos diseños modernos en Barcelona llevan su sello personal o conjunto. Los pa-neles de protección sonora de la Gran Vía, uno de los grandes ejes de circulación en la ciudad, fueron instalados póstumamente en 2007. La forma de los paneles refleja el sonido hacia la propia Vía rodada, y los materiales empleados absorben parte del ruido en beneficio de los vecinos.

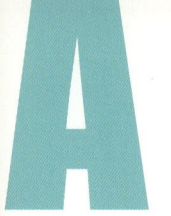

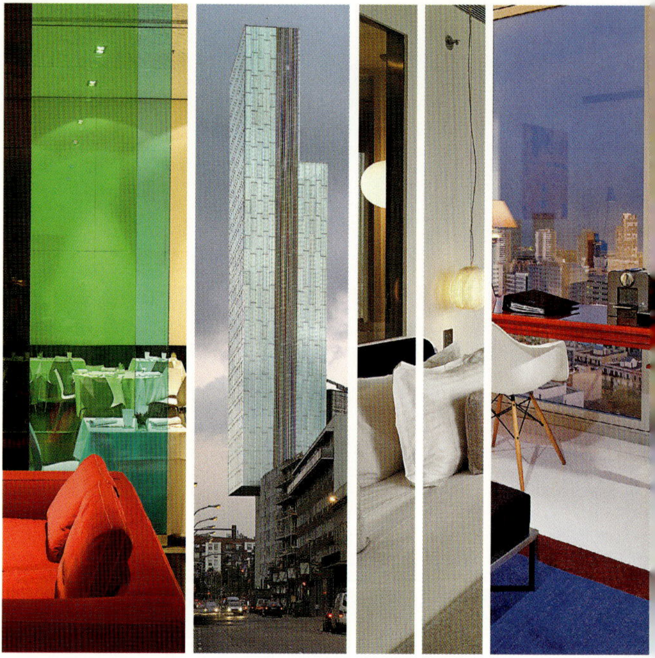

ME BARCELONA

Carrer de Pere IV, 272-286 // Sant Martí
Tel.: +34 93 672 05 0
www.me-barcelona.com

Metro L1 Glòries or L4 Poblenou

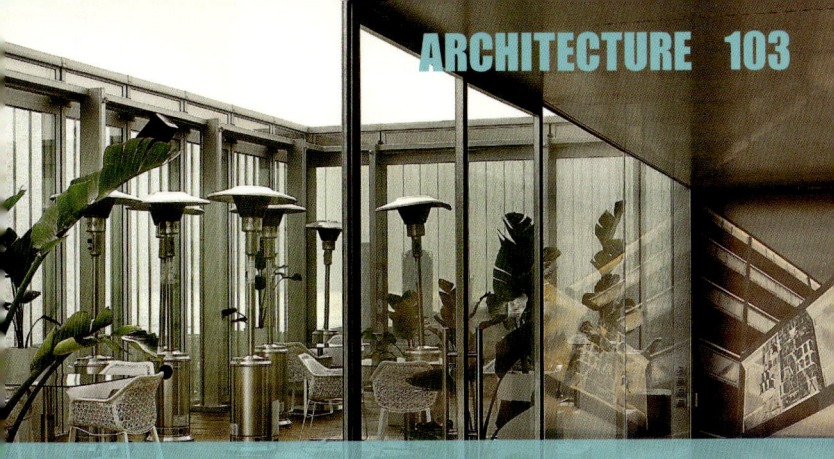

Architect Dominique Perrault's tower receives its dynamic character from the way the body of the building is fractured in the middle and thrust upward. The regular grid of the aluminum-clad façade emphasizes the resulting weightlessness. The expressiveness of the architecture is complemented on the inside by a commitment to vivid colors and strong shapes. Dos Cielos is the domain of chefs Sergio and Javier Torres who learned their craft from Santi Santamaria and Alain Ducasse.

Der Turm des Architekten Dominique Perrault besticht durch seine Dynamik, die der mittige Bruch des Baukörpers und die Verschiebung der Fassade nach oben erzeugen. Das gleichmäßige Raster der mit Aluminium verkleideten Fassade unterstreicht die so erzeugte Schwerelosigkeit. Der Ausdrucksstärke der Architektur entspricht im Inneren das Bekenntnis zu klaren Farben und starken Formen. Im Restaurant Dos Cielos kochen Sergio und Javier Torres, geschult bei Santi Santamaria und Alain Ducasse.

La tour de l'architecte Dominique Perrault séduit par sa dynamique symbolisée par un porte-à-faux, une partie de la façade étant décalée vers le haut. Le quadrillage régulier de la façade recouverte d'aluminium souligne cette impression d'apesanteur. Le caractère expressif de cette architecture se retrouve à l'intérieur grâce au choix de couleurs vives et de formes expressives. Sergio et Javier Torres, formés par Santi Santamaria et Alain Ducasse, ravissent le restaurant Dos Cielos.

La torre del arquitecto Dominique Perrault destaca por su dinamismo, potenciado por la interrupción del bloque y el desplazamiento hacia arriba de la fachada. La cuadrícula de la fachada recubierta de aluminio subraya la ingravidez así creada. En el interior, la fuerza expresiva de la arquitectura encuentra reflejo en la apuesta por colores fuertes y formas definidas. En el restaurante Dos Cielos cocinan Sergio y Javier Torres, alumnos de Santi Santamaria y Alain Ducasse.

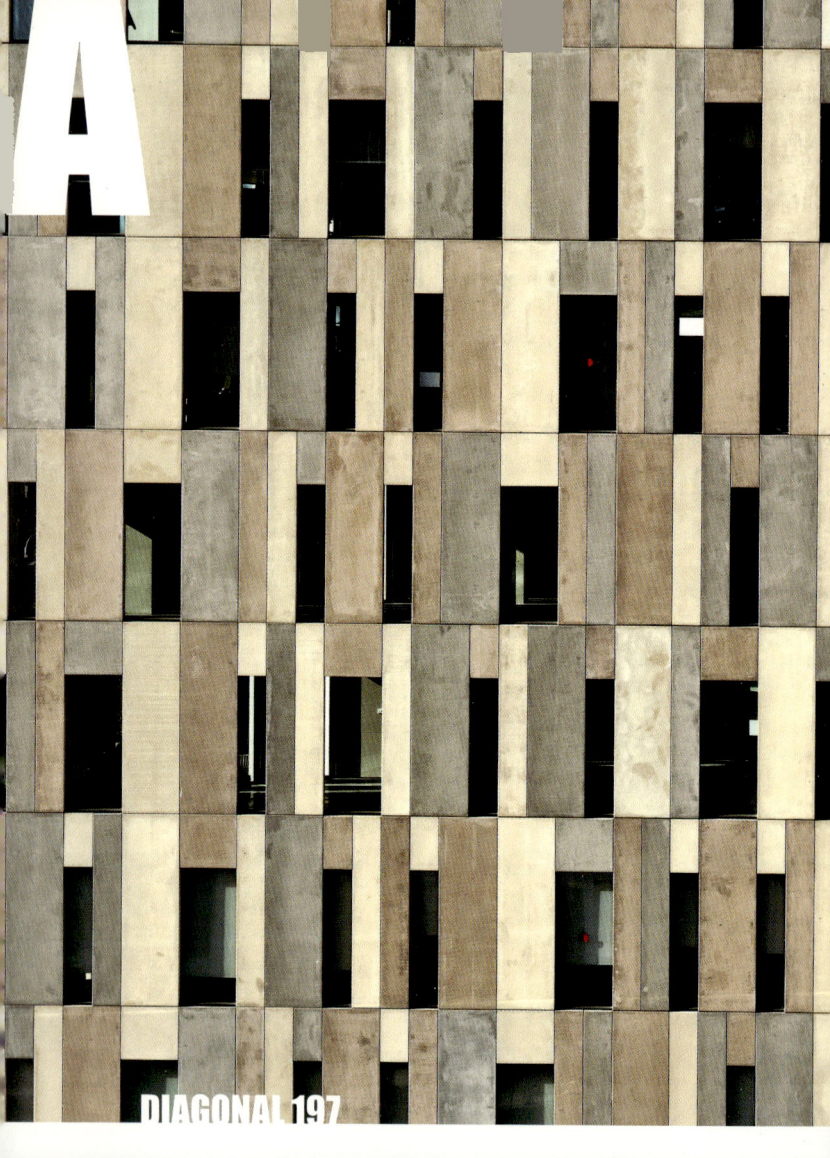

A

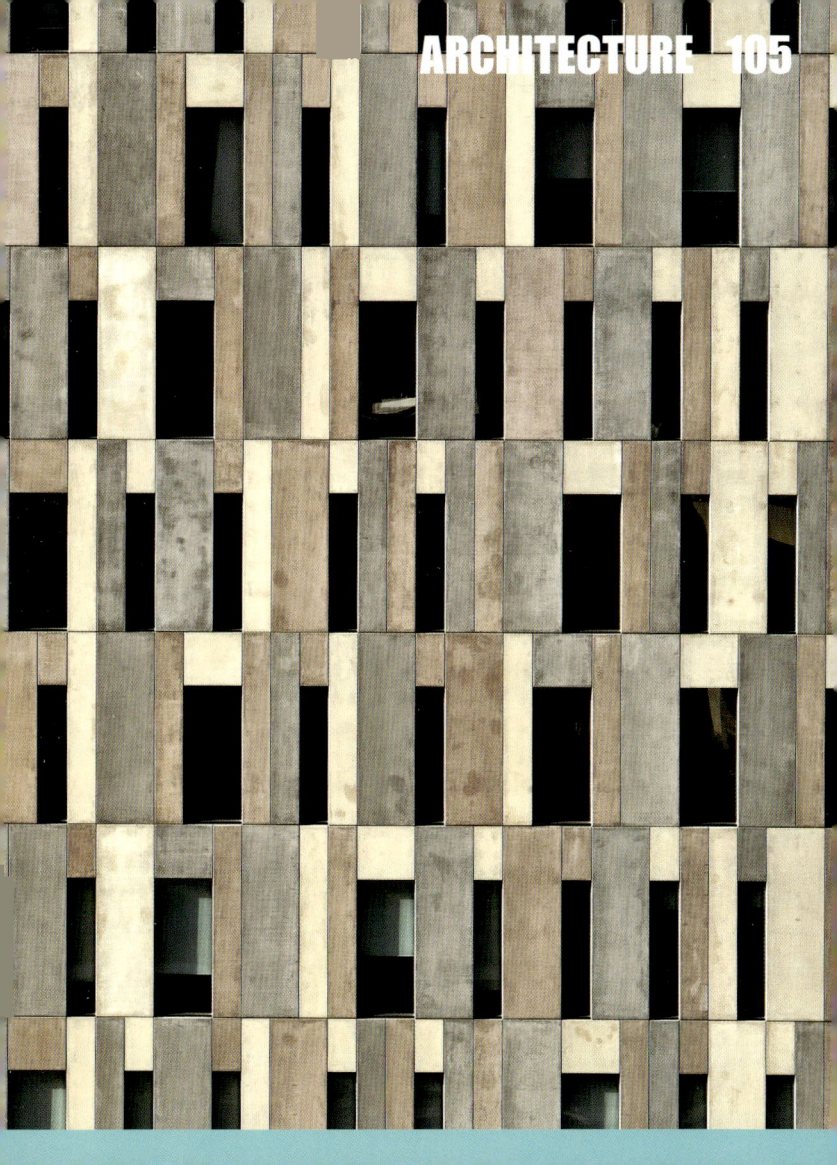

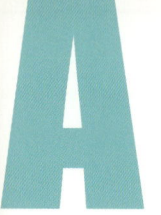

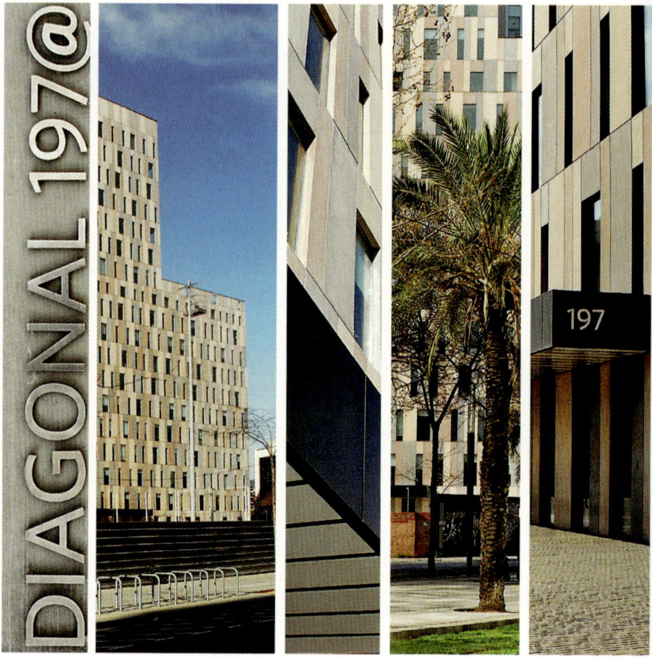

DIAGONAL 197

Avinguda Diagonal, 197 // Sant Martí / Poblenou / 22@
www.b720.com; www.davidchipperfield.co.uk

Metro L1 Glòries

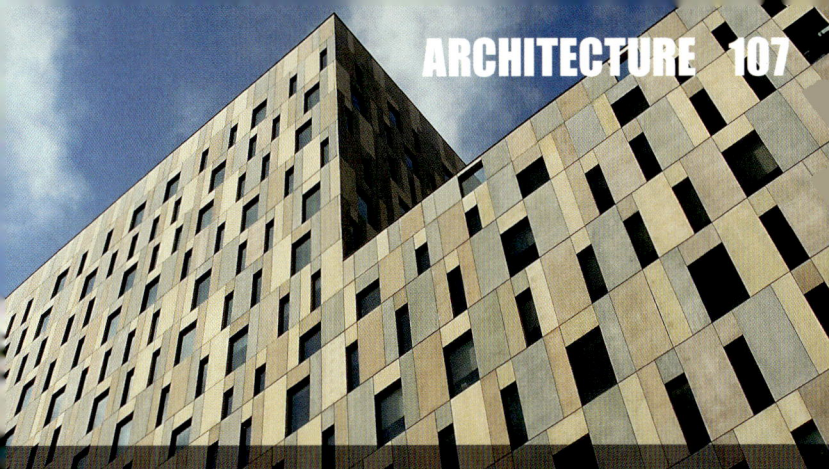

The industrial area between Plaça de les Glòries, Avinguda Diagonal, and the beach is structured by a new urbanism. Completed in 2008, the office high-rise designed by David Chipperfield and b720 Fermín Vázquez Arquitectos is part of the new Campus Audiovisual. What makes the building's skin unique are the seemingly random arrangement of room-height windows which give the façade an abstract character, as well as the vertical fiberglass-reinforced concrete panels colored in earth tones.

Ein neuer Urbanismus strukturiert das Industrieareal zwischen der Plaça de les Glòries, der Diagonal und der Küste. Das 2008 fertiggestellte Bürohochhaus von David Chipperfield und dem Büro b720 Fermín Vázquez Arquitectos ist Teil des neuen Campus Audiovisual. Interessant wird die Gebäudehülle durch die scheinbar zufällige Anordnung raumhoher Fensteröffnungen, die der Fassade einen abstrakten Charakter verleihen, sowie durch die vertikal ausgerichteten, in Erdtönen gefärbten und mit Glasfaser verstärkten Betonplatten.

Un nouveau plan d'urbanisme structure l'aire industrielle entre la Plaça de les Glòries, la Avinguda Diagonal et la côte. L'immeuble administratif, achevé en 2008 et conçu par David Chipperfield et le bureau d'architectes b720, fait partie du nouveau campus Audiovisual. Sa façade est remarquable grâce à l'agencement faussement aléatoire des fenêtres lui donnant un caractère abstrait, et aux plaques verticales de béton de fibre de verre, aux couleurs de la terre.

Un nuevo urbanismo estructura la zona industrial entre la Plaça de les Glòries, la Diagonal y la costa. La torre de oficinas creadas por David Chipperfield y el despacho b720 Fermín Vázquez Arquitectos en 2008 forma parte del nuevo Campus Audiovisual. La piel del edificio, con la distribución aparentemente aleatoria de las aberturas, da a la fachada un carácter abstracto tan interesante como las planchas de hormigón verticales de tonos pardos y reforzadas con fibra de vidrio.

A

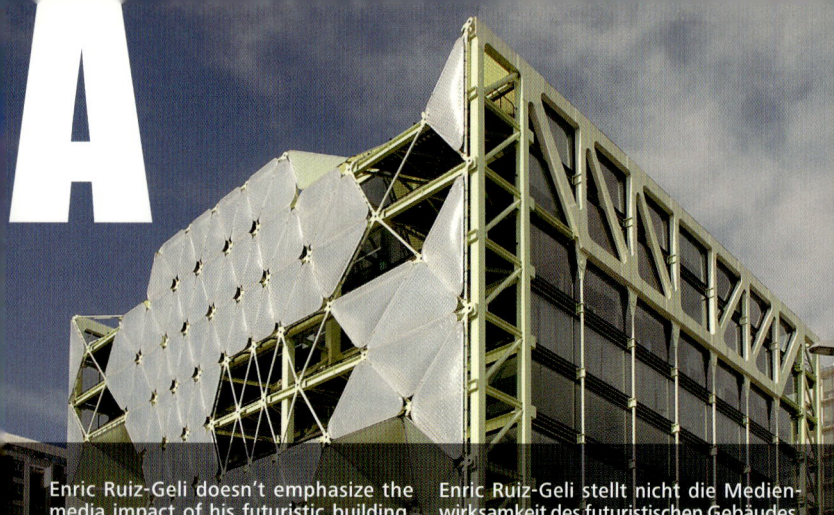

Enric Ruiz-Geli doesn't emphasize the media impact of his futuristic building, but instead its energy efficiency. Extensive studies formed the basis for the parametric design where the award-winning steel frame is on the outside and the interior offers flexible use of space. The patented cushions made of ETFE membranes are controllable, allowing the different façades to be insulated, opened, or shaded as needed. Media-TIC is a prime example of forward-looking architecture.

Enric Ruiz-Geli stellt nicht die Medienwirksamkeit des futuristischen Gebäudes, sondern seine Energieeffizienz in den Mittelpunkt. Ausführliche Studien ermöglichten die parametrische Konstruktion, bei der die preisgekrönte Stahlstruktur außen liegt und der Innenraum flexibel nutzbar ist. Die patentierten Kissen aus ETFE-Membranen sind steuerbar, um die unterschiedlich gestalteten Fassaden nach Bedarf zu isolieren, zu öffnen oder zu verschatten. Ein Musterbeispiel zukunftsweisender Architektur.

L'objectif d'Enric Ruiz-Geli n'est pas l'impact médiatique de ce bâtiment futuriste, mais sa consommation d'énergie. Des études poussées ont permis cette construction paramétrique caractérisée par sa structure en acier primée placée à l'extérieur et sa surface intérieure modulable. La position des coussins brevetés à membrane en ETFE est modifiable, afin d'isoler, ouvrir ou protéger les façades, toutes différentes, selon les besoins. Un avant-goût de l'architecture du futur.

Para Enric Ruiz-Geli, lo importante no es el efecto mediático de su futurista edificio, sino su eficiencia energética. Estudios exhaustivos permitieron una construcción paramétrica en la que la premiada estructura de acero se sitúa en el exterior y el espacio interior se presta a un uso flexible. Las membranas patentadas de ETFE son regulables para así aislar, abrir u oscurecer a voluntad las distintas fachadas. Un ejemplo paradigmático de arquitectura futurista.

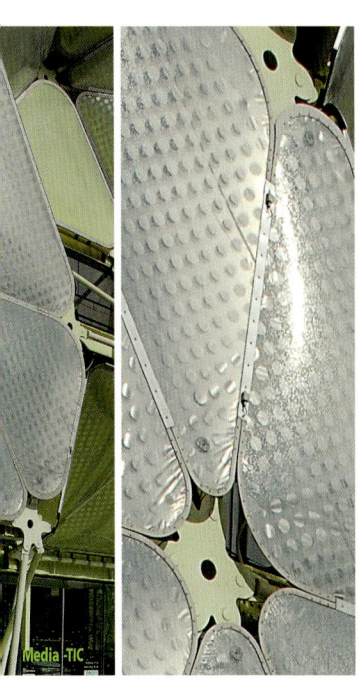

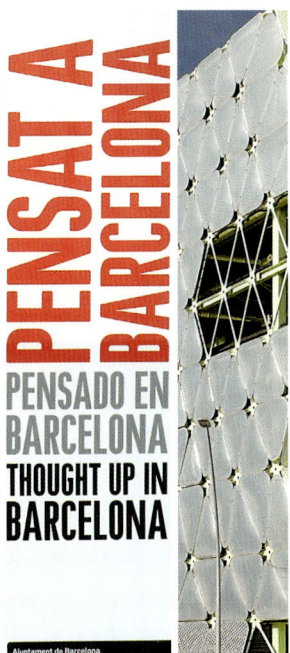

MEDIA-TIC

Carrer de Roc Boronat, 117 // Sant Martí /
Poblenou / 22@
www.ruiz-geli.com

Metro L4 Llacuna

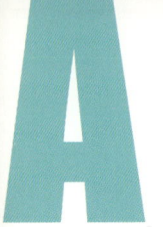

![Museum interior and exterior views]

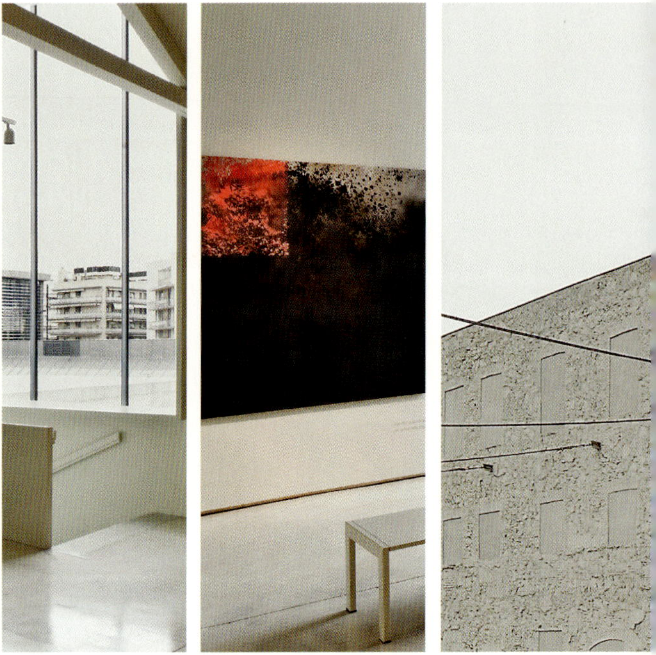

MUSEU CAN FRAMIS

Carrer de Roc Boronat, 116-126 // Sant Martí / Poblenou / 22@
Tel.: +34 93 320 87 36
www.fundaciovilacasas.com

Tue–Sat 11 am to 6 pm
Closed holidays and Aug
Metro L1 Glòries or L4 Llacuna

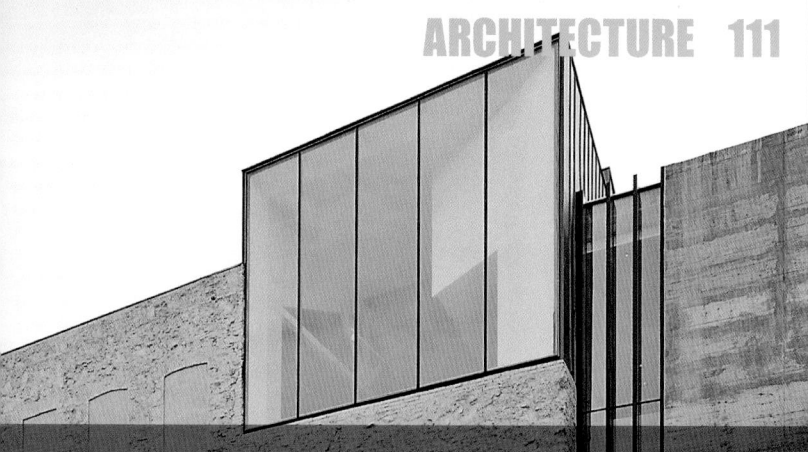

In the 22@ district, former industrial facilities are gradually being transformed into sites for new technologies and innovative companies. Can Framis, the Museum of Contemporary Catalan Painting, opened here in 2009. BAAS Architects clad two buildings of an old wool mill in gray paint so the existing structures form a harmonious whole with the new construction made of exposed concrete. Visitors start on the top level and move downwards as they explore the exhibitions.

Im Distrikt 22@ werden ehemalige Industrieanlagen schrittweise in Standorte für neue Technologien und innovative Unternehmen umgewandelt. Seit 2009 liegt hier auch das Museum für zeitgenössische katalanische Malerei. Das Studio BAAS hüllte zwei Gebäude einer alten Wollspinnerei in graue Farbe, sodass der Bestand mit dem Neubau aus Sichtbeton eine harmonische Einheit bildet. Als ununterbrochener Spaziergang erschließt sich die Ausstellung vom Obergeschoss nach unten.

D'anciennes usines du district 22@ sont petit à petit réaménagées en sites économiques pour nouvelles technologies et entreprises novatrices. Depuis 2009 s'y trouve également le musée de la peinture catalane contemporaine. Le studio BAAS a recouvert deux bâtiments d'une ancienne filature de laine d'une couleur grise afin de former un ensemble harmonieux avec le nouvel édifice en béton apparent. L'exposition se déroule de haut en bas, telle une promenade ininterrompue.

En el distrito 22@ se transforman paso a paso antiguas instalaciones industriales en espacios para nuevas tecnologías y empresas innovadoras. Desde 2009 se encuentra aquí el museo de pintura contemporánea catalana. El estudio BAAS recubrió dos edificios de una antigua fábrica de lana en tono gris, de modo que el bloque se integra armónicamente con la nueva construcción de cemento visto. La exposición se visita como un paseo continuado desde el piso superior a la planta baja.

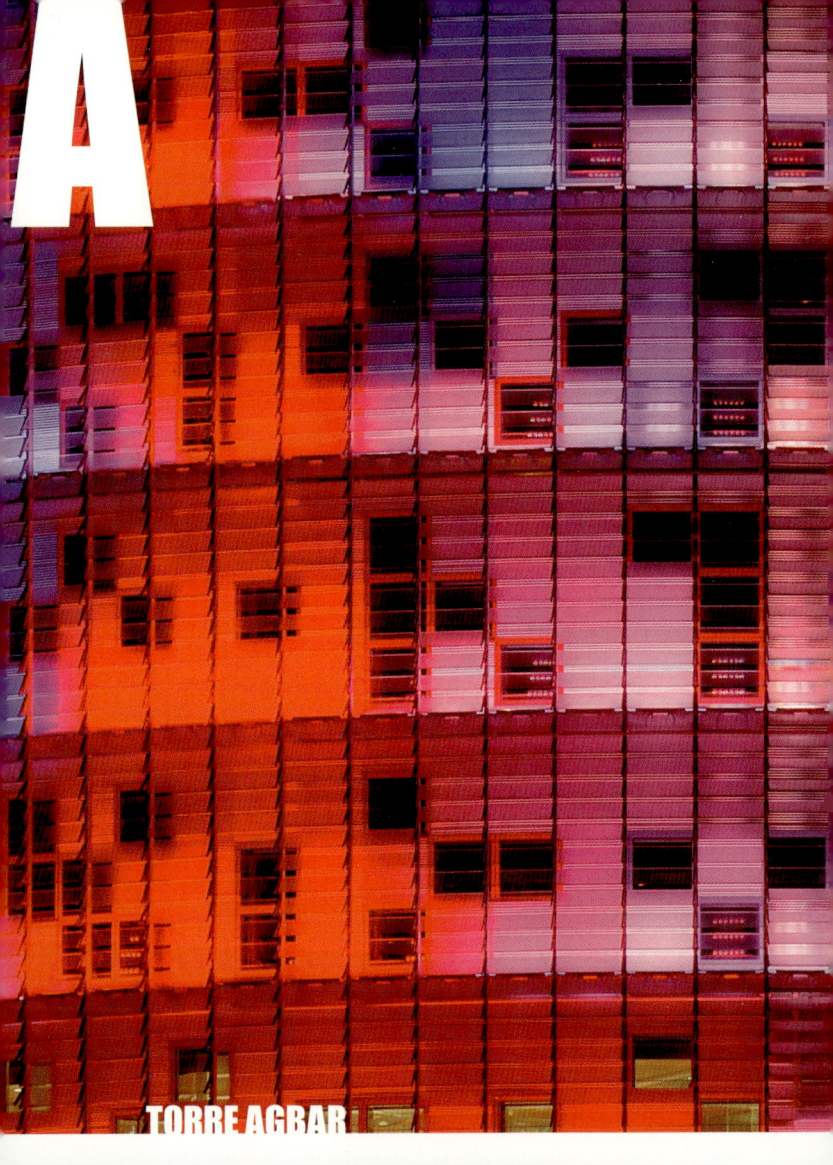

A

TORRE AGBAR

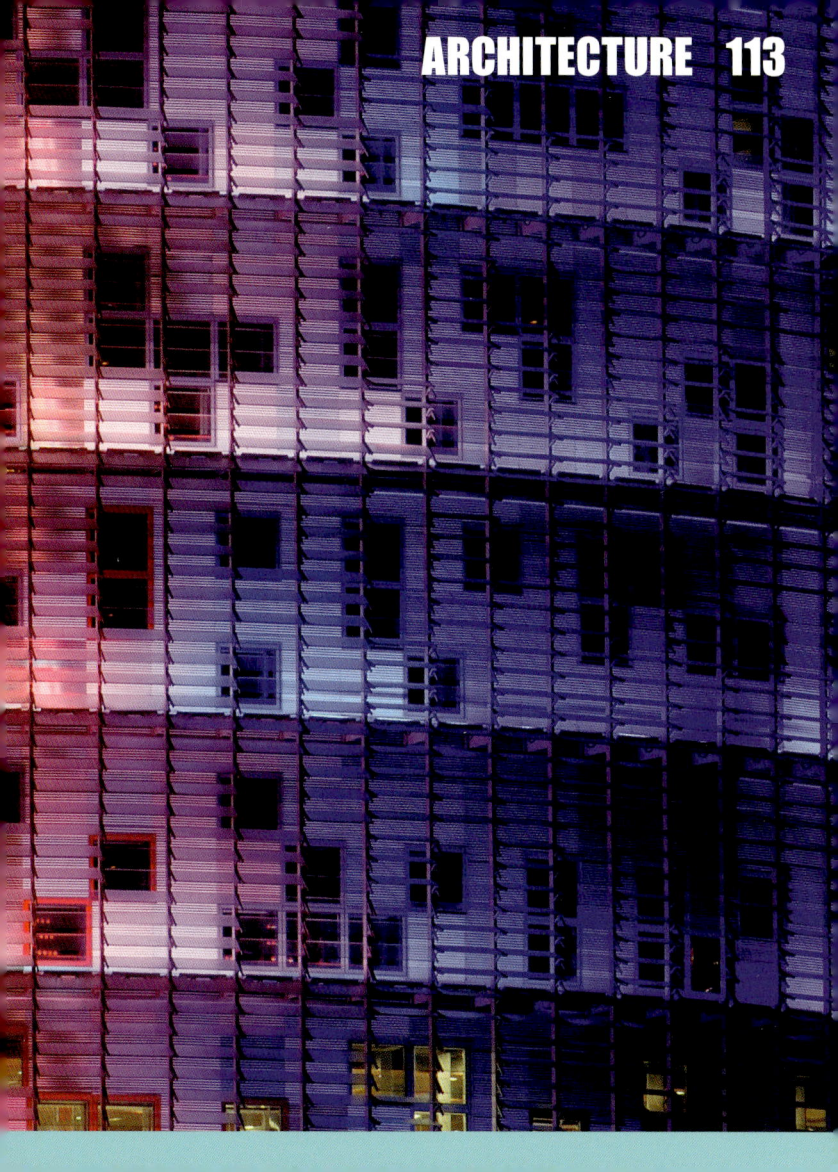

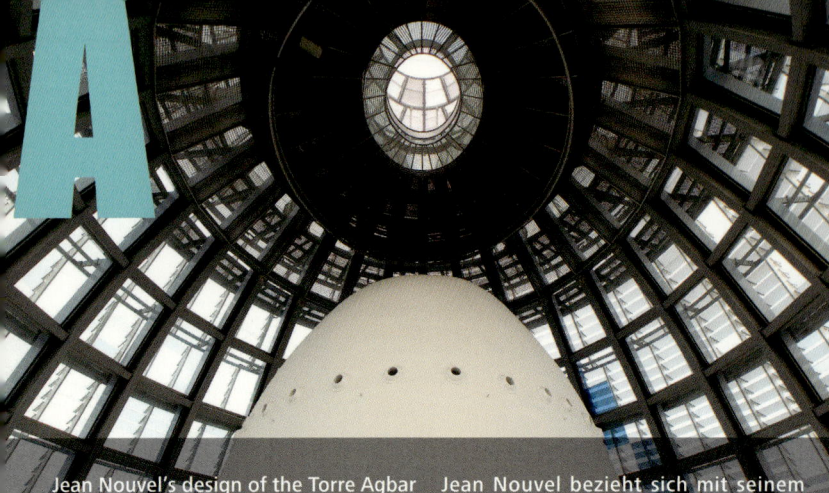

Jean Nouvel's design of the Torre Agbar (2005) brings to mind the distinctive shape of the mountains of Montserrat or the eruption of a geyser. The bioclimatic building is surrounded by a skin of aluminum painted in shades of red, brown and blue, overlaid by a glass façade with more than 59,000 louvers. A concrete core contains all service installations and emergency stairwells, resulting in 35 stories with flexible floor plans and no internal partition walls.

Jean Nouvel bezieht sich mit seinem Entwurf des Torre Agbar (2005) auf die markante Form der Berge von Montserrat und das Aufschäumen eines Geysirs. Eine doppelte Hülle aus in Rot-, Braun- und Blautönen lackiertem Aluminium und einer vorgeschalteten Glasfassade aus über 59 000 Luftklappen umschließt das bioklimatische Gebäude. Ein Betonkern bündelt die Installationen und vertikalen Erschließungen, sodass die 35 Geschosse von flexiblen Grundrissen ohne Zwischenwände profitieren.

En concevant la Torre Agbar en 2005, Jean Nouvel s'est inspiré des formes particulières du massif de Montserrat et de l'éruption d'un geyser. Une couche d'aluminium laqué de rouge, de marron et de bleu sous une façade de verre offrant plus de 59 000 volets d'aération entourent ce bâtiment bioclimatique. Une structure en béton armé protège les installations et équipements verticaux afin que les 35 étages bénéficient de plans flexibles, sans cloisons.

Con el diseño de la Torre Agbar (2005), Jean Nouvel alude a las inconfundibles formas de Monserrat y al agua borboteante de un géiser. Una cubierta doble de aluminio esmaltado en tonos rojos, pardos y azules y una fachada compuesta por 59 000 lamas de vidrio envuelven este edificio bioclimático. Un núcleo de hormigón engloba las instalaciones y accesos verticales, de modo que los 35 pisos gozan de una planta flexible desprovista de tabiques.

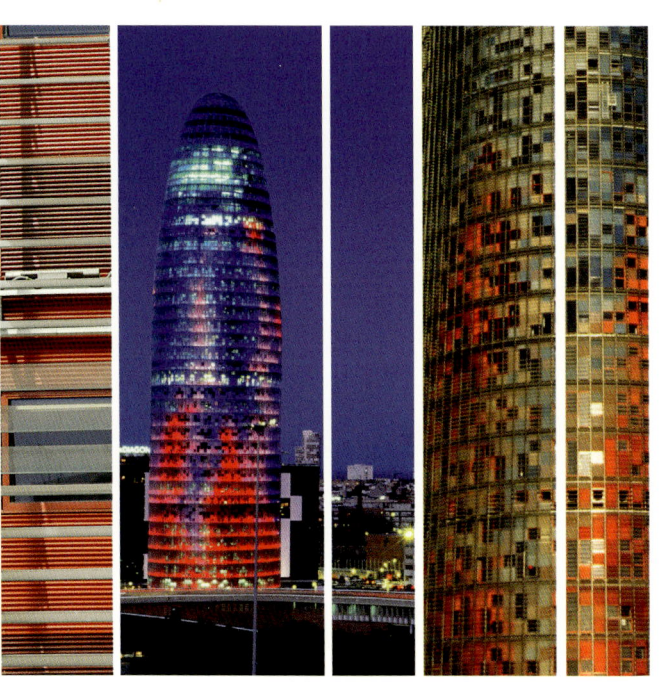

TORRE AGBAR

Plaça de les Glòries Catalanes / Avinguda Diagonal, 211
Sant Martí / Poblenou / 22@
www.torreagbar.com; www.jeannouvel.com

Metro L1 Glòries

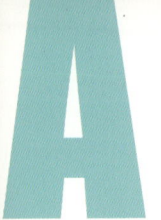

![Ciutat de la Justícia building photographs]

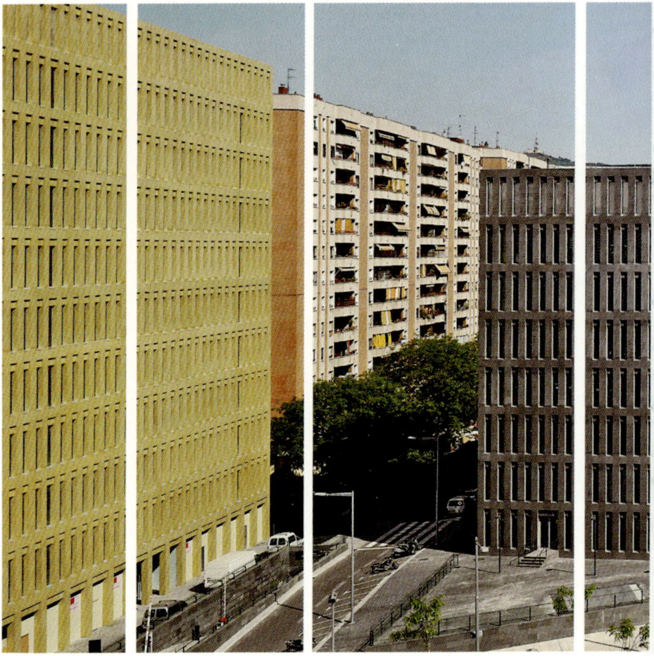

CIUTAT DE LA JUSTÍCIA

Gran Via de les Corts Catalanes, 111 // Sants-Montjuïc
www.ciutatdelajusticia.com

Metro L1 Santa Eulàlia

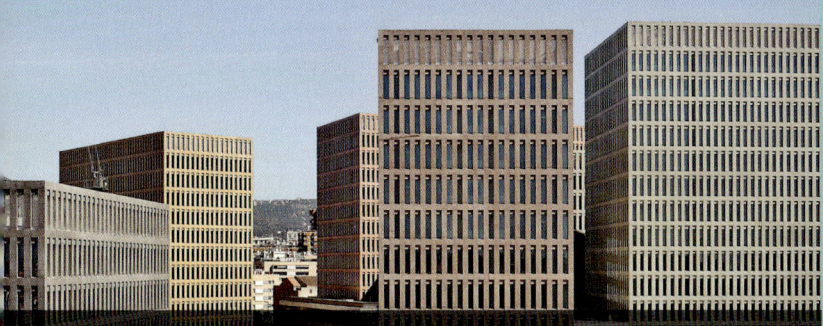

Inaugurated in 2009, this law court complex on the border between Barcelona and L'Hospitalet de Llobregat is characterized by the interplay between eight cubes of different volumes. David Chipperfield and the firm b720 Fermín Vázquez Arquitectos break up the monolithic structure by using varying building heights, different color pigments in the concrete façades, and arranging the buildings around an atrium. A total of 2.5 million sq. ft. is available for government agencies, stores, and offices.

Ein Spiel unterschiedlicher Volumina zwischen acht Kuben charakterisiert das 2009 eingeweihte Justizviertel auf der Grenze zwischen Barcelona und Hospitalet de Llobregat. David Chipperfield und das Büro b720 Fermín Vázquez Arquitectos brechen das Monolithische des Ensembles durch unterschiedliche Gebäudehöhen, verschiedene in die Betonfassaden eingearbeitete Farbpigmente und die Anordnung der Einheiten um ein Atrium auf. Mehr als 230 000 m² stehen den Behörden neben Geschäfts- und Büroflächen zur Verfügung.

Le quartier judiciaire, inauguré en 2009 à la frontière entre Barcelone et L'Hospitalet de Llobregat, se caractérise par ses huit cubes de dimensions différentes. David Chipperfield et le bureau b720 Fermín Vázquez Arquitectos brisent l'aspect monolithique de l'ensemble grâce à la différence de hauteur des édifices, de couleur des façades de béton et l'agencement des bâtiments autour d'un atrium. L'administration dispose de plus de 230 000 m² en plus des surfaces de bureaux et de commerces.

La relación que establecen los ocho cubos de diferentes volúmenes caracteriza el barrio judicial inaugurado en 2009 sobre la zona misma que separa Barcelona de L'Hospitalet de Llobregat. David Chipperfield y el despacho b720 Fermín Vázquez Arquitectos quiebran el monolítico conjunto con las diversas alturas de los edificios, diferentes pigmentos de las fachadas de hormigón y la ordenación de los elementos en torno a un patio. Los funcionarios disponen de más de 230 000 m², además de espacios para tiendas y oficinas.

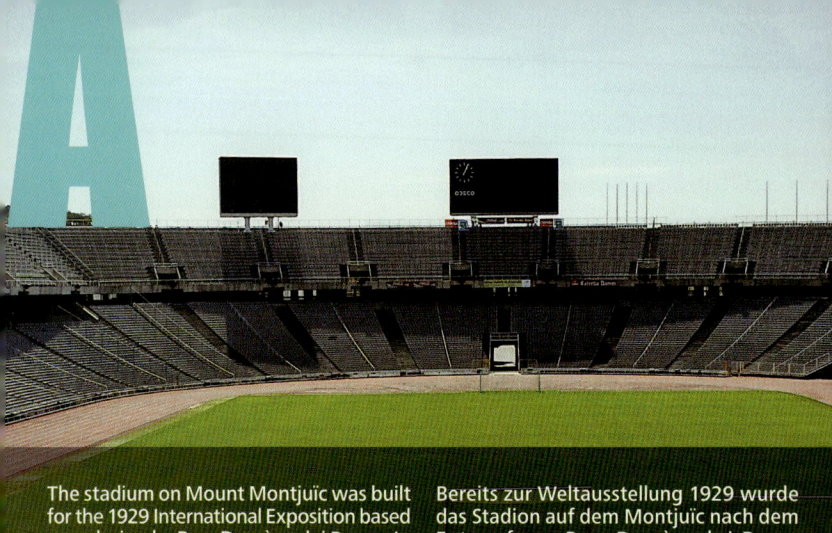

The stadium on Mount Montjuïc was built for the 1929 International Exposition based on a design by Pere Domènech i Roura. In preparation for the 1992 Olympic Games, the dilapidated stadium was completely gutted and rebuilt in the mid 1980s by Vittorio Gregotti and the architectural team of Correa-Milà-Margarit-Buxadé. They dug down 36 ft. to create an arena with seating for 55,000; the high-quality stone that was excavated was reused for the Sagrada Família.

Bereits zur Weltausstellung 1929 wurde das Stadion auf dem Montjuïc nach dem Entwurf von Pere Domènech i Roura errichtet. Im Hinblick auf die Olympiade 1992 konnte das marode Stadion in den 80er Jahren von Vittorio Gregotti und dem Architektenteam Correa-Milà-Margarit-Buxadé entkernt und saniert werden. Durch einen Aushub von 11 m bietet die Arena heute 55 000 Zuschauern Platz, während der so gewonnene hochwertige Stein für den Bau der Sagrada Família verwendet werden konnte.

Le stade fut construit à Montjuïc dès 1929 pour l'exposition universelle selon les plans de Pere Domènech i Roura. En prévision des Jeux Olympiques de 1992, celui-ci, en piteux état, fut entièrement rénové et agrandi par Vittorio Gregotti et l'équipe d'architectes Correa-Milà-Margarit-Buxadé. Grâce à une fosse de 11 m, le stade peut désormais accueillir 55 000 spectateurs, tandis que la pierre excavée, de très bonne qualité, a pu être utilisée pour la construction de la Sagrada Família.

Con ocasión de la Exposición Universal de 1929 se construyó el estadio de Montjuïc según el diseño de Pere Domènech i Roura. Durante los preparativos de los Juegos Olímpicos de 1992, el ruinoso estadio fue completamente renovado por Vittorio Gregotti y el equipo de arquitectos Correa-Milà-Margarit-Buxadé. La excavación de 11 m en el terreno hizo posible que el recinto pueda acoger hoy a 55 000 espectadores. La piedra obtenida en la obra se utilizó en la construcción de la Sagrada Família.

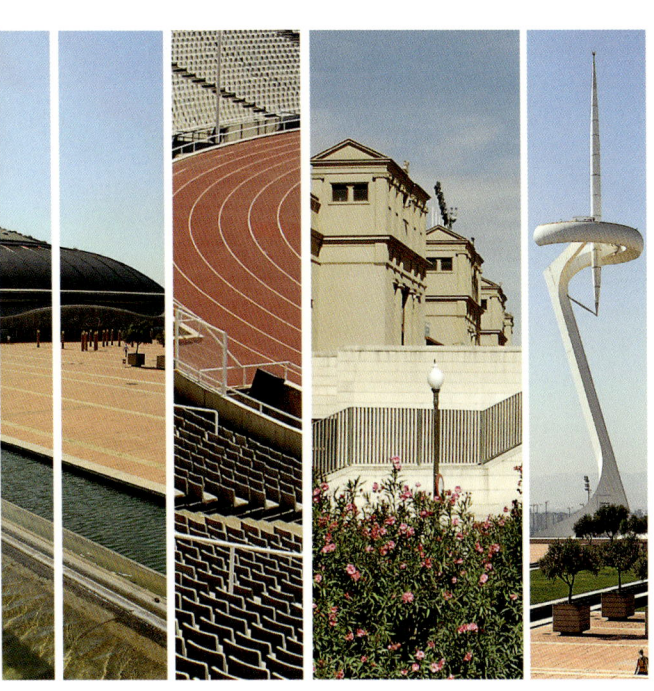

ESTADI OLÍMPIC LLUÍS COMPANYS

Avinguda de l'Estadi // Sants-Montjuïc
Tel.: +34 93 426 20 89
www.agendabcn.com

Metro L1, L3 Espanya
Bus 50, 61 Estadi Olímpic de
Montjuïc-MNAC or 55, 193
Av. de l'Estadi-Pg. Olímpic

Summer daily 10 am to 8 pm
Winter daily 10 am to 6 pm

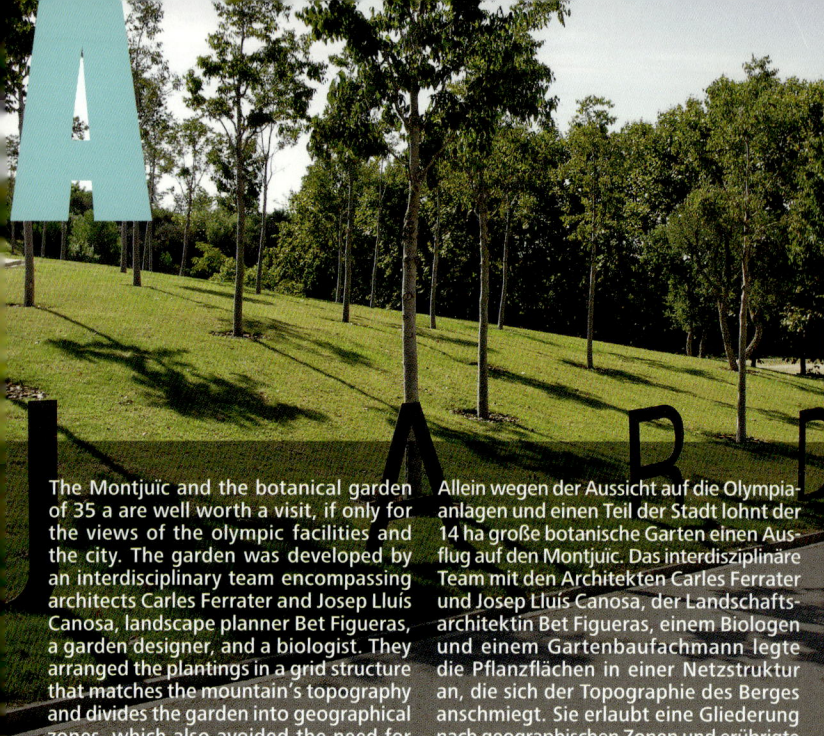

The Montjuïc and the botanical garden of 35 a are well worth a visit, if only for the views of the olympic facilities and the city. The garden was developed by an interdisciplinary team encompassing architects Carles Ferrater and Josep Lluís Canosa, landscape planner Bet Figueras, a garden designer, and a biologist. They arranged the plantings in a grid structure that matches the mountain's topography and divides the garden into geographical zones, which also avoided the need for extensive soil cutting.

Allein wegen der Aussicht auf die Olympia-anlagen und einen Teil der Stadt lohnt der 14 ha große botanische Garten einen Aus-flug auf den Montjuïc. Das interdisziplinäre Team mit den Architekten Carles Ferrater und Josep Lluis Canosa, der Landschafts-architektin Bet Figueras, einem Biologen und einem Gartenbaufachmann legte die Pflanzflächen in einer Netzstruktur an, die sich der Topographie des Berges anschmiegt. Sie erlaubt eine Gliederung nach geographischen Zonen und erübrigte umfassende Erdbewegungen.

La magnifique vue sur les installations olympiques et une partie de la ville depuis le jardin botanique de 14 ha vaut déjà une visite au Montjuïc ! L'équipe interdiscipli-naire avec les architectes Carles Ferrater et Josep Lluís Canosa, la paysagiste Bet Figueras, un biologiste et un horticulteur, a établi les zones de plantation dans une structure de réseau qui épouse la topo-graphie de la colline. Elle permet une répartition par zones géographiques et a épargné des déblaiements extensifs.

Las vistas de las instalaciones olímpicas y de parte de la ciudad hacen por sí mismas que valga la pena acercarse a las 14 ha del jardín botánico de Montjuïc. El equipo interdisciplinario formado por los arquitec-tos Carles Ferrater y Josep Lluís Canosa, la paisajista Bet Figueras, un biólogo y un experto en jardinería ha dispuesto los espacios vegetales en una estructura en red que se adapta a la topografía de la montaña, lo que permite distribuirlos por regiones geográficas e hizo innecesarias grandes obras.

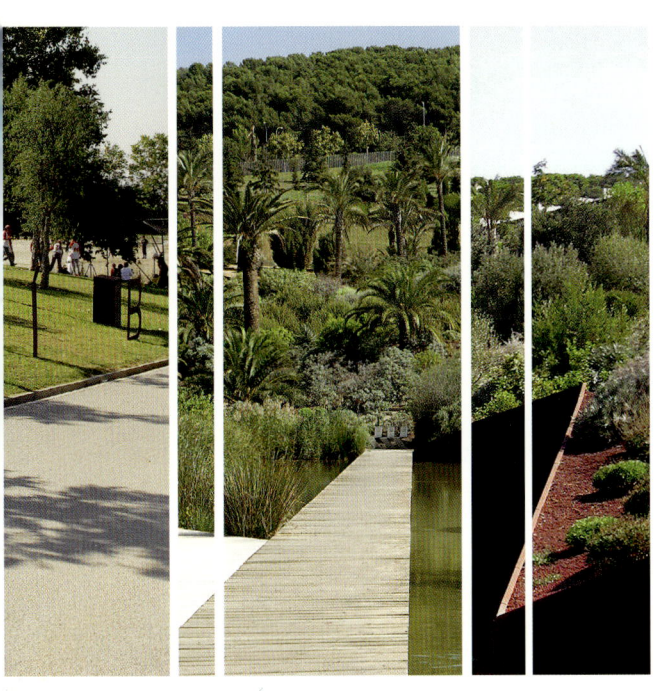

JARDÍ BOTÀNIC

Carrer del Doctor Font i Quer, 2
Sants-Montjuïc
Tel.: +34 93 256 41 60
www.jardibotanic.bcn.es

Oct–Mar Mon–Sun 10 am to 6 pm
Apr, May and Sep Mon–Sun 10 am to 7 pm
Jun–Aug Mon–Sun 10 am to 8 pm

Closed Jan 1st and Dec 25th
Free admission the last Sun of every
month and every Sun from 3 pm
Metro L1, L3 Espanya
Bus 193 Jardí Botànic
Railroad Montjuïc funicular, connected
with Metro L3 and L2

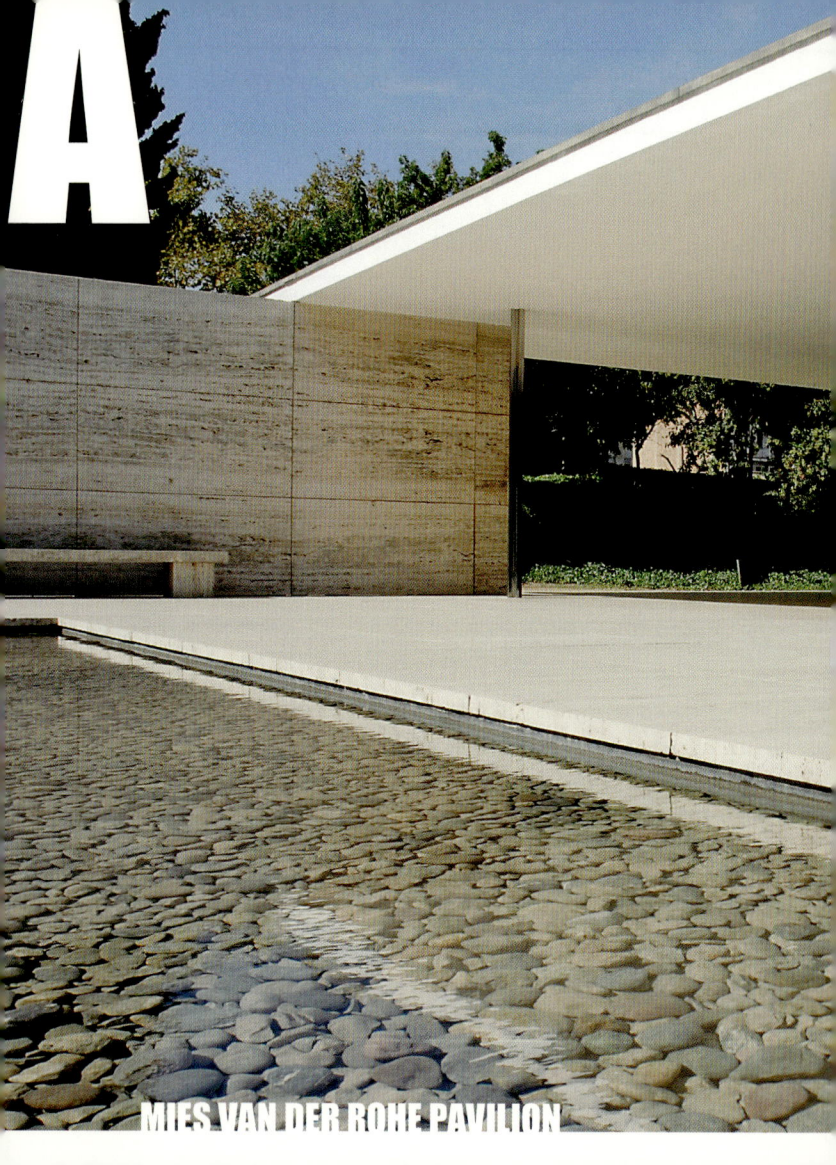

MIES VAN DER ROHE PAVILION

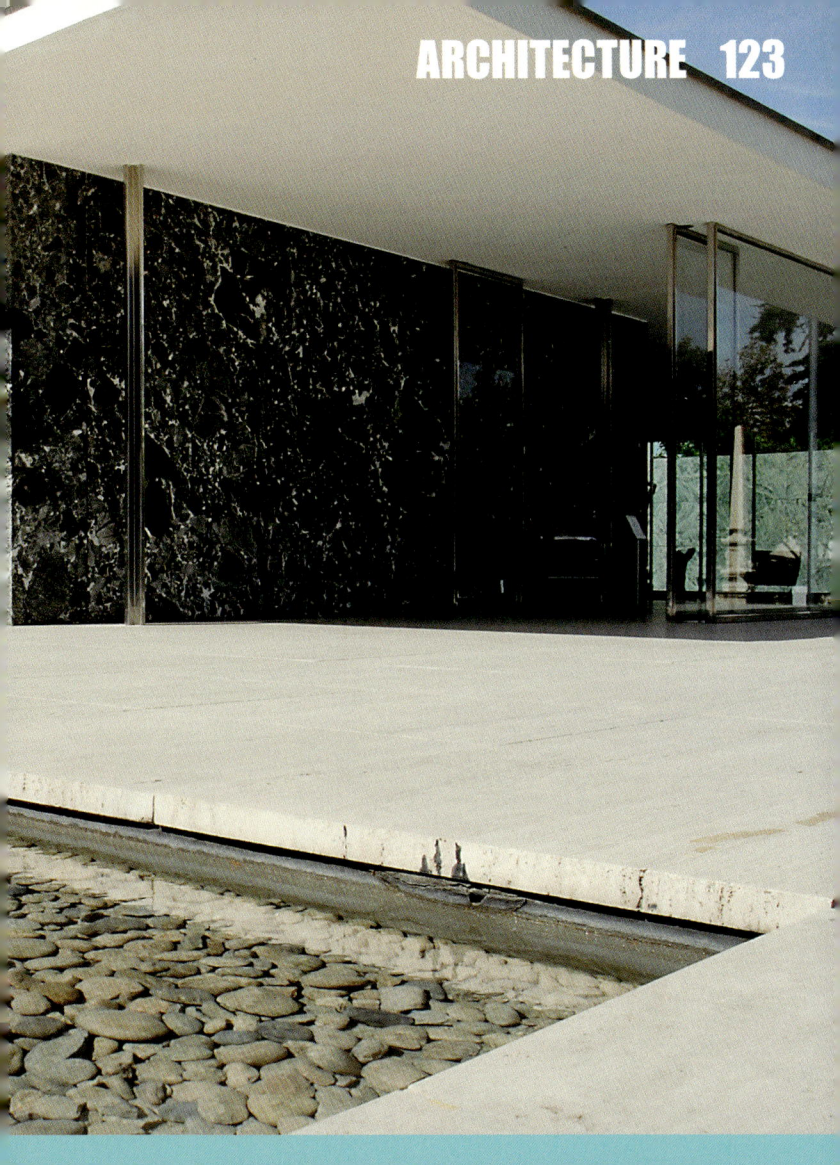

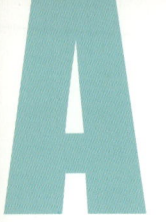

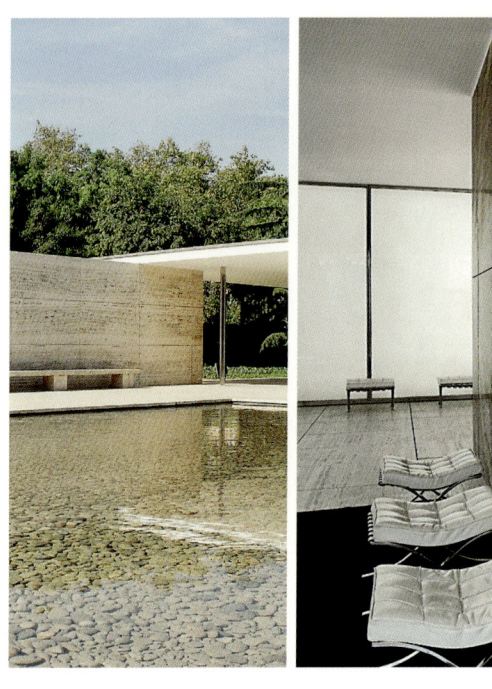

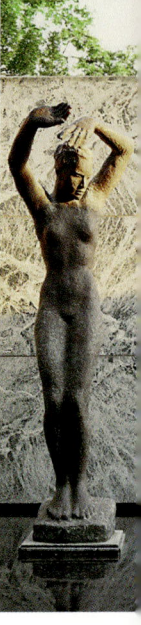

MIES VAN DER ROHE PAVILION

Avinguda de Francesc Ferrer i Guàrdia, 7 // Sants-Montjuïc
Tel.: +34 93 423 40 16
www.miesbcn.com

Mon 4 pm to 8 pm
Tue–Sun 10 am to 8 pm
L1, L3 Espanya
Bus 13, 50, 61 Av. Ferrer i Guàrdia or 193 Av. Reina Maria Cristina

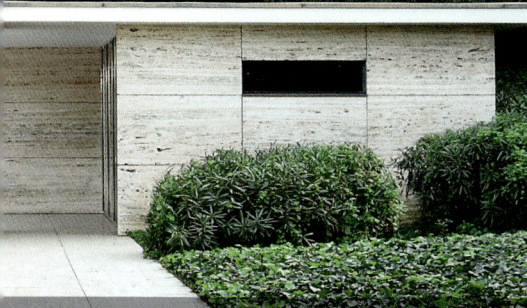

The Barcelona Pavilion is a reconstruction of the Weimar Republic's contribution to the 1929 International Exhibition. Built in 1986 at the original location at the base of Montjuïc, its light, non-load bearing walls and large expanses of glass embody two of Mies van der Rohe's design principles: floating room and free plan. Specially designed for the Barcelona Pavilion, the Barcelona chair made of curved stainless steel and leather cushions became famous in its own right.

Der stilbildende Pavillon ist eine Rekonstruktion des Beitrags der Weimarer Republik zur Weltausstellung 1929. Er wurde 1986 am ursprünglichen Standort am Fuße des Montjuïc errichtet und verkörpert mit den leichten, da nicht tragenden Wandscheiben und großen Glasflächen zwei von Mies van der Rohes Entwurfsprinzipien: fließender Raum und freier Grundriss. Weltberühmt wurde auch der für den Pavillon entworfene Barcelona-Sessel aus geschwungenem Edelstahlband mit Lederkissen.

Ce pavillon est une reproduction de celui de la République de Weimar à l'exposition universelle de 1929. Construit en 1986 à son emplacement original, au pied du Montjuïc, il incarne deux des grands principes de Mies van der Rohe, de part son absence de murs porteurs et ses larges façades en verre : la fluidité de l'espace et le plan libre. Conçue pour ce pavillon, la chaise Barcelone, avec sa fine structure en acier et ses coussins en cuirs, est également mondialement connue.

El pionero pabellón es una reconstrucción de la aportación de la república de Weimar a la Exposición Universal de 1929. Erigido de nuevo en 1986 en su ubicación original en la falda de Montjuïc, los livianos tabiques y grandes cristaleras encarnan dos de los principios del diseño de Mies van der Rohe: espacios fluidos y planta libre. La silla Barcelona, de curvilínea estructura metálica con almohadón de cuero, fue diseñada para el pabellón y es mundialmente conocida.

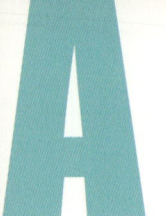

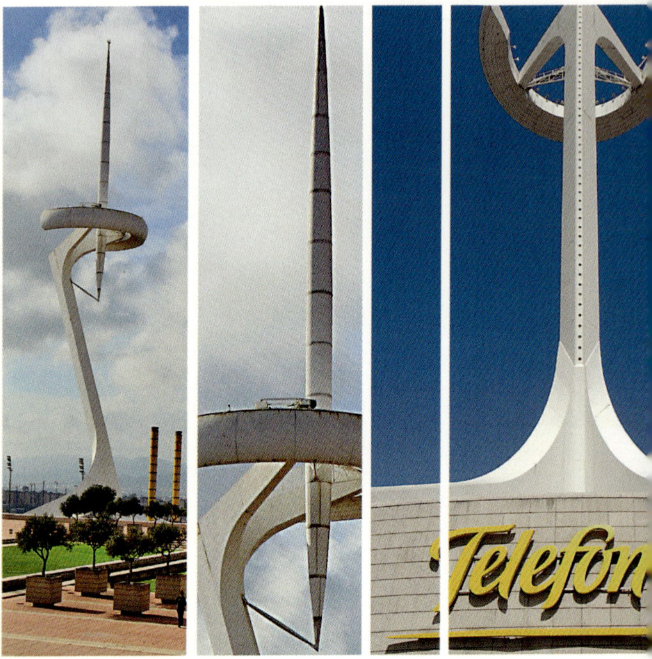

TORRE DE COMUNICACIONS DE MONTJUÏC

Plaça d'Europa, Parc de Montjuïc // Sants-Montjuïc

L1 Espanya or L8 Magòria-La Campana
Bus 50, 61 Av. de l'Estadi-Pl. Europa

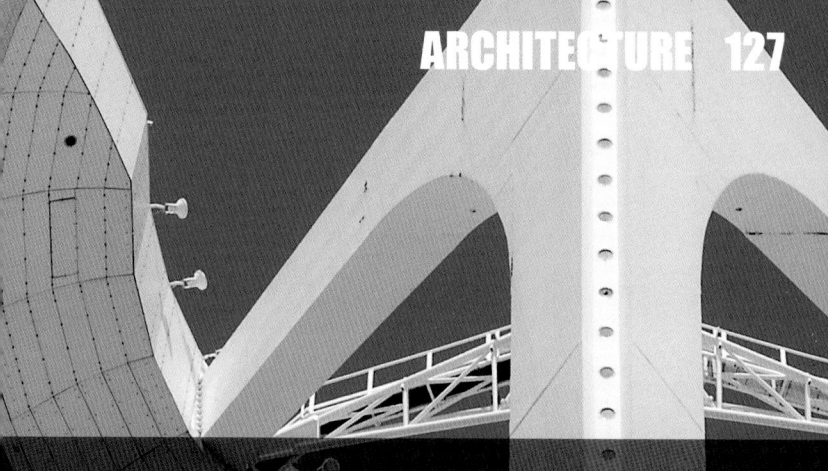

Located on Mount Montjuïc close to the Olympic Stadium and Arata Isozaki's Palau Sant Jordi, this transmission tower was built for the 1992 Olympic Games by telecommunications company Telefónica. Santiago Calatrava's dynamic interpretation of an athlete holding the Olympic torch has been an icon of the city since then. A white mosaic at the base of this white structure of metal and concrete explicitly references the architectural work of Gaudí.

Anlässlich der olympischen Spiele errichtete die Telefongesellschaft 1992 diesen Sendeturm auf dem Berg Montjuïc in unmittelbarer Nähe des Stadions und des Palau Sant Jordi von Arata Isozaki. Santiago Calatravas dynamische Interpretation eines Athleten mit der olympischen Fackel ist längst zu einem Symbol der Stadt geworden. Am Fuß der weißen Struktur aus Metall und Beton stellt Calatrava mit einem weißen Mosaik ausdrücklich einen Bezug zum Architekturschaffen Gaudís her.

À l'occasion des Jeux Olympiques de 1992, la société de télécommunication Telefónica fit construire une tour sur la montagne de Montjuïc, à proximité du stade olympique et du Palau Sant Jordi de Arata Isozaki. La représentation de Santiago Calatrava d'un athlète portant la flamme olympique est devenue un des symboles de la ville. Une mosaïque blanche au pied de la structure faite de métal et de béton rend hommage à l'œuvre architecturale de Gaudí.

Tras serle adjudicados los Juegos Olímpicos a Barcelona, Telefónica construyó en 1992 una torre de comunicaciones sobre Montjuïc, a escasa distancia del estadio y del Palau Sant Jordi de Arata Isozaki. La dinámica interpretación de un atleta con la antorcha olímpica, obra de Santiago Calatrava, se ha convertido en símbolo de la ciudad. Al pie de la blanca estructura de metal y cemento, Calatrava traza un vínculo directo con el arte gaudiniano por medio de un mosaico blanco.

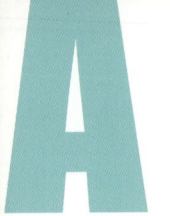

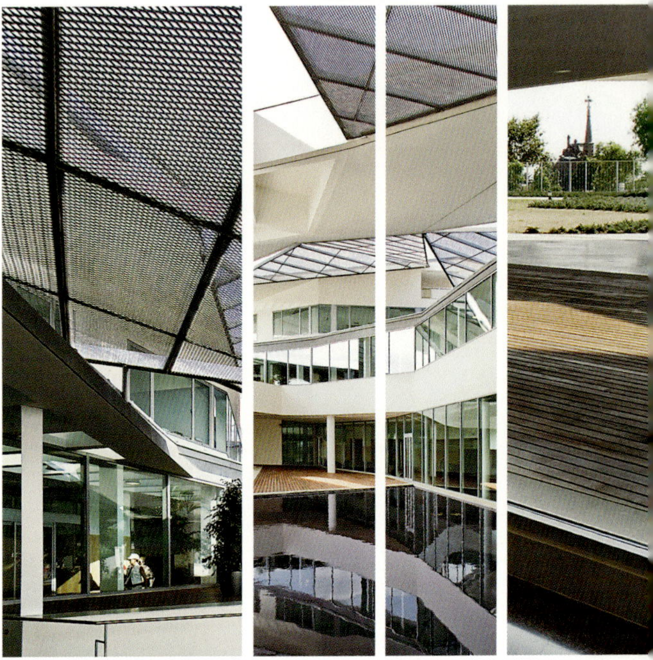

INSTITUTO DE
MICROCIRUGÍA OCULAR (IMO)

Carrer de Josep Maria Lladó, 3 // Sarrià-Sant Gervasi
www.imo.es

Bus 196 Josep Maria Lladó (Carles Riba-Benedetti)

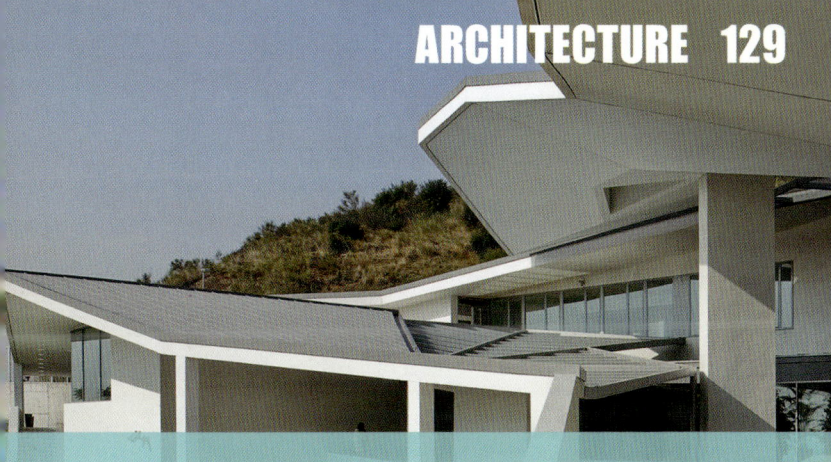

The white structure of the Institute of Ocular Microsurgery designed by Josep Llinás is nestled against Mount Tibidabo above the city, shielded from the road by green space. The southern façade is broad and inviting, allowing the offices and cafeteria to benefit from daylight and a view of the city, while protruding roof areas and the arrangement of openings and skylights contribute to a subdued interior light level that is appropriate for patients undergoing eye surgery.

Der weiße Bau der neuen Augenklinik des Architekten Josep Llinás fügt sich oberhalb der Stadt in die Topographie des Tibidabo-Berges ein, abgeschirmt von der Straße durch einen Grünraum. Die Südfassade öffnet sich weit und einladend, sodass Büros und Cafeteria vom Tageslicht und der Aussicht über die Stadt profitieren, während die vorgezogenen Dachflächen sowie die Anordnung der Öffnungen und Oberlichter dazu beitragen, dass das Licht im Inneren für die Patienten angenehm gedämpft ist.

La nouvelle clinique ophtalmologique réalisée par l'architecte Josep Llinás domine la ville depuis le mont Tibidabo. L'édifice de couleur blanche est protégé de la rue par un espace vert. La façade sud, large et accueillante, permet aux bureaux et à la cafétéria de profiter de la lumière du soleil et d'une superbe vue sur la ville. À l'inverse, le toit avancé ainsi que l'agencement des ouvertures et vasistas offrent aux patients une lumière intérieure agréable et tamisée.

El edificio blanco de la nueva clínica oftalmológica creada por el arquitecto Josep Llinás se integra en la topografía del Tibidabo, protegido de la calle por una zona ajardinada. La fachada sur, amplia y acogedora permite que las oficinas y la cafetería se beneficien de la luz solar y la vista sobre la ciudad. Los diversos tragaluces contribuyen a que la indirecta luz interior resulte tenue y agradable para los pacientes.

DESIGN

D

It is typical for Barcelona's Mediterranean lifestyle to meet in cafés, bars, and restaurants rather than at home. This custom has resulted in an impressive number of establishments that seem to be eternally vying for the trendiest design. Together with many new hotels, ranging from elegant business properties (ME, H1898, Mandarin Oriental) and ultra-modern luxury suites (El Palauet Living Barcelona) to casual hotels (Emma), they form a fertile laboratory where interior and product designers are free to experiment. The completion of a project is celebrated right on site as befits the city's party-friendly night life (Eclipse Bar, Ommsession Club). Projects that cross the boundaries between disciplines produce splendid results, as seen in Roca's flagship store where architecture, multimedia, and product and lighting design transform bathroom items into a fantastic art experience. In stores like Custo, Iguapop, or Vinçon, visitors find exquisitely shaped objects they can take home as Barcelona souvenirs.

Es ist typisch für die mediterrane Lebensart, sich nicht zu Hause, sondern in Cafés, Bars und Restaurants zu treffen. Dieser Brauch führt zu einem beeindruckend dichten Angebot an Lokalen, die sich einen ewigen Wettstreit um das trendigste Design liefern. Zusammen mit der großen Zahl brandneuer Hotels, von eleganten Businesshäusern (ME, H1898, Mandarin Oriental), über ultramoderne Luxussuiten (El Palauet Living Barcelona) bis zur Roommate-Atmosphäre (Emma), bilden sie ein breit gefächertes Experimentallabor für Innenarchitekten und Produktdesigner. Die Umsetzungen feiert man gleich vor Ort im Rahmen des partyfreundlichen Nachtlebens (Eclipse Bar, Omm Session Club). Grenzüberschreitungen zwischen den verschiedenen Spezialisierungen führen zu solch leuchtenden Beispielen wie dem Flagshipstore von Roca: Architektur, Multimedia, Produkt- und Lichtdesign stilisieren Badezimmerelemente zu einem fantastischen Kunsterlebnis. Und Besucher finden in Shops wie Custo, Iguapop oder Vinçon formvollendete Objekte, um sich ein Stück Barcelona-Design mit nach Hause zu nehmen.

Les Méditerranéens se rencontrent plutôt dans des cafés, bars et restaurants qu'à la maison. On observe donc une offre prodigieuse d'établissements rivalisant depuis toujours pour proposer le design le plus tendance. S'ajoutant au grand nombre d'hôtels flambant neufs, d'hôtels d'affaires élégants (ME, H1898, Mandarin Oriental), de suites de luxe ultra modernes (El Palauet Living Barcelona) et de room mates (Emma), ils constituent un laboratoire expérimental très diversifié pour les architectes d'intérieur et les designers de produits. Les réalisations sont fêtées sur place au rythme de la vie nocturne (Eclipse Bar, Ommsession Club). Les extravagances artistiques différentes forment des exemples brillants comme le magasin phare Roca : architecture, multimédia, design de produits et design lumineux transforment la salle de bain en une expérience artistique fantastique. Et dans des boutiques comme Custo, Iguapop ou Vinçon, les visiteurs y trouvent des objets aux lignes parfaites pour ramener un peu de design barcelonais à la maison.

Es muy propio del modo de vida mediterráneo encontrarse con los amigos no en casa, sino en cafés, bares y restaurantes. Esta costumbre motiva la sorprendente abundancia de locales que compiten sin cesar por ofrecer el diseño más a la moda. Junto al gran número de novísimos hoteles –que van desde las elegantes residencias para ejecutivos (ME, H1898, Mandarin Oriental), hasta las ultramodernas suites de lujo (El Palauet Living Barcelona) y el ambiente distendido de un piso compartido (Emma)– constituyen un amplio laboratorio de experimentos para interioristas y diseñadores de productos. Los resultados pueden disfrutarse en vivo, recorriendo la animada vida nocturna de la ciudad (Eclipse Bar, Ommsession Club). El solapamiento de las distintas especializaciones lleva a ejemplos tan majestuosos como el flagship store de Roca: arquitectura, multimedia y diseño de producto y de iluminación transforman la exposición de piezas de baño en una fantástica experiencia artística. Y los visitantes encontrarán en tiendas como Custo, Iguapop o Vinçon piezas de formas perfectas, un trocito de diseño barcelonés para llevarse a casa.

ROSA MARIA ESTEVA + TO ELLA

Grupo Tragaluz owns 13 restaurants and Hotel Omm. With their standards of quality and design, they are a major player in Barcelona's restaurant scene. Rosa Maria Esteva and her son Tomás Tarruella run the business with attention to detail. Grupo Tragaluz started in 1987 with Mordisco in the Eixample district. With its casual atmosphere, it quickly became a trendy hotspot, and a new concept was born. While each restaurant has a different character, they all embody the philosophy of this eternally curious, cosmopolitan, and art-loving restaurateur family: a cohesive concept, and excellent value. Sandra Tarruella, Tomás' sister, designs the modern interiors with their sleek tables and elegant materials. The design takes a backseat to the food, and the focus is on shared experiences. The desire to help others led to the creation of a foundation whose mission is to improve the living conditions, education, and health of children in poor countries. It also finds expression in live events and on their website, which resembles a magazine.

Zur Unternehmensgruppe Tragaluz gehören 13 Restaurants sowie das Hotel Omm. Mit ihren Qualitätsstandards und ihrem überzeugenden Design prägen sie die Gastronomieszene Barcelonas. Hinter den Kulissen geben Rosa Maria Esteva und ihr Sohn Tomás Tarruella mit viel Liebe zum Detail den Ton an. Die Anfänge des erfolgreichen Familienunternehmens gehen zurück auf das im Jahr 1987 eröffnete Mordisco im Eixample. Das kleine Lokal mit seiner lockeren Atmosphäre mauserte sich schnell zum In-Treffpunkt, ein neues Konzept war geboren. Die Restaurants, jedes mit einem eigenen Charakter, bringen die Philosophie der immer neugierigen, weltoffenen und Kunst liebenden Restauratorenfamilie zum Ausdruck: ein kohärentes Gesamtkonzept und ein hervorragendes Preis-Leistungs-Verhältnis. Sandra Tarruella, Tomás Schwester, entwirft die nüchtern-modernen Einrichtungen mit meist geradlinigen Tischen und eleganten Materialien. Das Design stiehlt dem Essen nicht die Schau und gemeinsames Erleben steht im Vordergrund. Der Wunsch, mit anderen zu teilen, mündete in die Gründung einer Stiftung, deren Ziel die Verbesserung der Lebensbedingungen, Bildung und Gesundheit von Kindern in armen Ländern ist, und kommt auch in Liveevents sowie auf der magazinartigen Webseite zum Ausdruck.

MÁS TARRU-

Le groupe d'entreprises Tragaluz est composé de 13 restaurants et de l'hôtel Omm. Avec leurs standards de qualité et leur design convaincant, ils imprègnent la scène gastronomique barcelonaise. En coulisse, Rosa Maria Esteva et son fils Tomás Tarruella donnent le la en affichant leur amour du détail. Les débuts de l'entreprise familiale florissante remontent à 1987, année de l'ouverture de Mordisco dans l'Eixample. Le petit local à l'atmosphère détendue se transforma rapidement en un lieu de rencontre tendance, un nouveau concept était né. Les restaurants, qui arborent chacun un caractère propre, traduisent la philosophie de cette famille de restaurateurs toujours curieuse, ouverte au monde et amatrice d'art : un concept global cohérent et un excellent rapport qualité-prix. Sandra Tarruella, la sœur de Tomás, conçoit des aménagements modernes et sobres avec la plupart du temps des tables aux lignes droites et des matériaux nobles. Le design ne vole pas la vedette à la cuisine. Leur désir de partage a donné naissance à une fondation dont l'objectif est d'améliorer les conditions de vie, l'éducation et la santé d'enfants de pays pauvres et se traduit également par des événements live et un site web type magazine.

El grupo empresarial Tragaluz cuenta con 13 restaurantes y es también propietario del hotel Omm. Con sus altos estándares de calidad y un diseño más que atractivo marca tendencias en la gastronomía barcelonesa. Entre bastidores, Rosa Maria Esteva y su hijo Tomás Tarruella llevan la batuta y prestan atención hasta al último detalle. Los orígenes del éxito de esta empresa familiar se remontan al Mordisco, inaugurado en 1987 en el Eixample. El pequeño local de ambiente distendido pronto se convirtió en obligado punto de encuentro: había nacido un nuevo concepto. Los restaurantes, cada uno con carácter propio, son expresión de la filosofía de esta familia de restauradores perennemente curiosa, cosmopolita y enamorada del arte: un concepto general coherente y una relación calidad-precio extraordinaria. Sandra Tarruella, la hermana de Tomás, diseña los interiores, discretos y modernos, con mesas de líneas rectas y elegantes materiales. El diseño, con todo, no desvía la atención de la comida, y lo que prima en el local es compartir una experiencia. El deseo de compartir con otros desembocó en la creación de una fundación que tiene por objetivo la mejora de la calidad de vida, la educación y la salud infantil en países pobres, y encuentra expresión tanto en eventos en vivo como en la página web del grupo, similar a una revista.

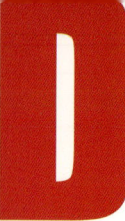

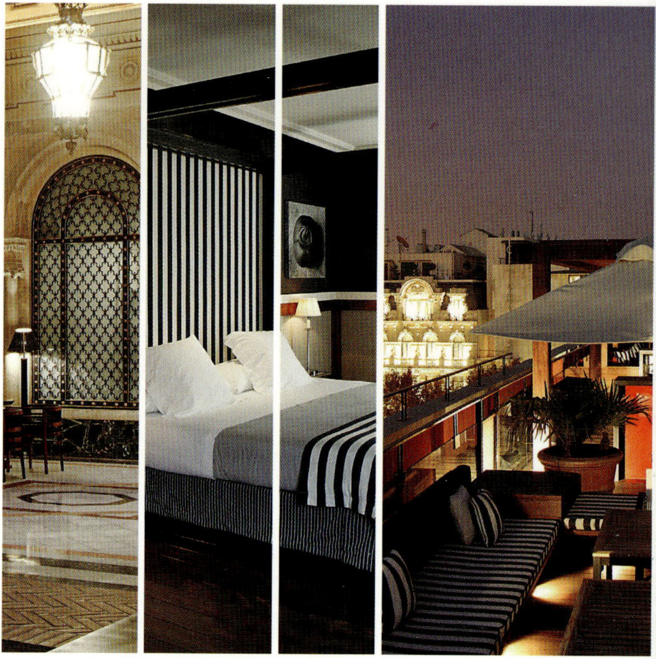

HOTEL 1898

La Rambla, 109 // Ciutat Vella / El Raval
Tel.: +34 93 552 95 52
www.hotel1898.com

Metro L1, L3, L6, L7 Catalunya

The sophisticated charm of the colonial style is found everywhere in this luxurious spa hotel located at the upper end of La Rambla. Dark woods, heavy armchairs, and muted colors invoke the 19th century when the tobacco industry was at its height thanks to colonies like Cuba and the Philippines. This 1881 building designed by Josep Oriol Mestres also houses two restaurants led by chef de cuisine Carles Boronat and a bar—all are well worth a visit.

Der mondäne Charme des Kolonialstils prägt den Geist dieses luxuriösen Hotels mit Spa, das am oberen Ende der Rambla liegt. Dunkle Edelhölzer, schwere Sessel und gedeckte Farben beschwören die Zeiten, als Kolonien wie Kuba und die Philippinen die Tabakindustrie im 19. Jahrhundert florieren ließen. In dem von Josep Oriol Mestres 1881 errichteten Gebäude sind auch die beiden Restaurants unter der Ägide von Küchenchef Carles Boronat sowie die Bar einen Besuch wert.

Cet hôtel luxueux avec spa, qui se trouve sur La Rambla, est emprunt du charme mondain propre au style colonial. Bois sombres précieux, fauteuils massifs et couleurs neutres témoignent d'une époque où les colonies telles que Cuba et les Philippines participaient à l'essor de l'industrie du tabac, au XIXe siècle. À l'intérieur de ce bâtiment réalisé par Josep Oriol Mestres en 1881, les deux restaurants placés sous l'égide du chef Carles Boronat et le bar sont à recommander.

El encanto mundano del estilo colonial es omnipresente en este lujoso hotel con spa en el extremo superior de La Rambla. Maderas nobles, pesados sillones y colores apagados conjuran una época en la que las colonias cubanas y filipinas hacían florecer la industria tabaquera del siglo XIX. En el edificio erigido por Josep Oriol Mestres en 1881 se encuentran también los dos restaurantes del chef Carles Boronat y un bar: todos valen la pena.

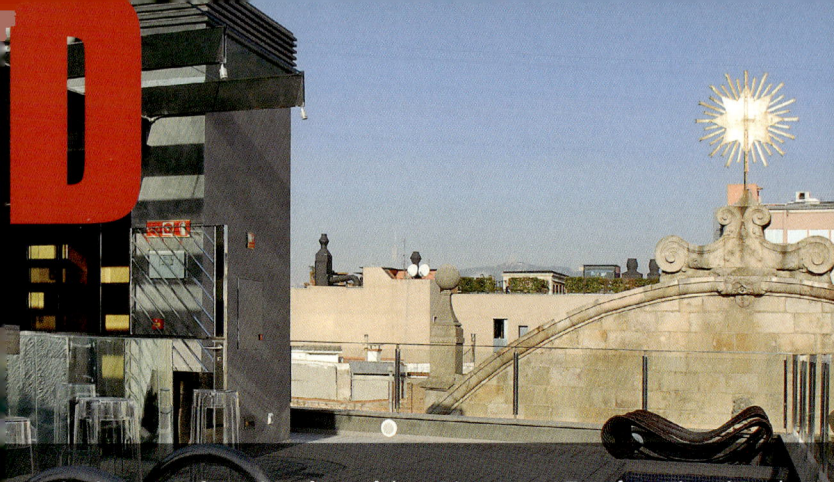

The daring transformation of one of the best known city palaces on La Rambla into a modern 5-star hotel has been a rousing success. Jordi Clos, art collector, patron, and president of Derby Hotels Collection, merges art, luxury, and culture into a jewel where stairs become sculptures and indirect lighting highlights the structures and textures of stone, metal, and satin—as well as wood and leather in the guest rooms. An exhibition shows creations by Modernista jeweler Masriera.

Die gewagte Transformation eines der bekanntesten Stadtpaläste an der Rambla in ein modernes 5-Sterne-Hotel ist genial geglückt. Jordi Clos, Kunstsammler, Mäzen und Präsident der Derby Hotels Collection, vereint Kunst, Luxus und Kultur zu einem Juwel, in dem Treppen zu Skulpturen werden und die indirekte Beleuchtung die Strukturen und Texturen von Stein, Metall und Satin – in den Zimmern auch Holz und Leder – hervorheben. Eine Ausstellung zeigt Arbeiten des Jugendstiljuweliers Masriera.

La transformation d'un des palais les plus connus de Les Rambles en un hôtel moderne cinq étoiles est une réussite. Jordi Clos, collectionneur, mécène et président de Derby Hotels Collection, réunit art, luxe et culture en un seul joyau dans lequel les escaliers deviennent des sculptures et l'éclairage indirect fait ressortir les structures et textures de pierre, de métal et de satin, ainsi que de bois et de cuir dans les chambres. Des œuvres du joaillier Masriera y sont exposées.

La atrevida transformación de uno de los palacetes urbanos más conocidos de Les Rambles en un moderno hotel de cinco estrellas ha sido un éxito sin paliativos. Jordi Clos, coleccionista de arte, mecenas y presidente de Derby Hotels Collection, ha combinado arte, lujo y cultura en una joyita en las que las escaleras son esculturas y la luz indirecta subraya la nobleza de estructuras y texturas: piedra, metal, satén, y cuero y madera en las habitaciones. Una exposición muestra obras del joyero modernista Masriera.

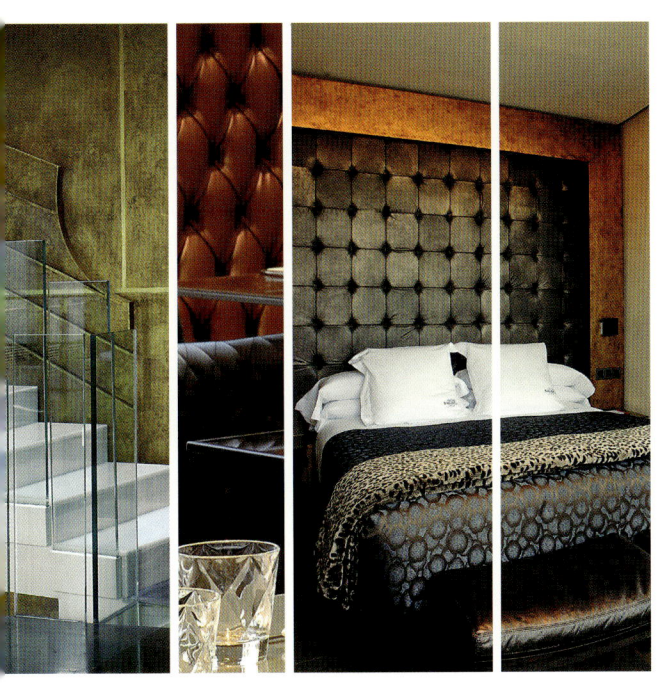

HOTEL BAGUÉS

La Rambla, 105 // Ciutat Vella / El Raval
Tel.: +34 93 343 50 00
www.derbyhotels.com/Hotel-Bagues-Barcelona

Metro L1, L3, L6, L7 Catalunya or L4 Jaume I

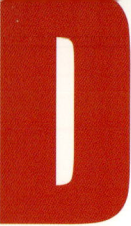

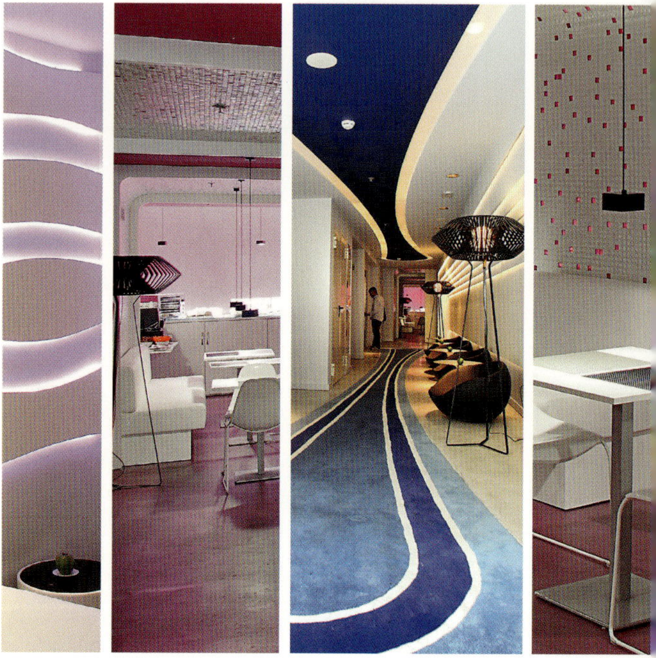

EMMA

Carrer del Rosselló, 205 // Eixample
Tel.: +34 93 238 56 06
www.room-matehotels.com

Metro L3, L5, L6, L7 Diagonal

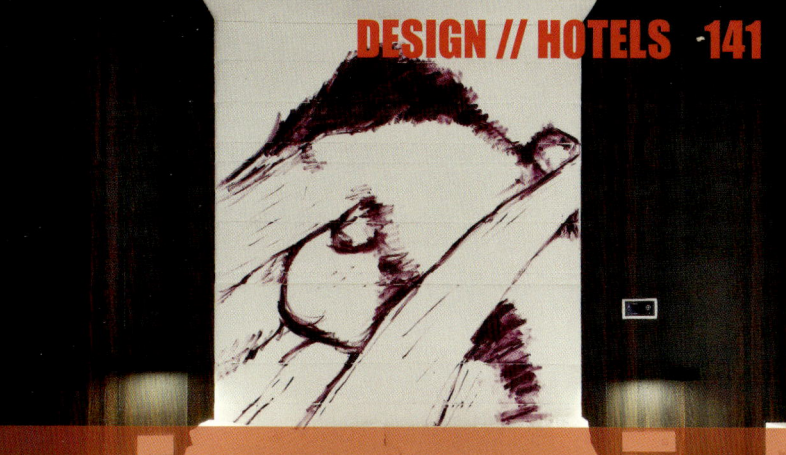

Hip, dynamic, uncomplicated, and beautiful: Emma embodies some of the same attributes that draw visitors to Barcelona from all over the world. While the modern façade designed by Nadal Moneo Architects integrates the building into its surroundings, Tomás Alía's interiors with their organic elements and subtle lighting are decidedly futuristic. Its location in Eixample and breakfast until noon make it the ideal base for visitors who are into shopping, culture, and nightlife.

Hip, dynamisch, unkompliziert und dabei wunderschön – das Hotel verkörpert einige der Attribute, die Barcelona zum Magneten für Besucher aus allen Teilen der Welt machen. Während die moderne Fassade des Studios Nadal Moneo das Gebäude in seine Umgebung einbindet, weist Tomás Alía im Innenraum mit organischen Elementen und subtiler Beleuchtung den Weg in die Zukunft. Die Lage in Eixample und Frühstück bis 12 Uhr machen es zum idealen Ausgangspunkt für Shopping, Kultur und Nachtleben.

Branché, dynamique, simple mais magnifique : l'hôtel symbolise ce qui fait de Barcelone une ville si appréciée des visiteurs du monde entier. Tandis que la façade réalisée par le studio d'architecte Nadal Moneo intègre parfaitement le bâtiment à l'environnement du quartier Eixample, Tomás Alía donne à l'intérieur une pointe de futurisme grâce à des éléments organiques et un éclairage subtil. Sa situation et le petit-déjeuner servi jusq'à 12 h permettent de choisir entre shopping, culture et nuit festive.

Moderno, dinámico, sencillo y maravilloso: en el hotel toman forma muchos de los atributos que hacen de Barcelona un imán para visitantes de todo el mundo. Así como la moderna fachada del estudio del arquitecto Nadal Moneo integra el edificio en su entorno, Tomás Alía marca sendas de futuro en el interior con elementos orgánicos y una iluminación sutil. Su situación en el Eixample y el desayuno servido hasta mediodía lo hacen un punto de partida ideal para compras, visitas culturales y salidas nocturnas.

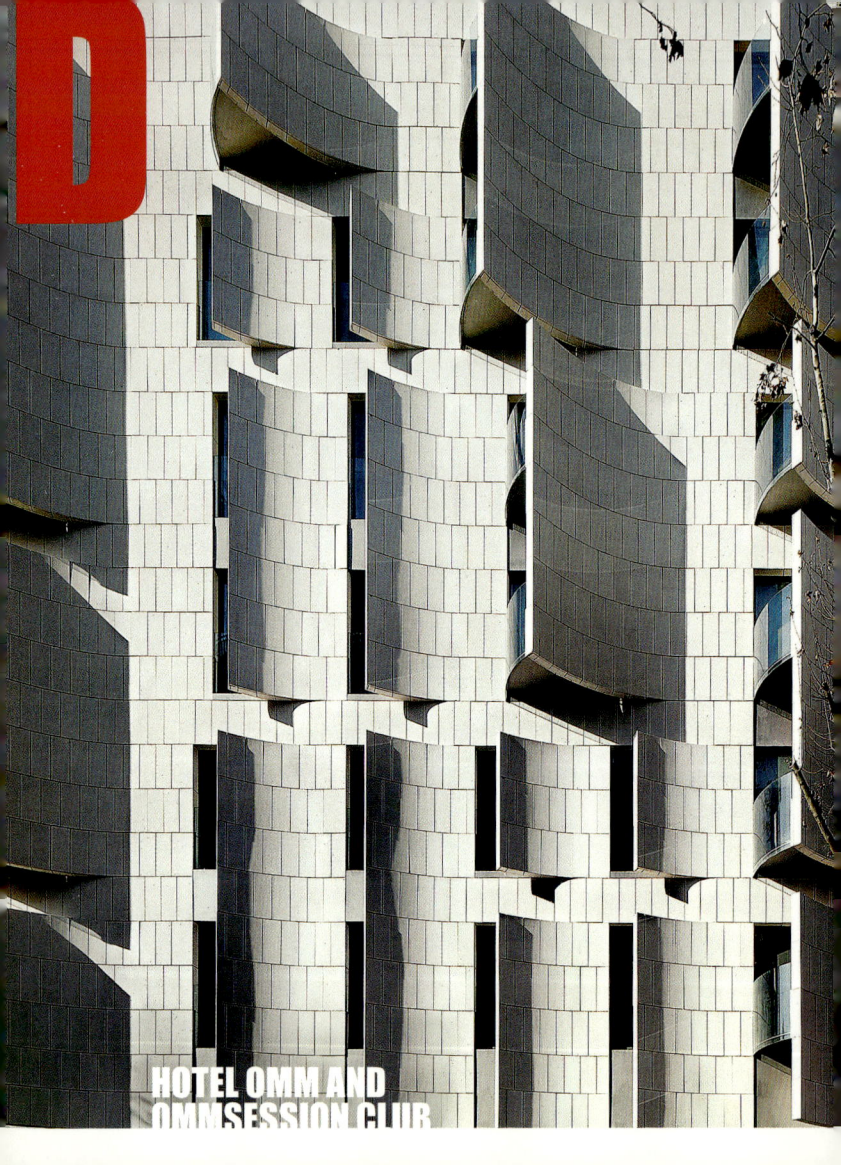

D

HOTEL OMM AND OMMSESSION CLUB

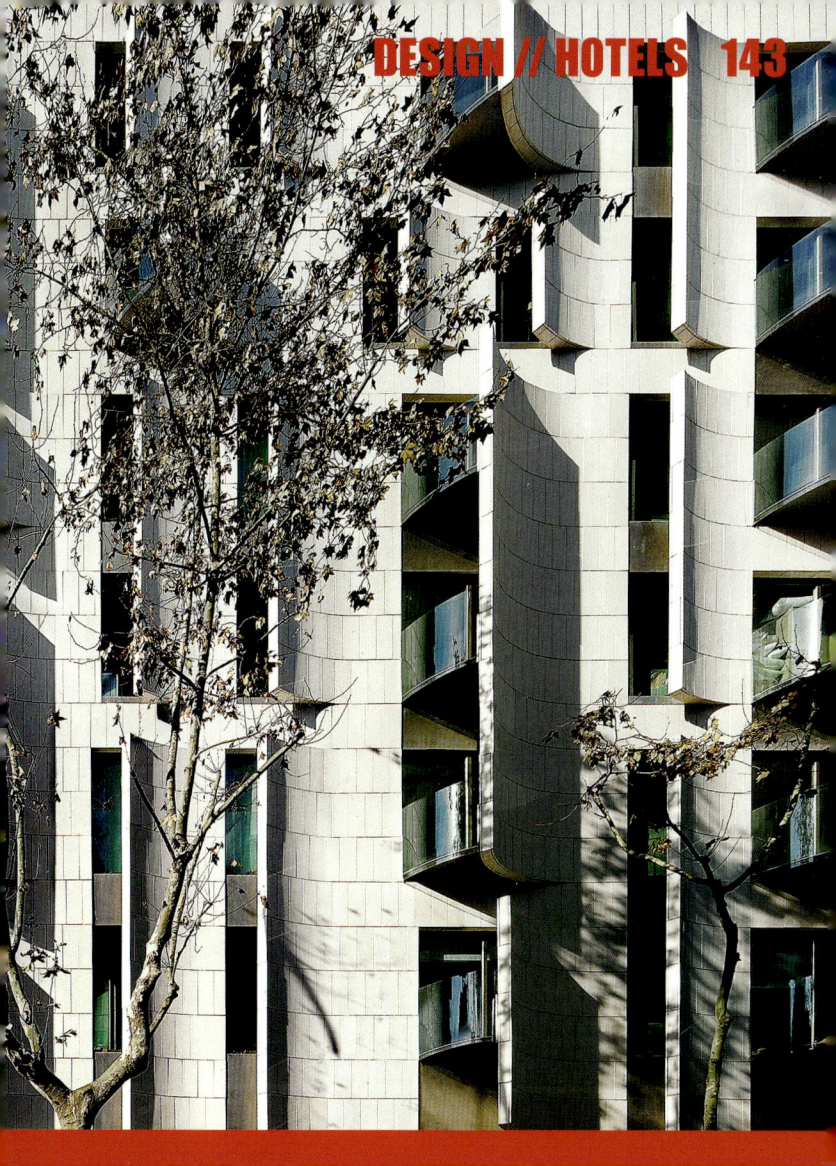

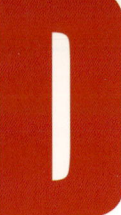

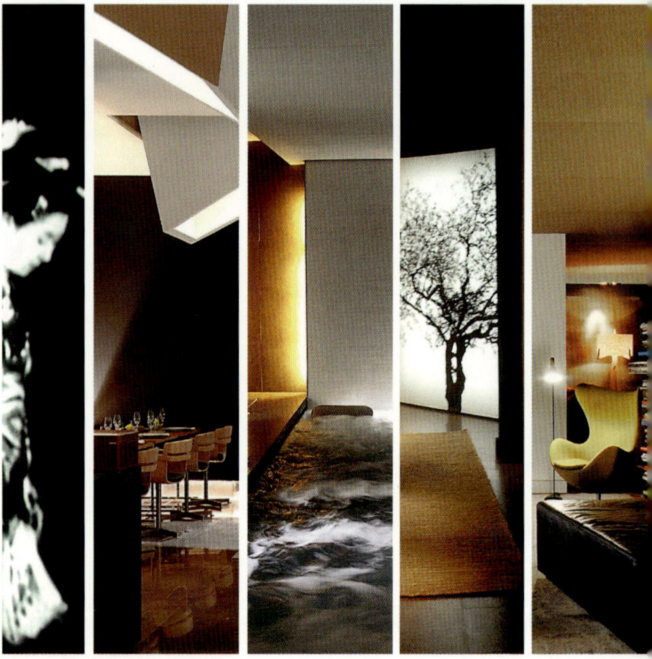

HOTEL OMM AND OMMSESSION CLUB

Carrer del Rosselló, 265 // Eixample
Tel.: +34 93 445 40 00
www.hotelomm.es

Metro L3, L5, L6, L7 Diagonal

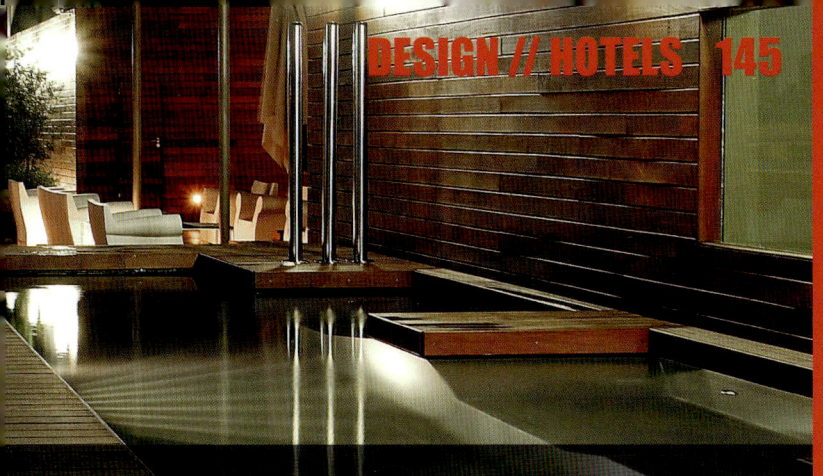

91 rooms, sleekly decorated by interior designers Sandra Tarruella and Isabel López Vilalta, are behind the unique exterior created by Juli Capella. Resembling pages in a book, the openings in the façade overlook the elegant Passeig de Gràcia. White stone discreetly integrates the 2003 building into the Modernista architecture of the Eixample district. The basement houses the ultra trendy Ommssession Club, and the roof terrace offers views of the sculptural roof of Casa Milà.

91 von den Innenarchitektinnen Sandra Tarruella und Isabel López Vilalta gestaltete Zimmer liegen geschützt hinter der ausdrucksstarken Gebäudehülle von Juli Capella. Die wie Buchseiten aufgeblätterten Öffnungen in der Fassade bieten Ausblick auf die Prachtstraße Passeig de Gràcia. Weißer Stein integriert den Bau von 2003 diskret in das vom Jugendstil geprägte Viertel Eixample. Im Keller liegt der angesagte Ommssession Club, die Dachterrasse bietet einen Blick auf das skulpturenhafte Dach der Casa Milà.

Les 91 chambres décorées par les architectes d'intérieur Sandra Tarruella et Isabel López Vilalta se cachent derrière une enveloppe de caractère réalisée par Juli Capella. Les ouvertures de la façade, semblables aux pages d'un livre, donnent sur la Passeig de Gràcia. L'édifice de 2003 s'intègre discrètement au style Art nouveau du quartier Eixample. Vous trouverez au sous-sol le très en vogue Ommssession Club, et la terrasse du toit permet d'admirer le toit sculptural de la Casa Milà.

Tras la expresiva cubierta del edificio, diseñada por Juli Capella, se encuentran 91 habitaciones diseñadas por las interioristas Sandra Tarruella e Isabel López Vilalta. La fachada, sobre la que se abren las ventanas como hojas de un libro, da al prestigioso Passeig de Gràcia. La piedra blanca integra discretamente el edificio de 2003 en el barrio del Eixample, marcadamente modernista. En el sótano se encuentra el popular Ommssession Club y desde la azotea puede observarse el escultural tejado de la Casa Milà.

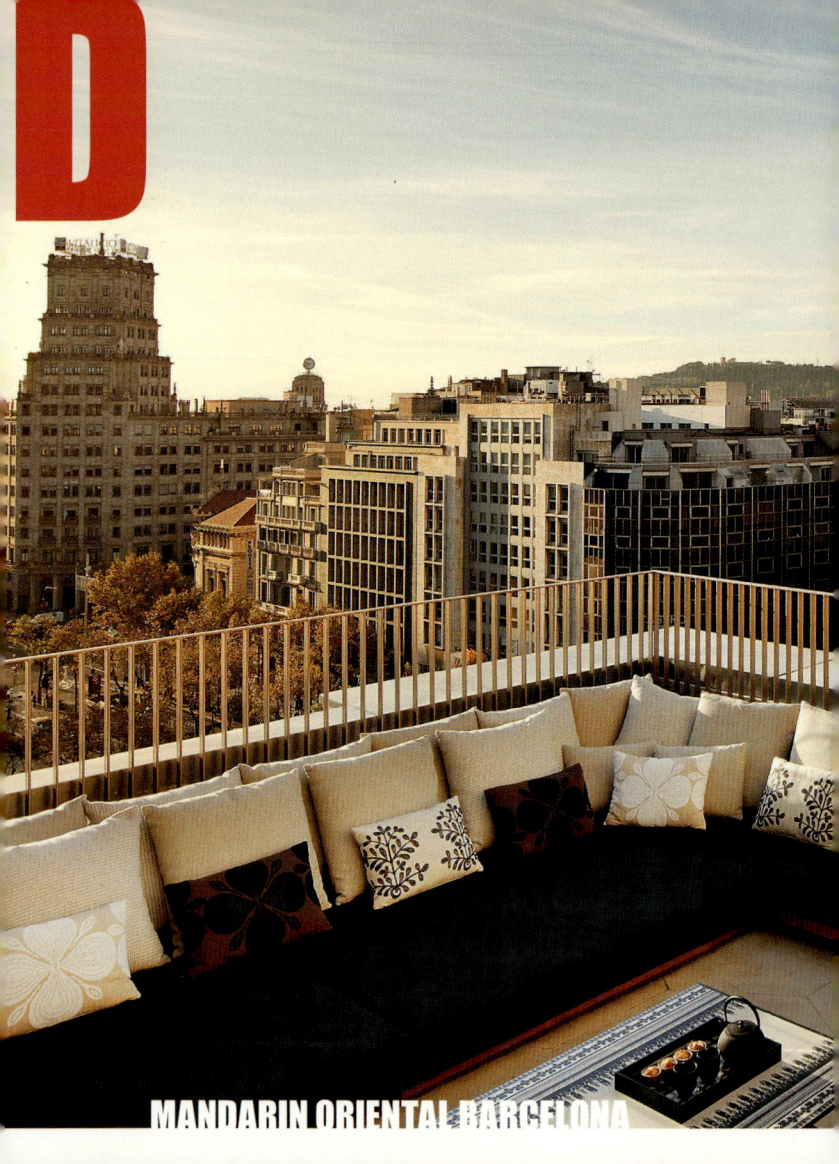

D

MANDARIN ORIENTAL BARCELONA

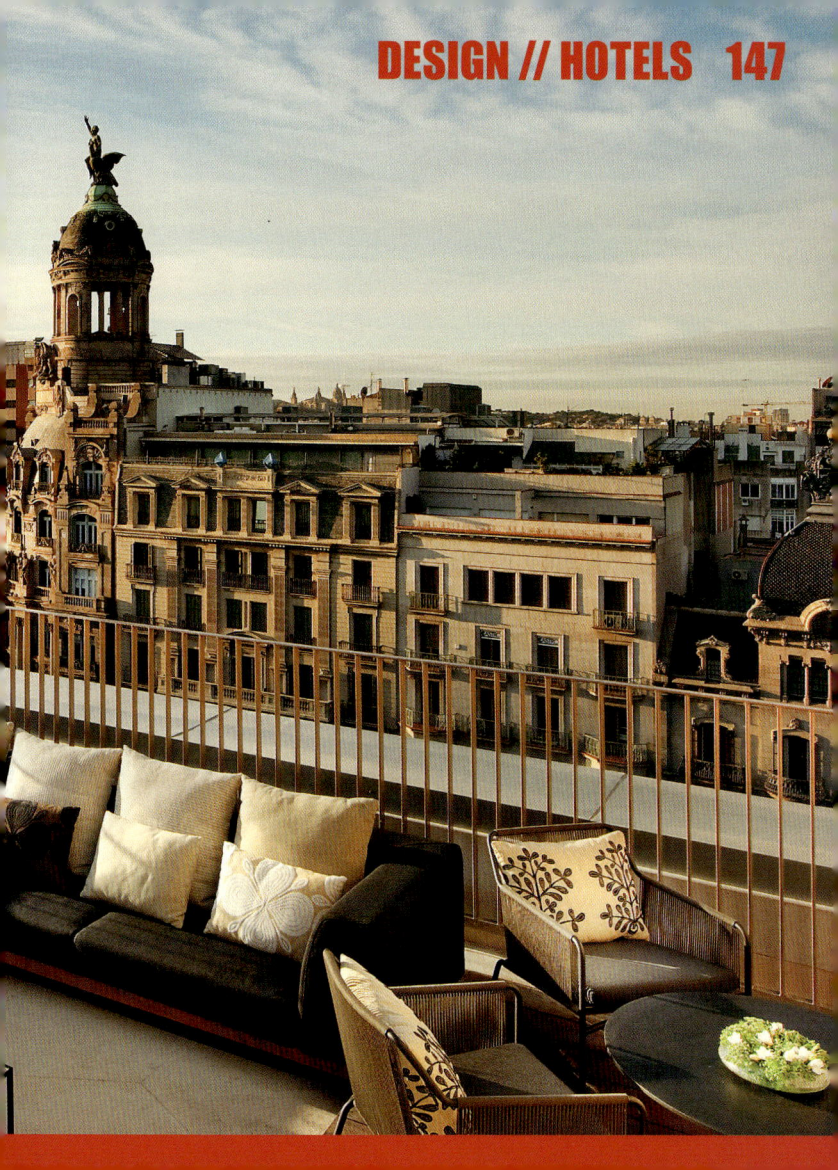

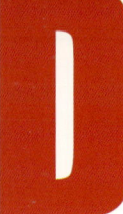

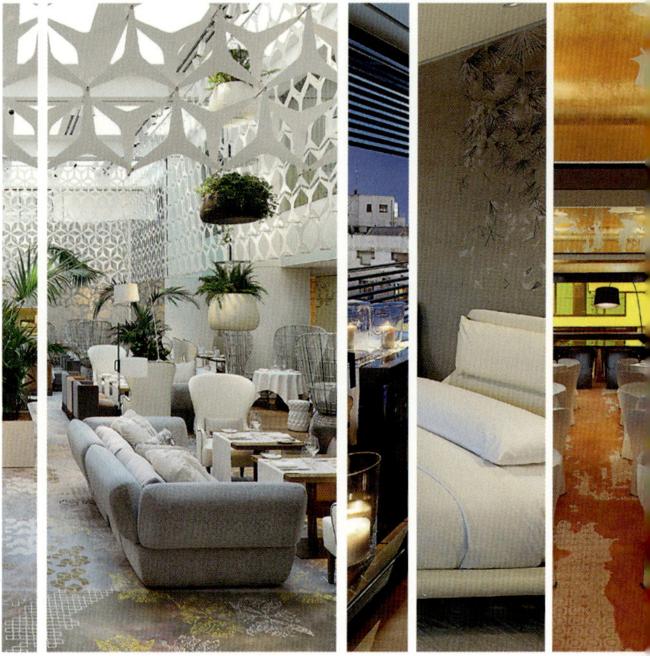

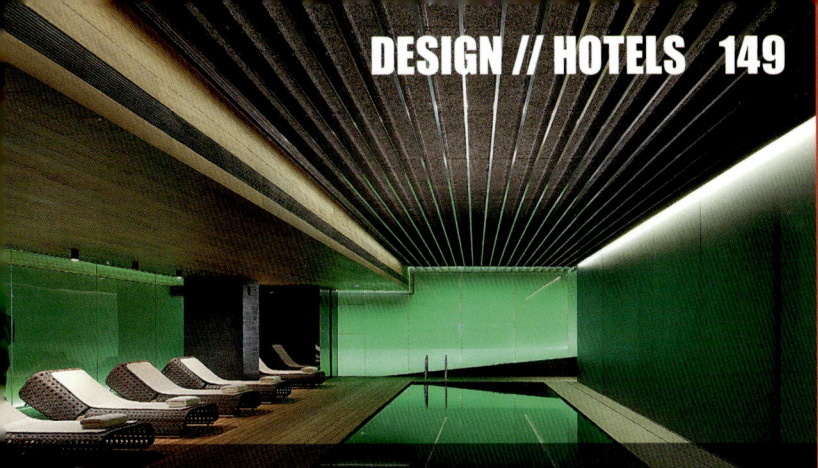

Milan-based Spanish architect and designer Patricia Urquiola, known for her work for brands like Cassina and B&B Italia, created a very soft, sophisticated, and comfortable atmosphere in this luxury hotel, using light colors and shades of gold. Constructed in the middle of the 20th century, the elegant building is centrally located on Passeig de Gràcia. Carme Ruscalleda, chef de cuisine at Moments Restaurant, was recently awarded her sixth Michelin star.

Die in Mailand ansässige spanische Architektin und Designerin Patricia Urquiola, bekannt unter anderem durch ihre Entwürfe für Marken wie Cassina und B&B Italia, schuf in diesem Luxushotel mit hellen Farbtönen und Gold eine sehr sanfte, raffinierte und behagliche Atmosphäre. Das elegante, Mitte des 20. Jahrhunderts errichtete Gebäude liegt zentral am Passeig de Gràcia. Carme Ruscalleda wurde als Küchenchefin des Restaurants Moments mit ihrem sechsten Michelin-Stern ausgezeichnet.

L'architecte et designer espagnole Patricia Urquiola, vivant à Milan, est connue entre autres pour ses réalisations pour des marques telles que Cassina et B&B Italia. C'est elle qui a créé l'atmosphère douce, raffinée et agréable de cet hôtel de luxe, grâce à des couleurs claires et or. Cet édifice élégant, construit au milieu du XXe siècle, se trouve sur la Passeig de Gràcia. Carme Ruscalleda, chef de cuisine du restaurant Moments, y a remporté sa sixième étoile Michelin.

La arquitecto y diseñadora española Patricia Urquiola, afincada en Milán y conocida por sus creaciones para marcas como Cassina y B&B Italia, creó en este hotel de lujo una atmósfera refinada y acogedora en tonos luminosos y dorados. El elegante edificio de mediados del siglo XX se encuentra en pleno Passeig de Gràcia. Carme Ruscalleda obtuvo su sexta estrella Michelin como cocinera jefe del restaurante Moments.

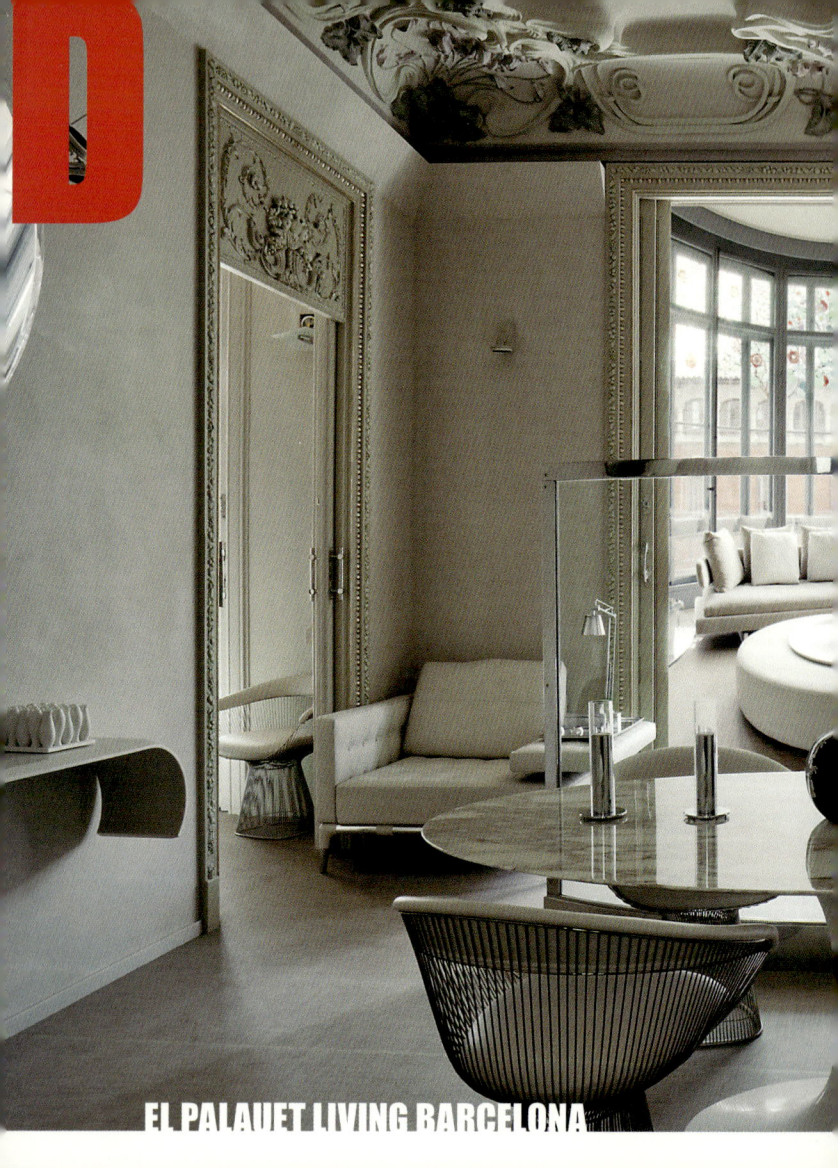

EL PALAUET LIVING BARCELONA

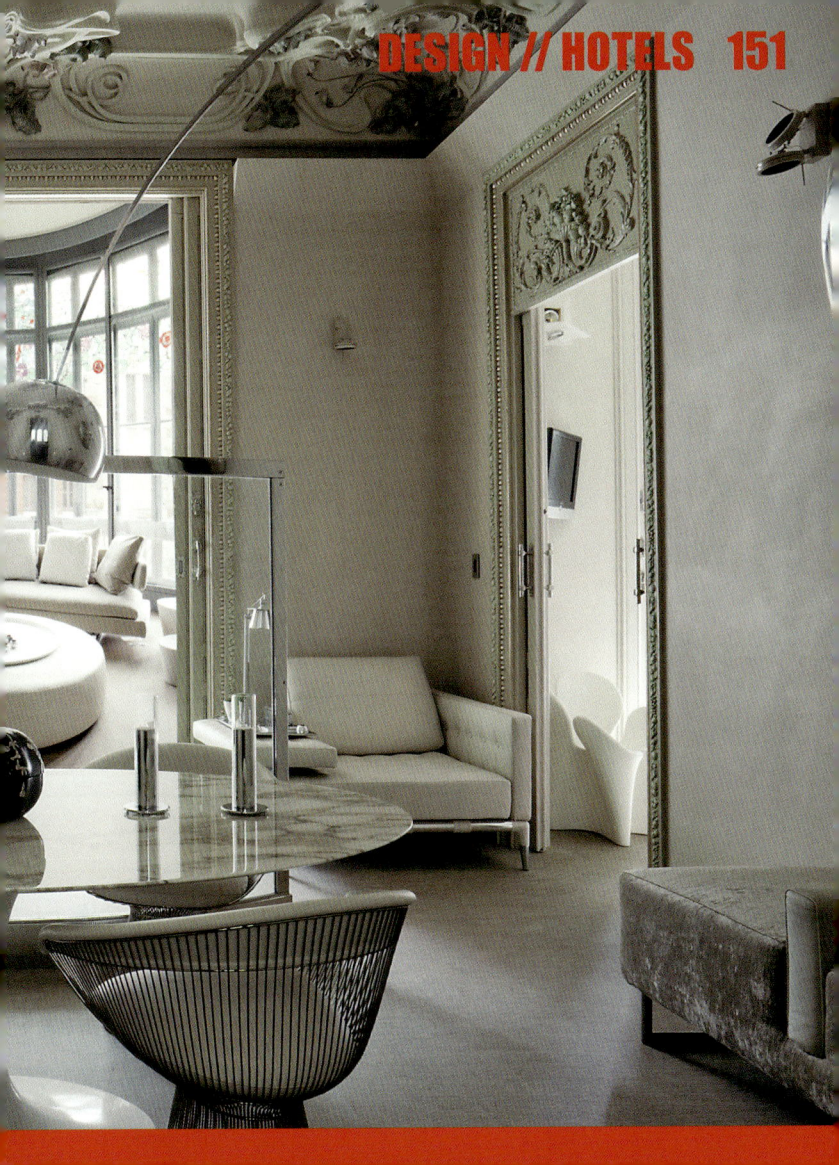

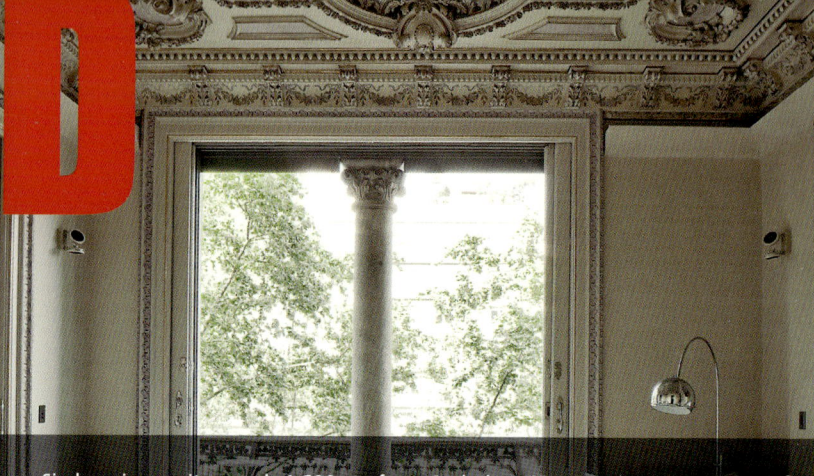

Six luxurious suites, each 1,600 sq. ft., offer all modern amenities, from discreetly integrated sound systems to a spa on the roof terrace. The centrally located Modernista palace from 1906 was renovated with great care, preserving original features such as stucco ceilings, doors, and windows. Decorative elements typical of Modernisme were reproduced in custom-made Corian furniture pieces. Lit from the inside, they embody a perfect fusion of the traditional and contemporary.

Sechs luxuriöse Suiten mit jeweils 150 m² verfügen über alle modernen Annehmlichkeiten: vom diskret integrierten Soundsystem bis zum Spa auf der Dachterrasse. Der zentral gelegene Jugendstilpalast aus dem Jahre 1906 mit Stuckdecken, dekorativen Türen und Verglasungen wurde mit großer Sorgfalt restauriert. Einige Jugendstilornamente finden sich in maßgefertigten Möbeln aus Corian wieder. Sie werden von innen beleuchtet und verkörpern eine perfekte Fusion von Tradition und Moderne.

Six suites de luxe de 150 m² chacune disposent de tout le confort moderne : de la sonorisation discrètement intégrée au spa sur le toit. Situé dans le centre, ce palais Art nouveau de 1906, avec plafonds en stuc, portes décoratives et vitrages, a été restauré avec grand soin. Certains ornements Art nouveau se retrouvent dans les meubles en Corian, taillés sur mesure. Ils bénéficient d'un éclairage intérieur et symbolisent le mariage parfait de la tradition et du modernisme.

Seis lujosas suites de 150 m²: cada una dispone de todas las amenidades modernas, desde un discreto equipo de sonido hasta un spa en la azotea. El palacio modernista de 1906, de techos de estuco, puertas decorativas y hermosas vidrieras ha sido restaurado con gran cuidado. En los muebles de Corian a medida se aprecian algunos elementos modernistas. Iluminados desde dentro, suponen la fusión perfecta de tradición y modernidad.

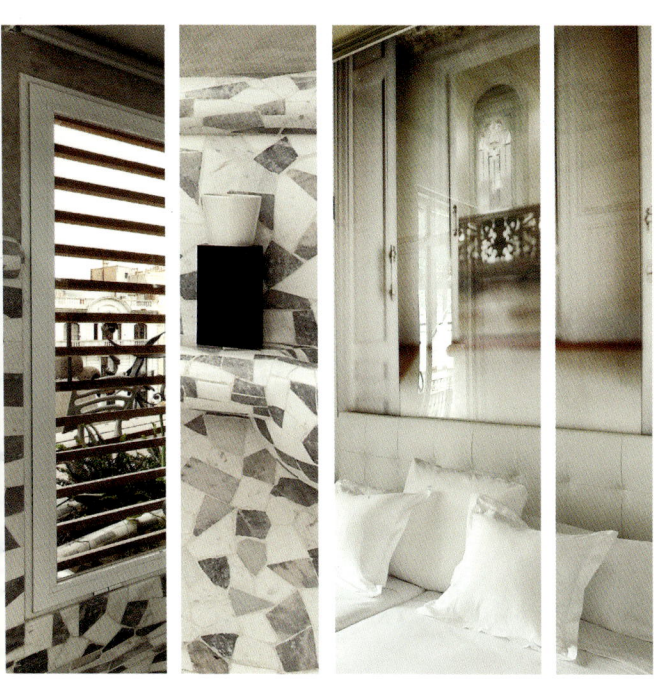

EL PALAUET LIVING BARCELONA

Passeig de Gràcia, 113 // Gràcia
Tel.: +34 93 218 00 50
www.elpalauet.com

Metro L3, L5, L6, L7 Diagonal

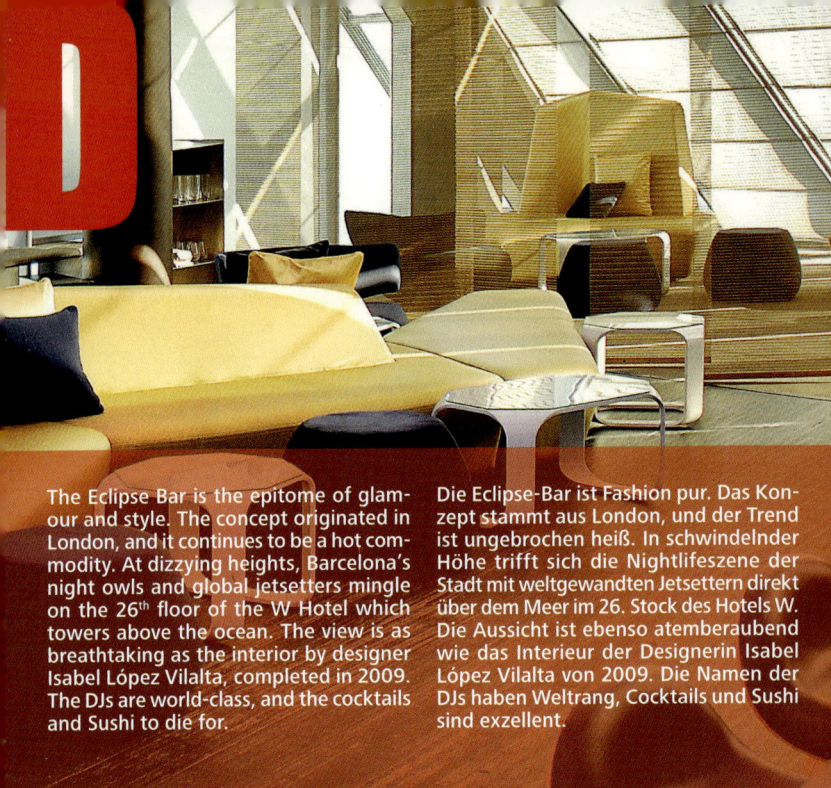

The Eclipse Bar is the epitome of glamour and style. The concept originated in London, and it continues to be a hot commodity. At dizzying heights, Barcelona's night owls and global jetsetters mingle on the 26th floor of the W Hotel which towers above the ocean. The view is as breathtaking as the interior by designer Isabel López Vilalta, completed in 2009. The DJs are world-class, and the cocktails and Sushi to die for.

Die Eclipse-Bar ist Fashion pur. Das Konzept stammt aus London, und der Trend ist ungebrochen heiß. In schwindelnder Höhe trifft sich die Nightlifeszene der Stadt mit weltgewandten Jetsettern direkt über dem Meer im 26. Stock des Hotels W. Die Aussicht ist ebenso atemberaubend wie das Interieur der Designerin Isabel López Vilalta von 2009. Die Namen der DJs haben Weltrang, Cocktails und Sushi sind exzellent.

L'Eclipse Bar, né d'un concept londonien toujours branché, représente la mode à l'état pur. La jet-set et les acteurs de la vie nocturne aiment se retrouver à une hauteur à donner le tournis, au 26e étage de l'hôtel W qui surplombe la mer. La vue y est aussi fabuleuse que l'intérieur réalisé en 2009 par la designer Isabel López Vilalta. Les DJs qui s'y produisent sont mondialement connus, les cocktails et les sushis y sont excellents.

Si hay algo "fashion", eso es el Eclipse Bar. De inspiración londinense, la tendencia no ha perdido su frescura. A una altura vertiginosa sobre el mar se encuentran los noctámbulos de la ciudad con lo más granado de la jet set, en el 26º piso del hotel W. Las vistas son tan asombrosas como el interior, diseñado por Isabel López Vilalta en 2009. DJs de fama mundial, cócteles y un sushi excelente...

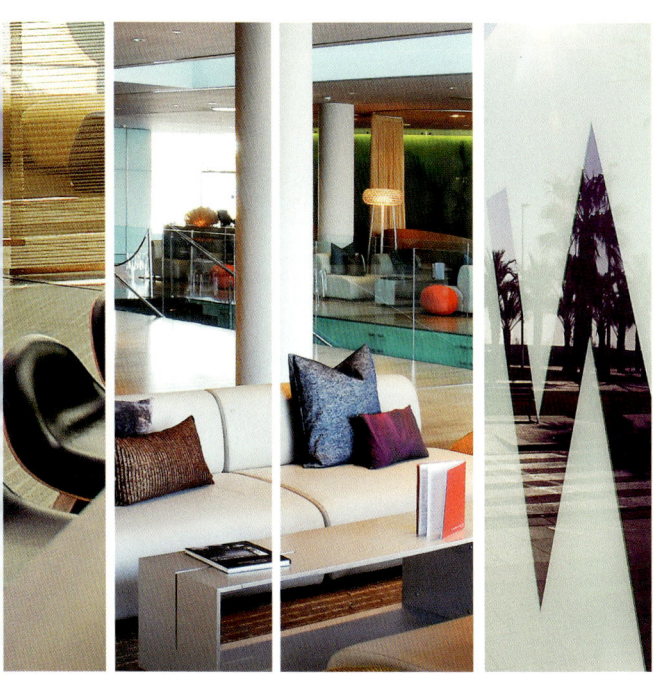

ECLIPSE W BARCELONA

Plaça de la Rosa dels Vents, 1 // Ciutat Vella
La Barceloneta
Tel.: +34 93 295 28 00
www.w-barcelona.com

Mon–Wed 7 pm to 2 am, Thu and Sun 7 pm to 3 am
Fri–Sat 7 pm to 4 am, Bus 17, 39, 64 W Hotel
Metro L4 Barceloneta

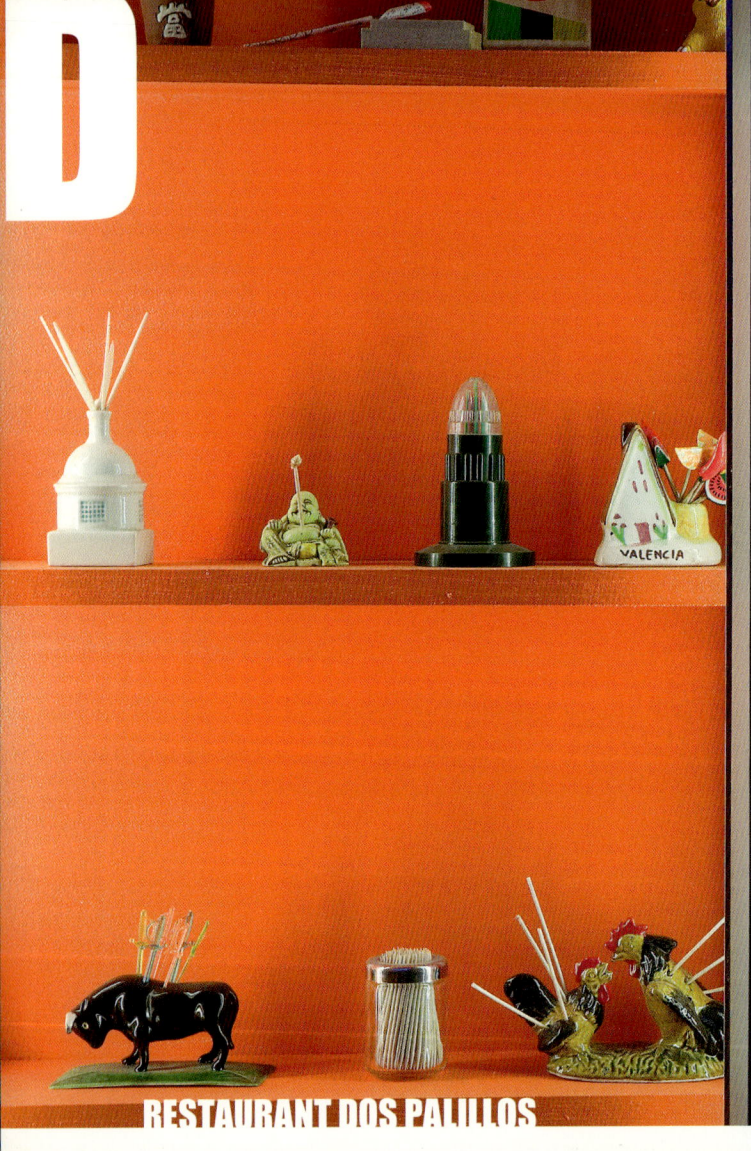

D

VALENCIA

RESTAURANT DOS PALILLOS

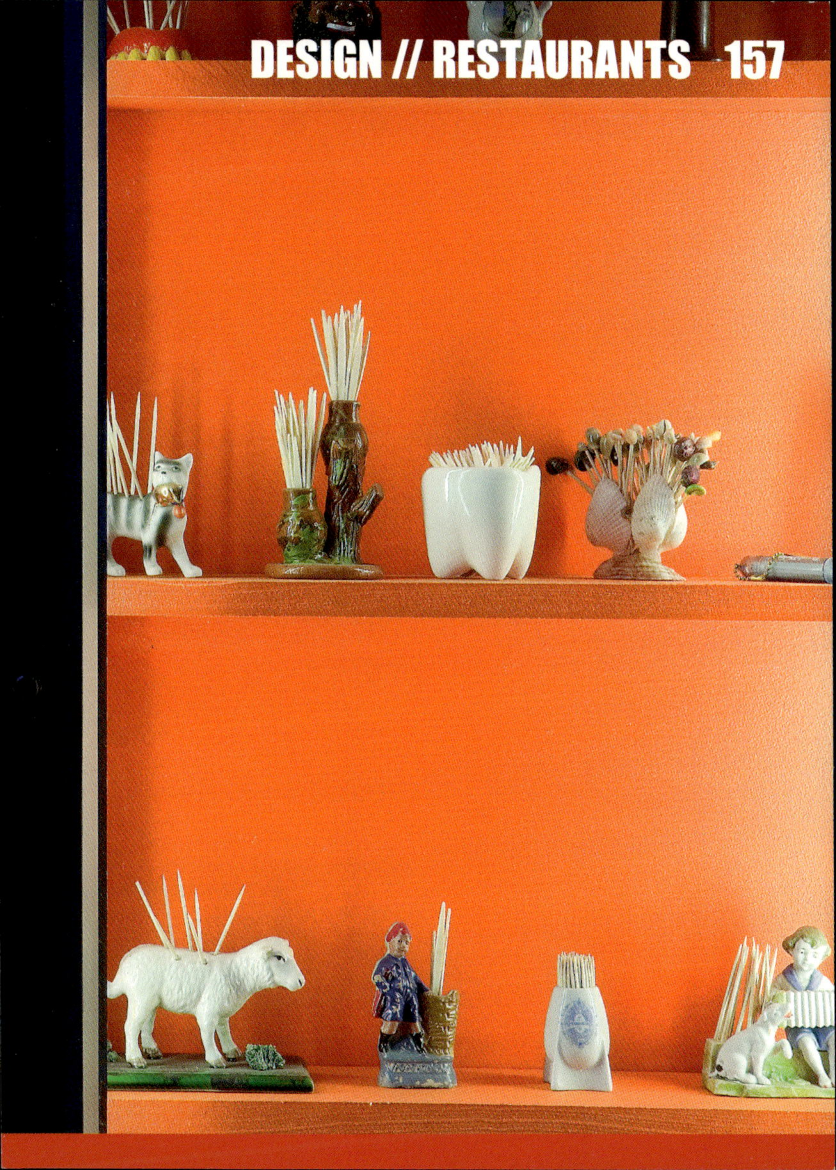

Chefs Takeshi Somekawa and Albert Raurich and sommelier Tamae Imachi spent three, four, and eleven years respectively at Ferran Adrià's elBulli, perfecting their craft. Raurich was chef de cuisine from 2001–2007. In 2008, they opened Dos Palillos in the trendy Casa Camper Hotel located in the heart of the city. Exquisite Asian tapas are served at two counters. "Palillos," referring both to Asian chopsticks and Spanish cocktail sticks, lend a humorous touch to the extravagant design.

Drei, vier und elf Jahre haben die Kochkünstler Takeshi Somekawa und Albert Raurich sowie die Sommelière Tamae Imachi ihre Talente im Restaurant elBulli von Ferran Adrià unter Beweis gestellt; Raurich als Küchenchef von 2001–2007. Im Jahr 2008 eröffneten sie im Szenehotel Camper in der Altstadt das Dos Palillos, wo an zwei Theken feinste asiatische Tapas angeboten werden. „Palillos", asiatische Essstäbchen und Zahnstocher, verleihen dem extravaganten Design einen humorvollen Touch.

Les maîtres cuisiniers Takeshi Somekawa et Albert Raurich ainsi que la sommelière Tamae Imachi ont exercé leur talent au elBulli de Ferran Adrià durant trois, quatre et onze ans. Raurich en a été le chef de cuisine de 2001 à 2007. En 2008, ils ont ouvert à l'hôtel Camper dans la vieille ville le restaurant Dos Palillos, où sont servis d'authentiques tapas asiatiques. Des « Palillos », baguettes asiatiques et cure-dents, ajoutent une touche d'humour au design extravagant.

Durante tres, cuatro y once años respectivamente, los cocineros Takeshi Somekawa y Albert Raurich y la "sommelière" Tamae Imachi demostraron su habilidad en el restaurante elBulli de Ferran Adrià, Raurich como jefe de cocina entre 2001 y 2007. En 2008 abrieron en el hotel Camper del casco antiguo Dos Palillos, en cuyas dos barras se ofrecen las mejores tapas asiáticas. Los palillos (tanto mondadientes como varillas) aportan un toque de humor al extravagante diseño.

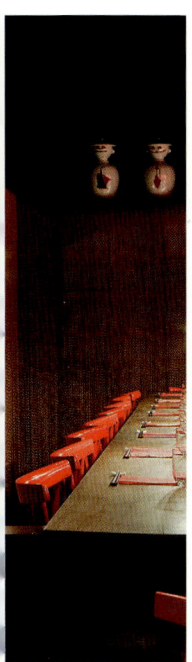
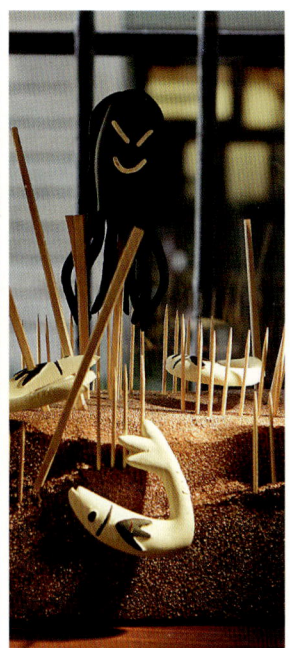
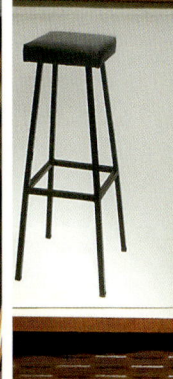
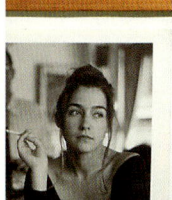

RESTAURANT
DOS PALILLOS

Carrer d'Elisabets, 9 // Ciutat Vella / El Raval
Tel.: +34 93 304 05 13
www.dospalillos.com

Tue–Wed 7.30 pm to 11.30 pm, Thu–Sat 1.30 pm
to 3.30 pm, 7.30 pm to 11.30 pm
Closed Dec 24th to Jan 10th and Aug 7th to Aug 29th
Metro L1, L3, L6, L7 Catalunya

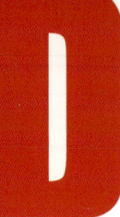

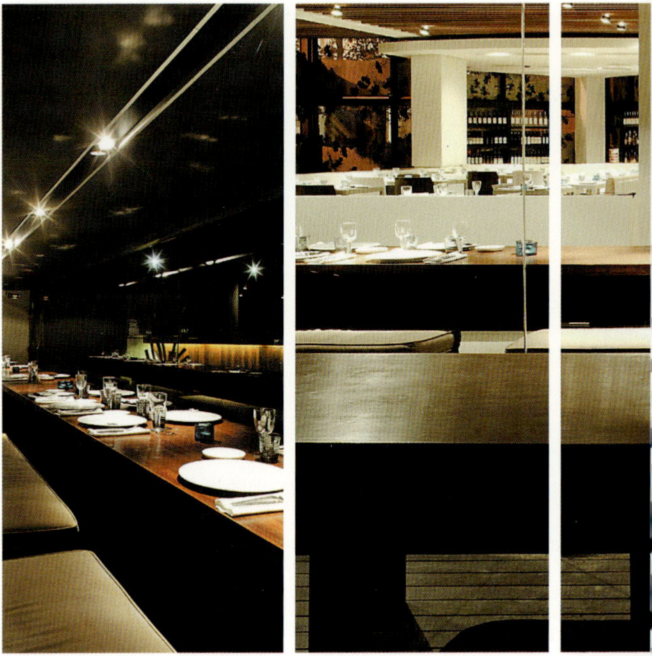

BESTIAL

Carrer de Ramon Trias Fargas, 2-4 // Ciutat Vella / La Barceloneta
Tel.: +34 93 224 04 07
www.bestialdeltragaluz.com

Lunch 1 pm to 3.45 pm
Dinner 8 pm to 11.30 pm

Metro L4 Ciutadella / Vila Olímpica

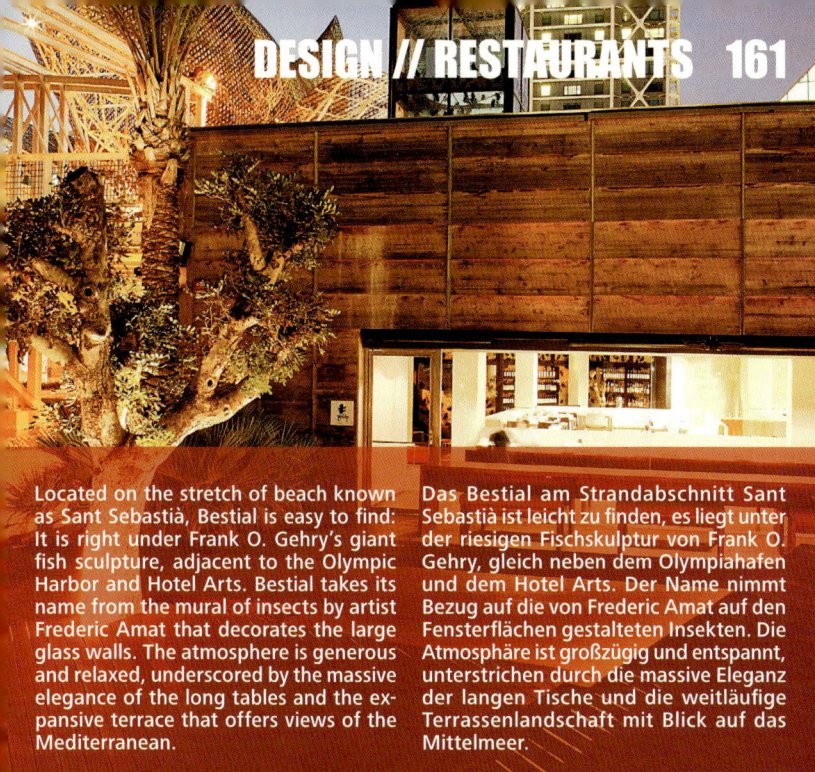

Located on the stretch of beach known as Sant Sebastià, Bestial is easy to find: It is right under Frank O. Gehry's giant fish sculpture, adjacent to the Olympic Harbor and Hotel Arts. Bestial takes its name from the mural of insects by artist Frederic Amat that decorates the large glass walls. The atmosphere is generous and relaxed, underscored by the massive elegance of the long tables and the expansive terrace that offers views of the Mediterranean.

Das Bestial am Strandabschnitt Sant Sebastià ist leicht zu finden, es liegt unter der riesigen Fischskulptur von Frank O. Gehry, gleich neben dem Olympiahafen und dem Hotel Arts. Der Name nimmt Bezug auf die von Frederic Amat auf den Fensterflächen gestalteten Insekten. Die Atmosphäre ist großzügig und entspannt, unterstrichen durch die massive Eleganz der langen Tische und die weitläufige Terrassenlandschaft mit Blick auf das Mittelmeer.

Vous n'aurez aucun mal à trouver le restaurant Bestial. Il se trouve en effet sur la plage de Sant Sebastià, sous l'énorme sculpture en forme de poisson de Frank O. Gehry, juste à côté du Port Olympique et de l'Hotel Arts. Son nom est un clin d'œil aux insectes dessinés par Frederic Amat sur les fenêtres du restaurant. L'atmosphère y est généreuse et décontractée, renforcée par l'élégance massive des longues tables et la vaste terrasse donnant sur la Mer Méditerranée.

El bestial, en el tramo de playa de Sant Sebastià, es fácil de encontrar: se encuentra bajo la enorme escultura del pez de Frank O. Gehry, junto al puerto olímpico y el hotel Arts. El nombre hace referencia a los insectos plasmados por Frederic Amat en las ventanas. La atmósfera es distendida y generosa, subrayada por la inmensa elegancia de las largas mesas y la extensa terraza abierta al Mediterráneo.

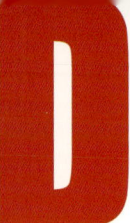

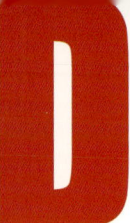

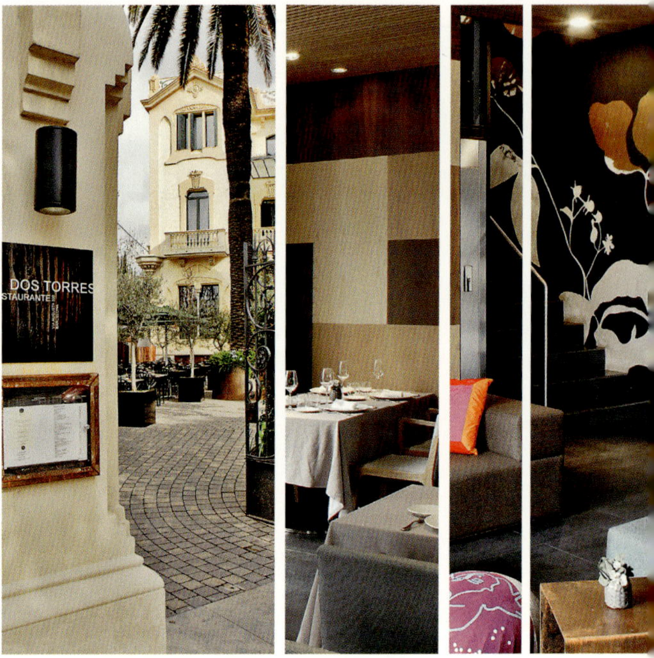

DOS TORRES

Via Augusta, 300 // Sarrià-Sant Gervasi
Tel.: +34 93 206 64 80
www.restaurantedostorres.com

Mon–Sat 1 pm to 4 pm
8.30 pm to 11.30 pm

Metro L6 Les Tres Torres

amore

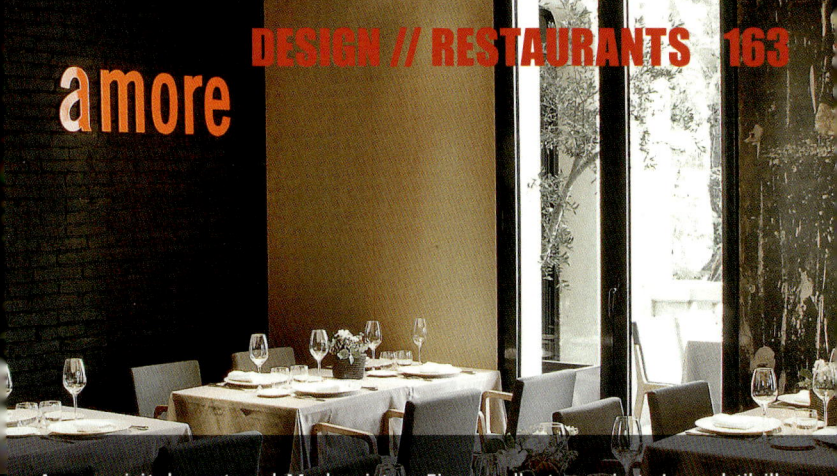

An exquisitely restored Modernista villa in uptown Barcelona is home to the creative Mediterranean cuisine of chef Carlos Casas. Fernando Salas has created a pleasantly sleek and modern interior. The elegant atmosphere of the café bar on the ground floor forms an effective backdrop for changing art exhibitions. Guests enjoy having breakfast on the terrace studded with palm trees or meeting for a casual drink before or after dinner.

Eine exzellent renovierte Jugendstilvilla steht Liebhabern der kreativen und mediterranen Küche des Küchenchefs Carlos Casas im oberen Teil der Stadt offen. Fernando Salas hat das Interieur angenehm schnörkellos und modern gestaltet. Wechselausstellungen an den Wänden der Café-Bar im Erdgeschoss kommen in der eleganten Atmosphäre besonders gut zur Geltung. Hier trifft man sich auch gern zum Frühstück auf der mit Palmen bepflanzten Terrasse oder am Abend auf einen Drink.

La villa rénovée dans le style Art nouveau est le lieu de rendez-vous des amoureux de la cuisine créative et méditerranéenne du chef Carlos Casas. Fernando Salas en a aménagé l'intérieur de façon moderne et sans fioritures, tandis que les expositions temporaires sur les murs du café-bar du rez-de-chaussée accentuent l'atmosphère élégante du lieu. L'on s'y retrouve également volontiers pour un petit-déjeuner au milieu des palmiers de la terrasse ou le soir autour d'un verre.

En la parte alta de la ciudad, una villa modernista excelentemente renovada abre sus puertas a los amantes de la cocina creativa y mediterránea de Carlos Casas, el cocinero jefe. Fernando Salas ha creado un agradable interior moderno y escueto. En las paredes del café-bar de la planta baja se exponen obras que realzan la elegancia del ambiente. Un local muy agradable, tanto para desayunar en la terraza adornada con palmeras como para disfrutar de una copa por la tarde.

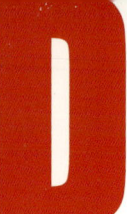

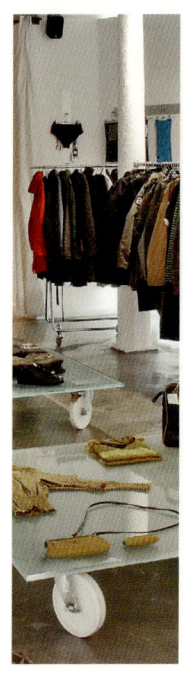
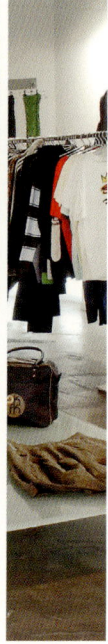
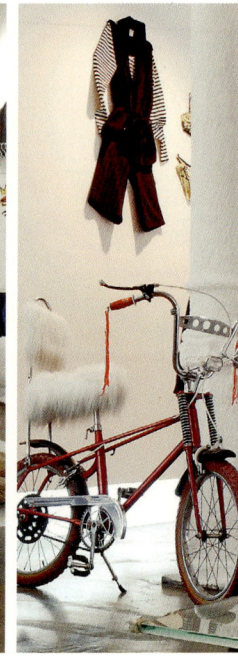
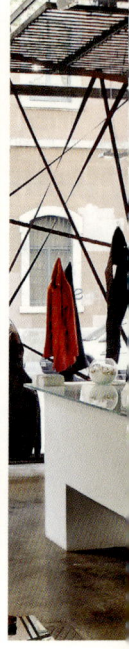

IGUAPOP SHOP

Carrer del Comerç, 15 // Ciutat Vella / El Born
Tel.: +34 93 319 68 13
www.iguapop.net

Mon 5 pm to 9 pm
Tue-Sat 11 am to 2.30 pm
5 pm to 9 pm
Metro L4 Jaume I or L1 Arc de Triomf

As a concert promoter, Iguapop has long shown an appetite for risk and a great instinct for trends. It is not surprising that the IguapopShop became an instant success after its opening in 2003. This shop offers urban fashion related to the world of art and picks up the latest trends of the city. It is a melting pot of the new tendencies in art and fashion, featuring presentations and events of commercial projects that rely on young artists.

Als Konzertagentur beweist Iguapop seit Jahren Mut zum Risiko und ein gutes Gespür für Trends. Es überrascht daher nicht, dass der im Jahr 2003 eröffnete IguapopShop unmittelbar Erfolg hatte. Dieser Shop vertreibt urbane Mode in Verbindung mit Kunst und greift die neuesten Strömungen der Stadt auf. Hier findet man aktuelle Kunst- und Modetrends und kann Präsentationen und Events kommerzieller Projekte in Verbindung mit jungen Künstlern beiwohnen.

Depuis des années, l'agence de concerts Iguapop démontre son goût du risque et son flair pour les nouvelles tendances. Le succès de l'IguapopShop, ouvert en 2003, n'a donc rien d'étonnant. Le concept réunit mode urbaine et art et s'inspire des toutes dernières impulsions de la ville. On y trouve les nouvelles tendances en matière d'art et de mode, ainsi que, à l'occasion, des présentations et évènements mettant en relation projets commerciaux et jeunes artistes.

La agencia de conciertos Iguapop demuestra desde hace años su pasión por el riesgo y un buen olfato para las nuevas tendencias. No sorprende, por tanto, el éxito del IguapopShop, inaugurado en 2003. Es tienda de moda urbana vinculada al mundo del arte que marca las últimas tendencias en la Ciudad Condal siendo un espacio referente de las nuevas corrientes artísticas y de ropa, celebrando eventos y presentaciones de colaboraciones comerciales con artistas emergentes.

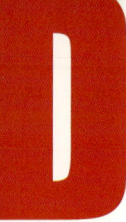

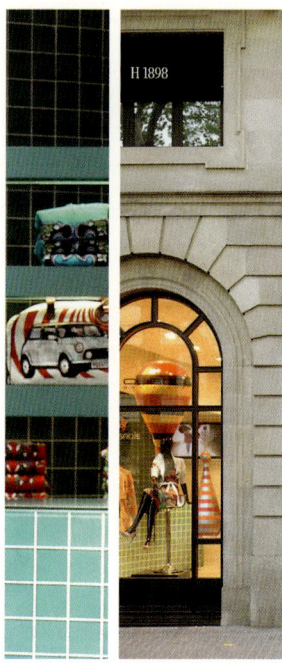

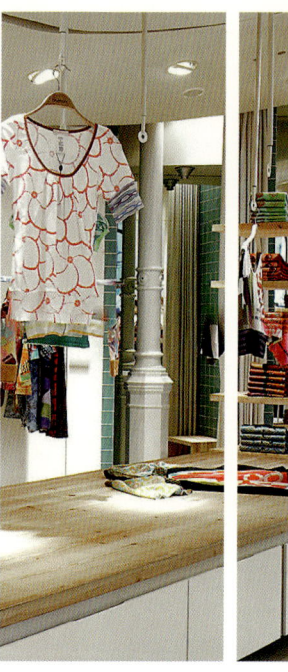

CUSTO BARCELONA

Les Rambles, 109 // Ciutat Vella / El Raval
Tel.: +34 93 481 39 30
www.custo-barcelona.com

Mon–Sat 10 am to 9 pm
Metro L1, L3, L6, L7 Catalunya

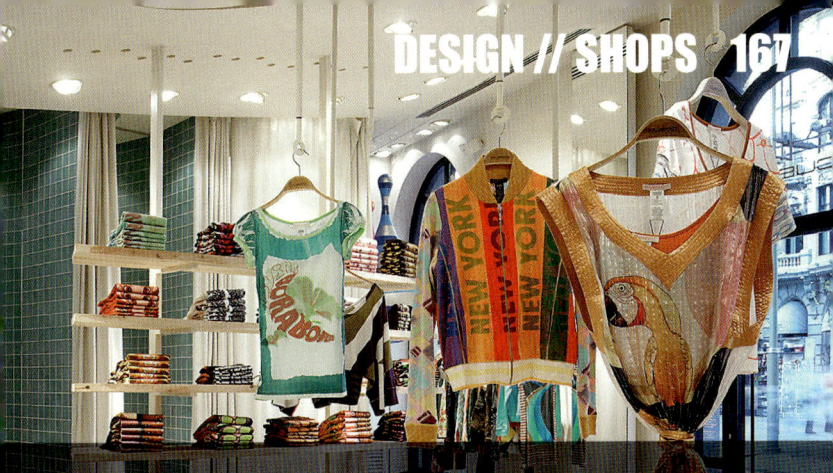

Custo and David Dalmau are the creative masterminds behind the fashion label which, since its start in the 1980s, has become an international success. The brothers were on a trip around the world when they discovered the California surfer look. This inspired them to create their shirts with a unique mix of patterns. They are particularly fond of graphic design and are masters at juggling colors and patterns. Their creations express innovation, daring, and sophistication.

Custo und David Dalmau stecken als kreative Köpfe hinter dem Modelabel, das seit seinen Anfängen in den 80er Jahren von Barcelona aus die Welt erobert. Die Brüder machten eine Weltreise, als sie den Look der kalifornischen Surfer entdeckten, der sie zu ihren Hemden mit dem charakteristischen Mustermix inspirierte. Sie fühlen sich dem Grafikdesign nahestehend und jonglieren meisterhaft mit Farben und Mustern. Ihre Kreationen stehen für Innovation, Wagemut und Raffinesse.

Custo et David Dalmau sont à la tête de ce label de mode dont le succès s'étend au monde entier depuis ses débuts dans les années 80. Ces deux frères effectuaient un tour du monde lorsqu'ils découvrirent le style des surfers californiens, dont ils s'inspirèrent pour leurs T-shirts. Ils accordent ainsi beaucoup d'importance à la conception graphique et jonglent parfaitement avec les couleurs et les modèles. Leurs créations sont symbole d'innovation, audace et sophistication.

Custo y David Dalmau son las dos cabezas pensantes de una marca que desde sus comienzos en los años 80 ha conquistado el mundo desde Barcelona. Los hermanos disfrutaban de un viaje por el mundo cuando descubrieron el "look" de los surferos californianos, que les inspiró la mezcla de dibujos características de sus camisas. Próximos siempre al diseño gráfico, saben combinar con destreza colores y patrones. Sus creaciones son sinónimo de innovación, atrevimiento y clase.

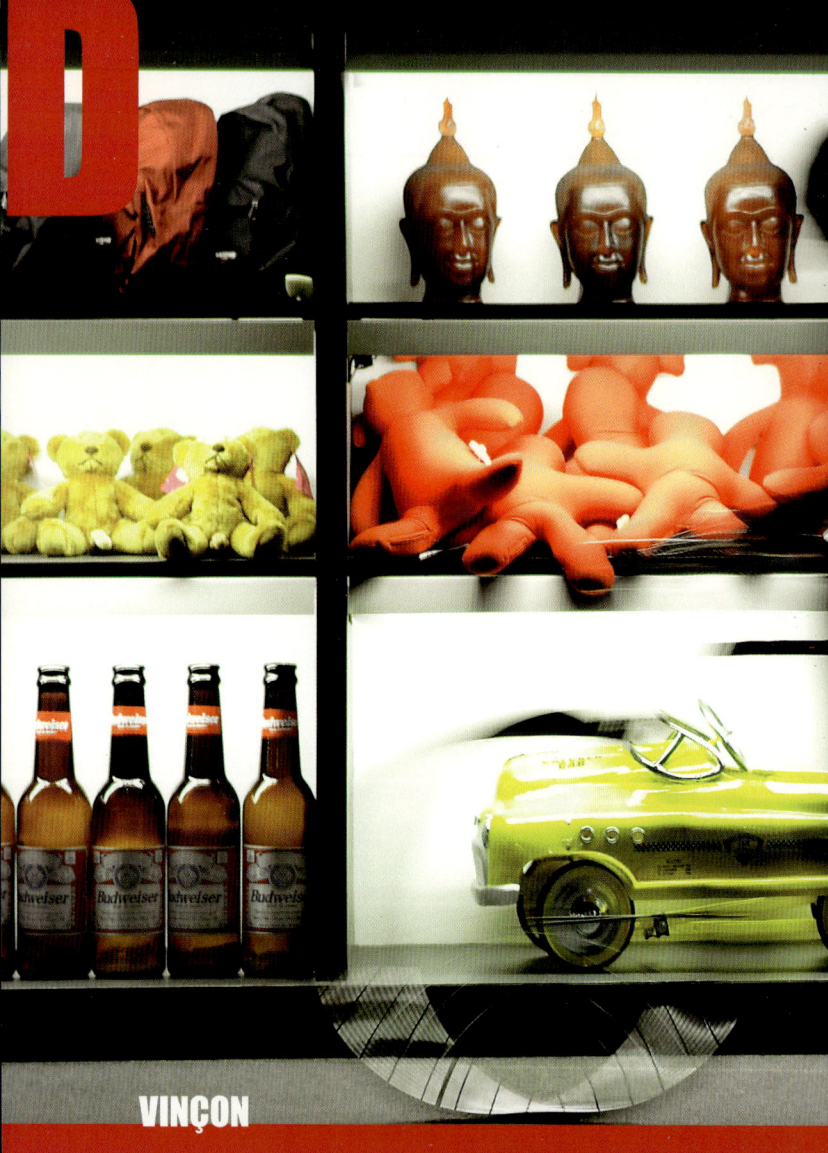

D

VINÇON

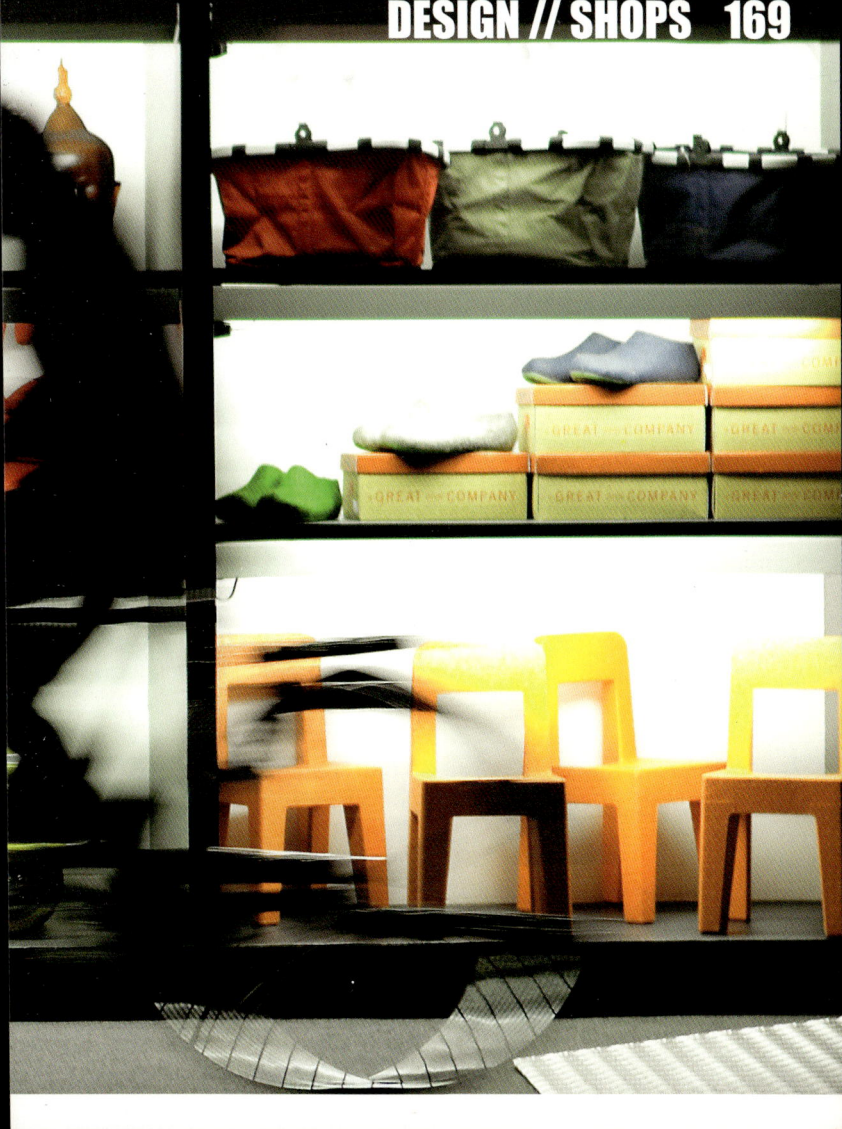

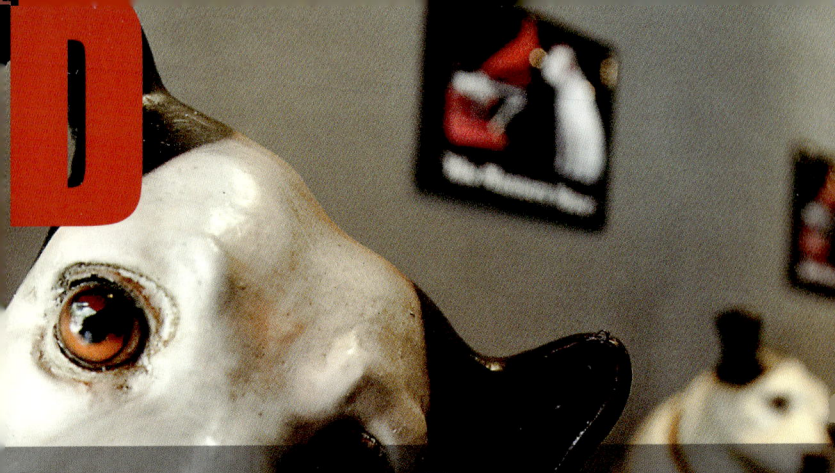

If you appreciate great design, be sure to allow plenty of time for a visit to Vinçon. Outside, you will love the always creative window displays. Inside, Gallery Sala Vinçon exhibits the finest graphic and industrial design, and you can choose from a huge selection of practical and whimsical items as well as everything you need to outfit the perfect kitchen. Don't miss the upper floor with its courtyard terrace which offers a view of the rear façade of La Pedrera.

Wer ein Faible für gutes Design hat, sollte für einen Besuch im Vinçon ausreichend Zeit einplanen. Mit der immer sehenswerten künstlerischen Dekoration der Schaufenster fängt es an. Innen zeigt die Galerie Sala Vinçon Grafik- und Industriedesign, und es gibt jede Menge praktische und witzige Objekte sowie alles für die Einrichtung der perfekten Küche zu kaufen. Tipp: Das herrschaftliche Obergeschoss mit Terrasse im Innenhof samt Blick auf die rückwärtige Fassade von La Pedrera.

Celui qui a un faible pour le design de qualité devra prévoir assez de temps pour cette visite. La décoration des vitrines vaut déjà le détour. À l'intérieur, la galerie Sala Vinçon expose du design graphique et industriel et des objets de décoration pratiques et amusants ainsi que tout l'attirail nécessaire à l'aménagement de la cuisine parfaite. L'étage majestueux du haut avec terrasse dans la cour intérieure offre une vue superbe sur la façade arrière de La Pedrera.

Quienes sientan debilidad por el buen diseño necesitarán mucho tiempo para visitar Vinçon. Todo comienza con la artística decoración de los escaparates, siempre vistosa. En el interior, la galería Sala Vinçon expone diseño gráfico e industrial y se pone a la venta todo tipo de objetos prácticos y divertidos, así como todo lo necesario para equipar la cocina perfecta. Muy recomendable: la señorial planta superior, con terraza interior y vistas a la fachada posterior de La Pedrera.

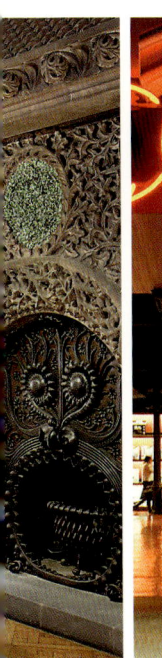
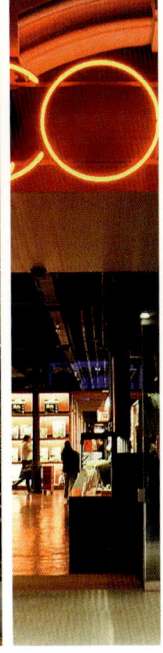
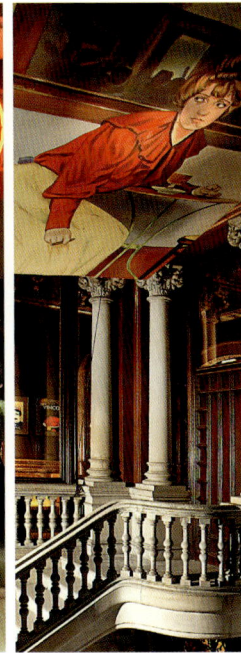
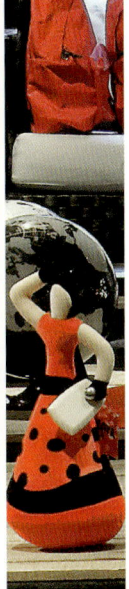

VINÇON

Passeig de Gràcia, 96 // Eixample
Tel.: +34 93 215 60 50
www.vincon.com

Mon–Sat 10 am to 8.30 pm

Metro L2, L3, L4 Passeig de Gràcia

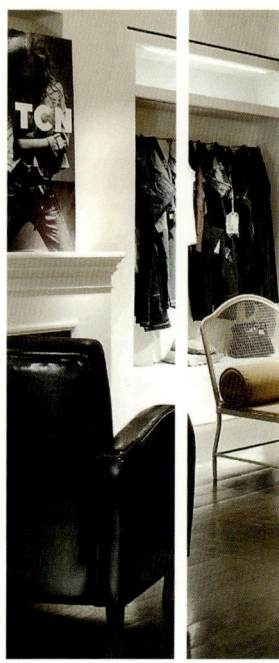

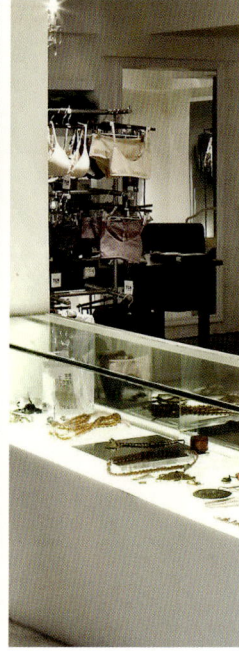

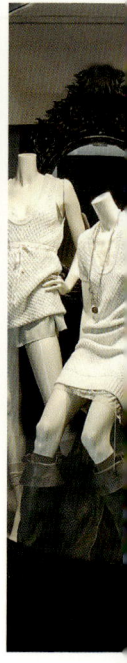

TCN

Carrer del Mestre Nicolau, 12 // Sarrià-Sant Gervasi
Tel.: +34 93 241 26 06
www.tcn.es

Mon–Sat 10 am to 8.30 pm
Bus 101 Pl. Francesc Macià
(Av. Josep Tarradellas)
Bus 14, 68 Calvet-Mestre Nicolau

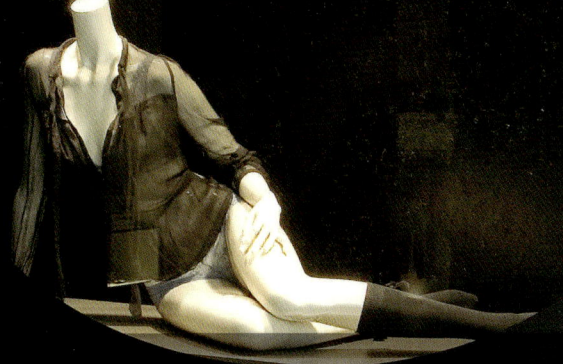

The creative mind behind the vanguard concept of TCN is Totón Comella, who started her career as a designer of underwear and beach fashion. Since the opening of this shop with an attached showroom of 3,300 sq. ft., the homewear label spread throughout Spain like wildfire. The sophisticated lighting brings out the spaciousness and intimity of the interior that was designed by the estudio p. libano, thus turning try-ons into a sensual experience.

Hinter dem avantgardistischen Konzept von TCN steckt die Designerin Totón Comella, deren Karriere mit dem Entwurf von Bademoden und Unterwäsche begann. Seit der Eröffnung dieses Ladenlokals mit angeschlossenem, 300 m² großem Showroom im Jahr 2001 expandiert das Homewear-Label mit großem Erfolg in Spanien. Die ausgefeilte Beleuchtung unterstreicht die Weitläufigkeit und Intimität des Interieurs aus der Feder des estudio p. libano, sodass Auswahl und Anprobe zu einem sinnlichen Ereignis werden.

Le concept d'avant-garde de TCN a été développé par la designer Totón Comella, qui a débuté sa carrière par la conception de maillots de bain et de sous-vêtements. Depuis l'ouverture de ce local commercial avec un showroom adjacent de 300 m² en 2001, l'expansion du label Homewear a rencontré beaucoup de succès en Espagne. L'éclairage sophistiqué met en évidence l'ampleur et l'intimité de l'intérieur créé par l'estudio p. libano, afin que choisir et essayer deviennent une expérience et un événement sensoriels.

Cabe agradecer el vanguardista concepto de TCN a la diseñadora Totón Comella, cuya carrera comenzó con el diseño de trajes de baño y lencería. Desde que en 2001 se inaugurara el local (que cuenta con una sala contigua de exposición de 300 m²), la marca ha sabido expandirse con gran éxito por toda España. La sutil iluminación subraya la amplitud y el intimismo del interior, obra del estudio p. libano, y hace de la selección y prueba de las prendas toda una experiencia para los sentidos.

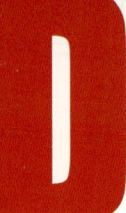

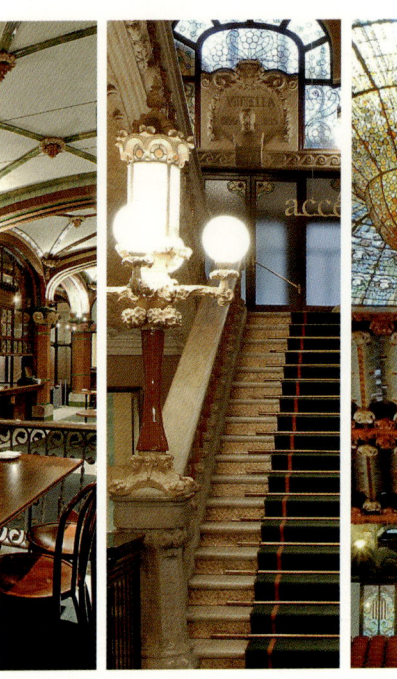

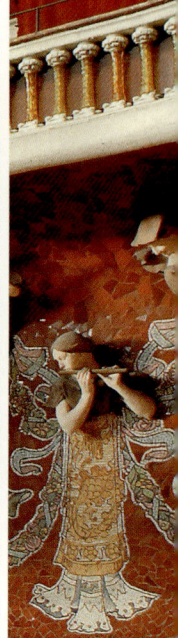

PALAU DE LA MÚSICA CATALANA

Carrer de Sant Pere Més Alt // Ciutat Vella / El Born
Tel.: +34 90 244 28 82
and +34 90 247 54 85 (ticket sales)
www.palaumusica.org

Daily guided tours 10 am to 3.30 pm
Aug and Easter Week 10 am to 6 pm
Metro L1, L4 Urquinaona

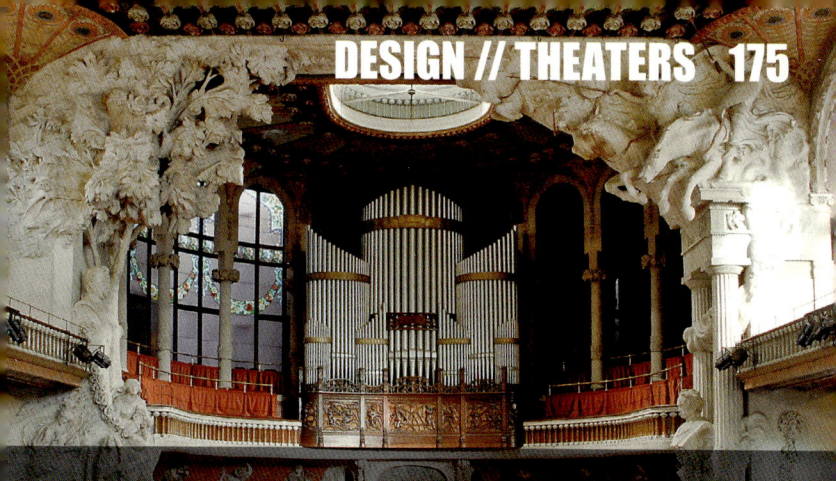

Barcelona loves its Palau de la Música, a masterwork of Modernisme designed by Lluís Domènech i Montaner and built between 1905 and 1908. The breathtaking concert hall with its inverted dome of glass has seen performances by the giants of classical music like Maurice Ravel, Igor Strawinsky, and Richard Strauss, as well as by artists like Duke Ellington, Paco de Lucía, and Norah Jones. The 1989 extension featuring light-red brick and glass was designed by Oscar Tusquets.

Die Barceloneser lieben ihren Palau de la Música, ein Meisterwerk des Modernisme, das 1905–1908 von Lluís Domènech i Montaner errichtet wurde. Die ganz Großen der klassischen Musik wie Maurice Ravel, Igor Strawinsky und Richard Strauss, aber auch Künstler wie Duke Ellington, Paco de Lucía oder Norah Jones sind in dem atemberaubenden Konzertsaal mit der hängenden Glaskuppel aufgetreten. Die moderne Erweiterung von 1989 mit hellrotem Backstein und Glas stammt von Oscar Tusquets.

Les Barcelonais aiment leur Palau de la Música, chef-d'œuvre du modernisme réalisé entre 1905 et 1908 par Lluís Domènech i Montaner. De grands noms de la musique classique, Maurice Ravel, Igor Strawinsky ou Richard Strauss, mais aussi des artistes tels que Duke Ellington, Paco de Lucía ou Norah Jones ont eu l'honneur de jouer dans cette fabuleuse salle de concert et sa coupole de vitraux suspendue. L'agrandissement de 1989, à base de briques rouges et de verre, est signé Oscar Tusquets.

Los barceloneses adoran su Palau de la Música, una obra maestra del modernismo construida por Lluís Domènech i Montaner entre 1905 y 1908. Grandes maestros de la música clásica como Maurice Ravel, Igor Strawinsky, Richard Strauss, pero también artistas como Duke Ellington, Paco de Lucía o Norah Jones han actuado en la espectacular sala de conciertos de cúpula vidriada suspendida. La moderna ampliación de 1989, en vidrio y ladrillo rojo, es obra de Oscar Tusquets.

ART

ARCHITECTURE

MAP 177

DESIGN

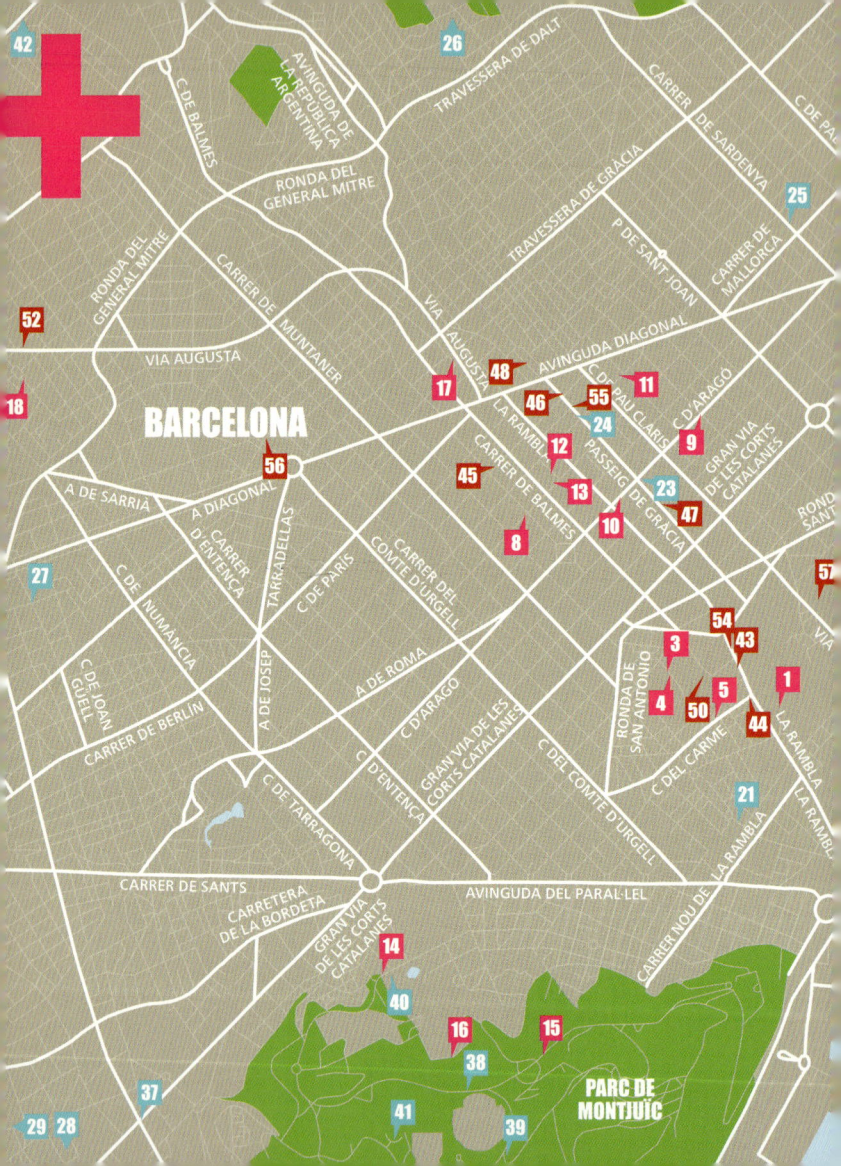

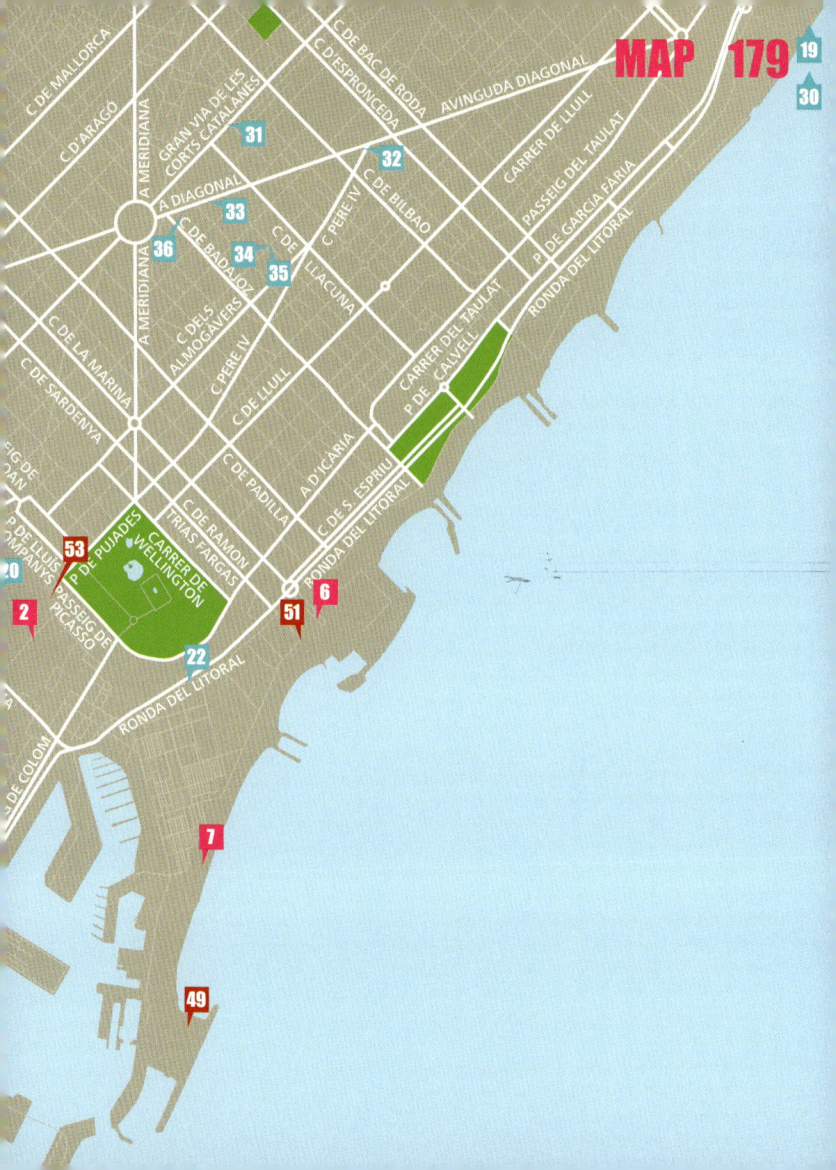

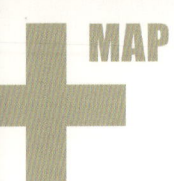

MAP

CIUTAT VELLA

Ciutat Vella—the old town—comprises four administrative neighborhoods: La Barceloneta, El Barri Gòtic, El Raval and Sant Pere, Santa Caterina i la Ribera which are better known as El Born. Geografically Ciutat Vella corresponds to the historic city center of Barcelona and as a consequence, most of the historic sights are located in this district.

EL BARRI GÒTIC, EL BORN

This is the center of the old city, still full of Roman ruins, Romanesque and Gothic buildings. Numerous small alleys form a giant open-air shopping center. Start your tour in the trendy stores of Barcelona's young fashion designers clustered around the Church of Santa María del Mar and then check out the many hip bars and restaurants.

EL RAVAL

La Rambla, the city's main artery that never sleeps, runs between El Raval and the Gothic Quarter all the way to the old harbor. El Raval is shaped by a heady mix of cultures, sometimes radical renovation projects, new squares in a maze of narrow streets, and a lively art and bar scene.

EIXAMPLE

Characterized by its Modernista architecture, this district has wide streets and paths that make it a paradise for walking, while elegant stores make it a paradise for shopping. Designer hotels, chic restaurants, established galleries, and streets known as "Gay-xample" attract foreign visitors and locals alike.

SARRIÀ-SANT GERVASI

The elegant district in the hills northwest of the city center is formed by the noble old villages Sarrià and others which have been added to the city at the beginning of the 20th century. It is still cultivating its elegant village atmosphere.

22@

22@ is an area in the Sant Martí district where innovative urban planning is completely transforming the former industrial zone. Spectacular architectural designs for companies developing the technologies of tomorrow, media and communication firms, and a campus of Pompeu Fabra University embrace this new pioneering spirit.

EMERGENCY

General emergencies 112
Ambulance 061
Fire 080
Guàrdia Urbana, local police 092

ARRIVAL

BY PLANE
AEROPORT DE BARCELONA –
EL PRAT DE LLOBREGAT (BCN)
Tel.: +34 91 321 10 00
www.aena.es – website also in English

10 km / 6 mi. southwest of the city center.
National and international flights.
2 Terminals 4 km / 2.5 mi. apart.
Free shuttle service (green buses)
between the 2 terminals. Bus stops outside
T1 and T2B (underneath the bridge).
Rodalies R10 commuter trains departing
from the airport every 30 min., going to
the railway stations Sants, Passeig de Gràcia,
and Estació de França (30 min.)

Airport bus "Aerobús A1" to and from city
center. Departing from Plaça de Catalunya
every 10 min.
www.aerobusbcn.com

BY TRAIN

ESTACIÓ BARCELONA SANTS
Barcelona's main railway station is
located in the Sants-Montjuïc district.
Access from Plaça dels Països Catalans
or Plaça de Joan Peiró.
Direct connection to Barcelona's Metro
lines L3 and L5, suburban commuter rail
(Cercanías and Rodalies), and long distance
trains.

ESTACIÓ DE FRANÇA
Barcelona's second important railway
station, located in the east of the city
close to the port. Accessible on the R10
line or by a 5 min. walk from Metro
Barceloneta L4.

PASSEIG DE GRÀCIA
Railway and Metro station located
in the Eixample district.
Served by Metro lines L2, L3, L4,
Catalunya Express, and Rodalies R2
and R10.

RENFE (OFFICIAL SPANISH RAIL COMPANY)
Tel.: +34 90 232 03 20
for information and tickets
www.renfe.es

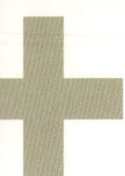

TOURIST INFORMATION

Turisme de Barcelona
www.barcelonaturisme.com
Official website of the city's tourist office
Tel.: +34 93 285 38 34

Service Mon–Fri 8 am to 8 pm
Sat and holidays 8 am to 2 pm

Information points located at Plaça de
Catalunya, Cabina Rambla, Rambla dels
Estudis, 115, Mirador de Colóm, Plaça
de Sant Jaume (in the City Hall), Estació
Central de Sants, Barcelona Airport,
Terminal A and B.
Opening hours of information points vary,
please check web or by phone.

www.bcn.cat
Official website of Barcelona's city
administration. Service, information
and interactive maps including transport
facilities.

www.barcelona-tourist-guide.com
Up-to-date information service and
interactive city map including photo guide,
accommodation service, city guides,
transportation, restaurants, weather
forecast (EN).

ACCOMMODATION

www.bcn.cat
Links from the official site to hotels,
apartments

www.sleepbcn.com
Rooms and apartments

www.barcelona-tourist-guide.com
www.oh-barcelona.com

www.barcelona30.com
Bed and breakfast, guest houses

www.cocoonbarcelona.com
Apartments

TICKETS

www.servicaixa.com
Servi-Caixa sells tickets for cultural and
sport events. Tickets can be purchased at
the cash machines in La Caixa banks.
Tel.: +34 90 233 22 11

www.articketbcn.org
Including entrance for 7 leading museums.
Available at participating museums or via
Telentrada.

www.telentrada.com
Tel.: +34 90 210 12 12
BARCELONA CARD
Free travel on public transport, various
discounts and free offers at museums,
cultural venues, leisure facilities, night-clubs,
shops, restaurants, and entertainments.

Booking at **www.barcelonaturisme.com**,
available at the city's travel agencies ACAV
or information points at Plaça de Catalunya,
Plaça de Sant Jaume and Airport Terminals
T1 and T2.

GETTING AROUND

PUBLIC TRANSPORTATION
www.tmb.cat
Official website of Barcelona Public
Transport
Tel.: +34 90 207 50 27
TMB information points at Metro stations
Diagonal, Sagrada Família, La Sagrera,
Sants Estació and Universitat

TAXI
www.taxibarcelona.cat
Information about fares and taxi stops
+34 93 225 00 00

Cooperativa Radio Taxi Metropolitana
+34 93 307 07 07 Mercedes Taxi
+34 93 358 11 11 ZBarna Taxi
+34 93 330 03 00 Servi Taxi
+34 93 420 80 88 Taxi Amic
(taxis adapted for people with disabilities)
BICYCLE RENTALS
Barcelona Bici
bcnshop.barcelonaturisme.com
Over 2,000 bicycles available from
7 rental points.

www.bicing.cat
website in Spanish only
413 rental points. A user card has to
be purchased in advance.
Tel.: +34 90 231 55 31

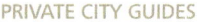

PRIVATE CITY GUIDES
www.bgb.es
Barcelona Guide Bureau
Via Laietana, 54
Tel.: +34 93 268 24 22

SIGHTSEEING FLIGHTS
www.barcelonahelicopters.com
Barcelona Helicopters
Tel.: +34 93 730 49 11

Cat Helicopters
Coastal flights, Sagrada Família,
and other sights
Tel.: +34 93 224 07 10

VIEWING THE CITY FROM ABOVE
El Corte Inglés, Plaça de Catalunya
Mirador de Colom
Plaça del Portal de la Pau
The viewing platform (60 m / 200 ft. high)
of the Christopher Columbus monument
offers a fantastic view over the harbor,
Les Rambles, and the old town.

Transbordador Aeri del Port
www.portvellbcn.com

Sagrada Família
www.sagradafamilia.com

Torre de Coll Serola
www.torredecollserola.com

The radio tower on the Tibidabo is
288 m / 945 ft. high, € 5,50 / pers.

ART & CULTURE

Museu Picasso
www.museupicasso.bcn.cat

Museu Marítim de Barcelona
www.mmb.cat

Museu d'Història de Catalunya
www.mhcat.net

MUHBA
Museu d'Història de Barcelona
Monestir de Pedralbes
www.museuhistoria.bcn.es

Culture and events
www.barcelonacultura.bcn.cat

GOING OUT

www.guiadelociobcn.com
Tips for theater, concerts, movies,
restaurants, bars, and clubs

www.agendabcn.com
Concerts, theater, sport events

www.lecool.com/barcelona
Exhibitions, cinema, theater, events

EVENTS
FASHION

www.080barcelonafashion.cat
Fashion Trade

FASHION TRADE

MACBA NITS
www.macba.cat
Open at night once a week during summer
Tel.: +34 93 412 08 10

www.dhub-bcn.cat
Disseny Hub Barcelona

www.artbarcelona.es
Art, events, festivals

www.bacfestival.com
Barcelona Festival of Contemporary Art

www.tnc.cat
Program of the Teatre Nacional de
Catalunya

MUSIC

www.atiza.com
Concerts, bars

www.barcelonarocks.com
Concerts, events

www.palaumusica.org
Opera and concert events in the Palau
de la Música Catalana

FILM

Loop Festival – Video Art
www.loop-barcelona.com

International Short Film Festival
www.mecalbcn.org

Cover photo (Hotel 1898 Barcelona)
by Martin Nicholas Kunz (further credited as mnk)

Back cover photos by Xavier Barbarro (2),
Mandarin Oriental Hotel Group

ART

p 10–11 (Sala Parés) artworks by Magí Puig,
Miquel Villa Bassols/VG Bild-Kunst, Bonn 2011 and
Ramon Pichot Soler/VG Bild-Kunst, Bonn 2011, all
photos by Xavier Barbarro (further credited as xb)
p 12–15 (Museu Picasso) all photos by xb
p 16–19 (Centro de Cultura Contemporànea de
Barcelona CCCB) all photos by xb
p 20–23 (Museu d'Art Contemporani de Barcelona
MACBA) p 20–21 "Rinzen 1992-1993" by Antoni
Tàpies, p 23 left middle "La ola 1998" by Jorge Oteiza
Embil/VG Bild-Kunst, Bonn 2011, all photos by xb
p 24–25 (The Gallery at Carmelitas Restaurant) all
photos by xb
p 26–27 (Gehry's Fish) sculpture by Frank Gehry,
all photos by xb
p 28–29 (L'Estel Ferit – Platja de la Barceloneta)
all photos by mnk
p 30–33 (ADN Galería) p 30–31 by Bruno Pierre
Peinado/VG Bild-Kunst, Bonn 2011, p 32 by Igor
Eškinja, p 33 left by Eugenio Merino, middle by
Concha Pérez, right by Jean-Luc Moerman, all photos
courtesy of ADN Galería
p 34–37 (Fundación Alorda Derksen) p 34–35 bicycle
"barrio dramas" by Dzine, blue object "Invariant 3
X" by Gabriel Orozco, sculpture "sin titulo" by Fran
West, painting with dots "rot-geld-weiss-blau" by
Imi Knödel, p 36 left sculpture "fog rivets" by John
Chamberlain, middle sculpture in yellow "sin titulo"
by Tom Friedman, black painting "Trash" by Jason
Martin, sculpture "sin titulo" by Anish Kapoor/VG
Bild-Kunst, bonn 2011, all photos by xb
p 40–41 (Fundació Antoni Tàpies) by Antoni Tàpies/
Fundació Antoni Tapies Barcelona/VG Bild-Kunst,
Bonn 2011, photos p 40 left and left middle by
xb, p 41 Yolanda Baixeras, all other by José Hevia/
Fundació Antoni Tàpies, Barcelona 2011
p 42–45 (Fundació Joan Brossa) by Joan Brossa I
Cuervo/Fundació Joan Brossa/VG Bild-Kunst, Bonn
2011, all photos by xb
p 46–49 (Galería Estrany-de la Mota) p 46–47 by
Sergi Aguilar I Sanchis/VG Bild-Kunst, Bonn 2011,
p 48 left by Douglas Gordon, right by Ignasi Ahallí,
p 49 by Sara Ramo, all photos courtesy of Galería
Estrany-de la Mota
p 50–51 (Kowasa Gallery) all photos by xb
p 52–53 (CaixaForum Barcelona) sculpture by Henry
Moore, all photos by xb
p 54–55 (Fundació Joan Miró) courtesy of Successió
Miró/VG Bild-Kunst, Bonn 2011, all photos by xb
p 56–57 (Museu Nacional d'Art de Catalunya
(MNAC)) all photos by xb
p 58–59 (Galería Alejandro Sales) p 58 left and p 59
by Salvador Juanpere Huget/VG Bild-Kunst, Bonn
2011, p 58 middle by Jakob Mattner, all photos by xb
p 60–61 (Tasneem Gallery) by Ernesto Leal, all
photos by xb

ARCHITECTURE

p 66–67 (CAP Progrés Raval de Badalona) all photos
courtesy of CAP
p 70–73 (Mercat de Santa Caterina) p 70–71 by
Luigi Nifosi/shutterstock, p 73 right by xb, all other
by Duccio Malagamba
p 74–77 (Can Ricart Sport Complex) all photos by
Adria Goula Sarda
p 78–79 (Gas Natural Headquarters) all photos by xb
p 80–81 (Casa Batlló) all photos by xb
p 82–83 (Casa Milà) all photos by xb
p 84–87 (Sagrada Família) all photos by xb
p 88–89 (Park Güell) p 88 by xb, p 89 left by
Patrick Poendl/istockphoto, left middle by William
Fawcett/fotoVoyager.com/istockphoto, right middle
by Tatyana Strygina/istockphoto, right by mnk
p 90–93 (Roca Barcelona Gallery) all photos courtesy
of Alejo Bagué/Roca Barcelona Gallery
p 94–95 (Torres Porta Fira) p 95 right by Adria
Goula, all other by xb

p 96–97 (Law Courts, Sant Boi de Llobregat) all photos by xb
p 98–99 (Fòrum Esplanade and Photovoltaic Powerplant) p 98 by Francisco Nogueira/Fotolia, all other by xb
p 100–101 (Gran Via Acoustic Panels) all photos by xb
p 102–103 (ME Barcelona) p 102 right by Francisco Guerrero Tanco, all other by André Morin/Adagp
p 104–107 (Diagonal 197) p 104–105 by Adria Goula, all others by xb
p 108–109 (Media-TIC) all photos by xb
p 110–111 (Museu Can Framis) p 110 middle by Alfons Borrel/VG Bild-Kunst, Bonn 2011, all photos by Pedro Pegenaute
p 112–115 (Torre Agbar) p 112–113 by Alfredo Maiquez/istockphoto, p 114 by Rafael Vargas, p 115 left by xb, left middle and right by Marc Dozier/hemis.fr/laif
p 116–117 (Ciutat de la Justícia) photo by Christian Richters
p 118–119 (Estadi Olímpic Lluis Companys) all photos by xb
p 120–121 (Jardí Botànic) all photos by xb
p 122–125 (Mies van der Rohe Pavilion) by Mies van der Rohe/VG Bild-Kunst, Bonn 2011, Sculpture p 124 right by Georg Kolbe/VG Bild-Kunst, Bonn 2011, photos p 122–123 and 124 left by xb, p 124 middle and right courtesy of The Barcelona Pavilion, 125 by mnk
p 126–127 (Torre de Communicacions de Montjuïc) p 126 left and middle by mnk, all other photos by xb
p 128–129 (Instituto de Microcirugía Ocular IMO) all photos by Roger Subirà

DESIGN
p 136–137 (Hotel 1898) all photos by mnk
p 138–139 (Hotel Bagués) all photos by xb
p 140–141 (Emma) all photos by Vanessa Gonzales
p 142–145 (Hotel Omm and Ommsession Club)
p 144 right by xb, all other courtesy of Hotel Omm

p 146–149 (Mandarin Oriental Barcelona) all photos courtesy of Mandarin Oriental Hotel Group
p 150–153 (El Palauet Living Barcelona) all photos courtesy of El Palauet Living Barcelona
p 154–155 (Eclipse W Barcelona) all photos by xb
p 156–159 (Restaurant Dos Palillos) all photos courtesy of Restaurant Dos Palillos
p 160–161 (Bestial) all photos by mnk
p 162–163 (Dos Torres) all photos by xb
p 164–165 (Iguapop Shop) all photos by xb
p 166–167 (Custo Barcelona) all photos courtesy of Custo Barcelona
p 168–171 (Vinçon) all photos courtesy of Vinçon
p 172–173 (TCN) all photos courtesy of TCN
p 174–175 (Palau de la Música Catalana) all photos by xb

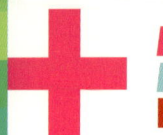

AAD
Art Architecture Design

+

LOOK UP

MY FAVORITES

INFO

SUBSCRIBE

SETTINGS

AAD
Art Architecture Design

+

BARCELONA

teNeues

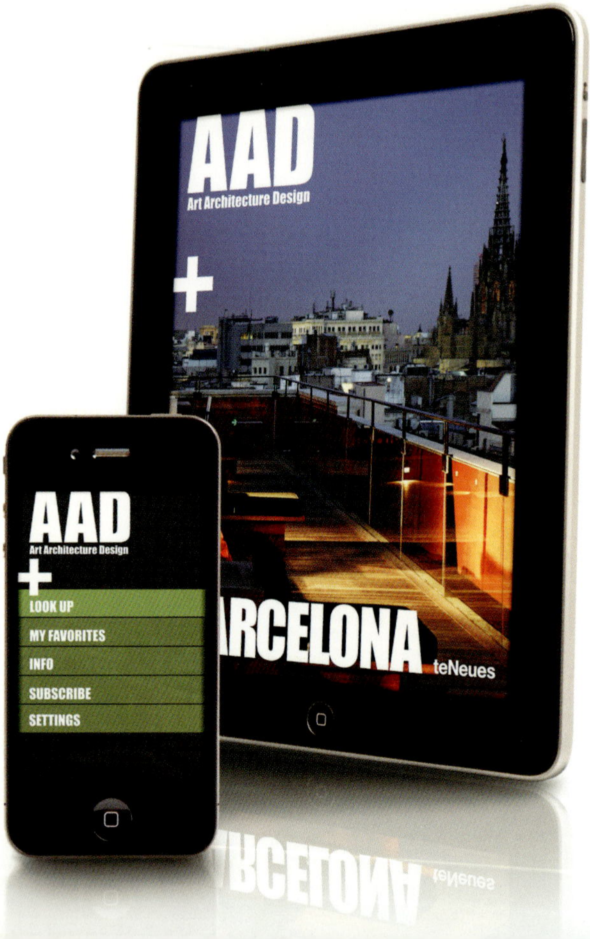

A NEW GENERATION

of multimedia travel guides featuring the ultimate selection of architectural icons, galleries, museums, stylish hotels, and shops for cultural and art conscious travelers.

VISUAL

Immerse yourself into inspiring locations with photos and videos.

APP FEATURES

Search by categories, districts, or geo locator; get directions or create your own tour.

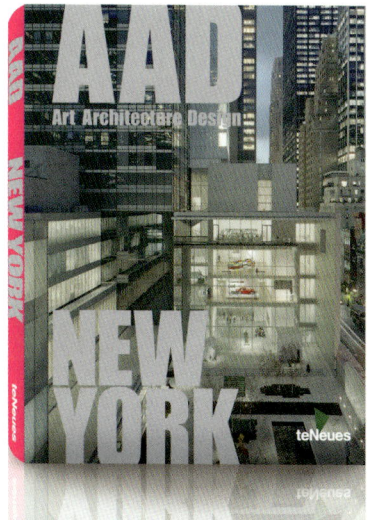

ISBN 978-3-8327-9435-4

COPENHAGEN
BARCELONA
SHANGHAI
TOKYO
SINGAPORE
BEIJING
VIENNA
PARIS
SYDNEY
HONG KONG
MUNICH
ZURICH
NEW YORK
SAO PAULO
AMSTERDAM
MIAMI
MEXICO CITY
HAMBURG
LONDON
ROME
EMIRATES
CHICAGO
MILAN
BERLIN

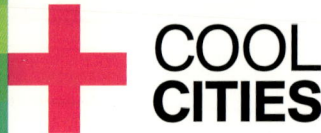

COOL
CITIES

**Pocket-size Book,
App for iPhone/iPad/iPod Touch**
www.cool-cities.com

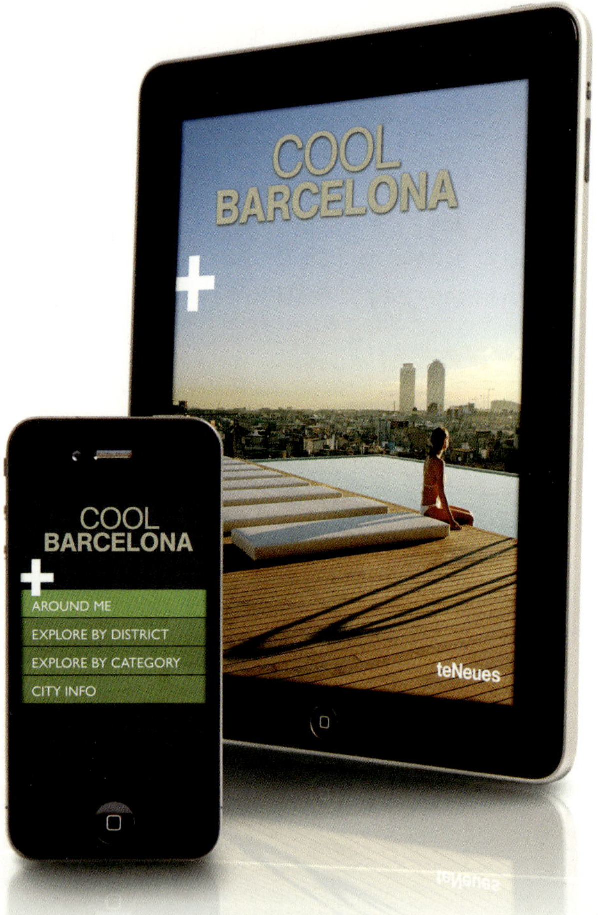

COOL
BARCELONA

COOL
BARCELONA

AROUND ME

EXPLORE BY DISTRICT

EXPLORE BY CATEGORY

CITY INFO

teNeues

A NEW GENERATION
of multimedia lifestyle travel guides
featuring the hippest most fashionable
hotels, shops, and dining spots for
cosmopolitan travelers.

VISUAL
Discover the city with tons
of brilliant photos and videos.

APP FEATURES
Search by categories, districts, or geo locator;
get directions or create your own tour.

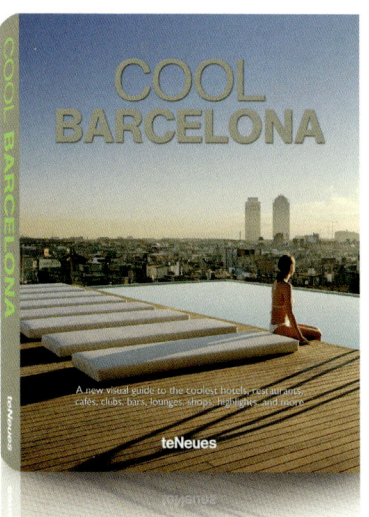

COOL
BARCELONA

A new visual guide to the coolest hotels, restaurants,
cafés, clubs, bars, lounges, shops, highlights, and more

teNeues

ISBN 978-3-8327-9495-8

BRUSSELS
VENICE
BANGKOK
MALLORCA+IBIZA
NEW YORK
AMSTERDAM
MIAMI
MEXICO CITY
HAMBURG
LONDON
ROME
MILAN
BERLIN
FRANKFURT
STOCKHOLM
BARCELONA
COPENHAGEN
LOS ANGELES
SHANGHAI
TOKYO
SINGAPORE
VIENNA
BEIJING
COLOGNE
PARIS
HONG KONG
MUNICH

© 2011 Idea & concept by Martin Nicholas Kunz, Lizzy Courage Berlin
Selected, edited and produced by Patricia Massó
Texts by Haike Falkenberg
Editorial coordination: Miriam Bischoff
Executive Photo Editor: David Burghardt, Photo Editor: Maren Haupt
Copy Editors: Dr. Simone Bischoff, Janosch Müller
Art Director: Lizzy Courage Berlin
Design Assistant: Christin Steirat
Imaging and pre-press production: Tridix, Berlin
Translations: Translations by Romina Russo, RR Communications
Heather Bock, Romina Russo (English), Alexandre Hubert, Samantha Michaux (French)
Pablo Álvarez, Romina Russo (Spanish)

© 2011 teNeues Verlag GmbH + Co. KG, Kempen

teNeues Verlag GmbH + Co. KG
Am Selder 37, 47906 Kempen // Germany
Phone: +49 (0)2152 916-0, Fax: +49 (0)2152 916-111
e-mail: books@teneues.de

Press department: Andrea Rehn
Phone: +49 (0)2152 916-202 // e-mail: arehn@teneues.de

teNeues Digital Media GmbH
Kohlfurter Straße 41–43, 10999 Berlin // Germany
Phone: +49 (0)30 700 77 65-0

teNeues Publishing Company
7 West 18th Street, New York, NY 10011 // USA
Phone: +1 212 627 9090, Fax: +1 212 627 9511

teNeues Publishing UK Ltd.
21 Marlowe Court, Lymer Avenue, London SE19 1LP // UK
Phone: +44 (0)20 8670 7522, Fax: +44 (0)20 8670 7523

teNeues France S.A.R.L.
39, rue des Billets, 18250 Henrichemont // France
Phone: +33 (0)2 4826 9348, Fax: +33 (0)1 7072 3482

www.teneues.com

While we strive for utmost precision in every detail, we cannot be held
responsible for any inaccuracies, nor for any subsequent loss or damage arising.
Bibliographic information published by the Deutsche Nationalbibliothek.
The Deutsche Nationalbibliothek lists this publication in the
Deutsche Nationalbibliografie; detailed bibliographic data are
available in the Internet at http://dnb.d-nb.de.

Printed in the Czech Republic
ISBN: 978-3-8327-9465-1

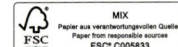